Mortar Gunner on the Eastern Front

The Memoir of Dr Hans Heinz Rehfeldt

Volume I: From the Moscow Winter Offensive to Operation Zitadelle

Hans Heinz Rehfeldt

Translated by Geoffrey Brooks

Introduction by Marc Rikmenspoel

Greenhill Books

Mortar Gunner on the Eastern Front:
The Memoir of Dr Hans Heinz Rehfeldt,
Volume I: From the Moscow Winter Offensive to Operation Zitadelle

Greenhill Books

Greenhill Books, c/o Pen & Sword Books Ltd,
47 Church Street, Barnsley, S. Yorkshire, S70 2AS, England
For more information on our books, please visit
www.greenhillbooks.com, email contact@greenhillbooks.com
or write to us at the above address.

Geoffrey Brooks English-language translation © Greenhill Books, 2019
Marc Rikmenspoel introduction © Greenhill Books, 2019
Hans Heinz Rehfeldt text © Verlagshaus Würzburg GmbH & Co. KG
Flechsig Verlag
Beethovenstr. 5 B
D-97080 Würzburg
Germany
www.verlagshaus.com

PUBLISHING HISTORY
Mortar Gunner on the Eastern Front by Hans Rehfeldt was first published in 2008 by
Verlagshaus Würzburg GmbH & Co. KG with the title *Mit dem Eliteverband des Heeres
"Großdeutschland" tief in den Weiten Russlands.* This is the first English-language translation
and publication. This edition has a new introduction by Marc Rikmenspoel. In 2019
Greenhill Books will also be publishing the second volume of Rehfeldt's memoirs.

CIP data records for this title are available from the British Library

ISBN 978-1-78438-361-9

Typeset and designed by JCS Publishing Services Ltd
Typeset in 11pt Adobe Caslon Pro
Printed and bound in Great Britain by TJ Books Limited

MIX
Paper from
responsible sources
FSC® C013056

Contents

Foreword

When, fifty years after I had written them, I read through my contemporary diary notes describing my four years in Russia and the Eastern Front, my coldness in those days shocked me. I had glossed over the most dreadful things as if they were mere everyday occurrences. These notes are a sign of those times, of the blunting and mental brutalization caused by war. Only in a few places in the notes did I mention my feelings. What impressed me most was the inhumanity of the military leaderships. The Bolshevists observed neither the Hague Convention on Land Warfare nor the Geneva Convention. We often found the bodies of our soldiers horrifically mutilated. Even those with the worst wounds were finished off in the most bestial manner. On our side we had the 'Commissar Order', i.e. the Führerbefehl in which Commissars and other political personnel taken prisoner were to be shot dead on the battlefield. I never saw it done during my four years in the East, but certainly many Commissars were liquidated in this way as a result of that order.

We of the Wehrmacht were harnessed to a powerful war machine in which too much was asked of us physically and mentally. We were always expected to keep making one more effort even when utterly exhausted. It left us with very little time to reflect. It was a struggle for survival. In the shortest breaks, even in battle (see my report on Rzhev, September 1942), one fell asleep immediately.

Looking back, it surprises me that under these conditions I still found the time to keep a diary. This was of course strictly forbidden, for these personal notes contained a great deal of information about us that would be useful to the enemy should they fall into their hands. Even when in 1942/43 doubts about a victorious conclusion to the struggle were being voiced increasingly loudly, we still felt ourselves part of an enormous war machine moving unstoppably eastwards against the global enemy, Bolshevism.

It was easier for those men who didn't think too deeply about things. They felt a certain liberation from the normality of everyday life and saw the opportunity to prove themselves. Even in the most difficult period, around the middle of 1943 after Operation *Zitadelle* when we had fought off Russian attacks and held our lines, I too had moments of pride upon seeing the masses of demoralized prisoners, the huge piles of captured weapons, tanks and vehicles. The experience of being at the Front – for years – changed me completely. Feelings of warmth and love were left at home with my parents and the girl in the homeland, for whom we risked our lives day after day. Compassion and pity were buried deep within oneself, only occasionally would one be overwhelmed by such sentiments. Without really noticing it, one became part of the steamroller. Even fear surfaced only rarely. 'Bravery consists of overcoming the inner coward!' To replace it there was comradeship – the feeling of being able to rely on one's comrades even in the worst situations. How else could one have slept peacefully in a trench only 100m from the enemy if one was not certain that alert comrades were watching over the group, the platoon, the company?

These were the conditions under which I made my notes. They were set down in writing, disjointed, incomplete, at the moment I experienced them; later in the military hospital, on leave and after the war I made some improvements and additions, for a man in a burning house has no time to ponder the circumstances.

Quite a few sentences of this foreword were taken verbatim from the book *Erinnerungen eines alten Ostpreussen* ('The Memoirs of an Old East Prussian') by Fürst zu Dohna-Schlobitten from the chapter 'Der Russlandfeldzug aus meinem Tagebuch' ('The Russian Campaign from my Diary'). His very lucid text describes that period of my life which I too spent on the Eastern Front.

Dr Hans Heinz Rehfeldt

Acknowledgements

My observations and the events I experienced were noted down directly on the day and at the place they occurred or in lulls in the fighting. I still have my diaries from that time! After the war I worked on the text, initially with a typewriter and in the years 2001 and 2002 with a computer.

I thank Michael Dürre and Gunther Grübler for having approached Verlagshaus Würzburg with the results of my editing. Furthermore I extend my thanks to my esteemed war comrade Josef Dörfler who placed at my disposal numerous photographs for publication in this book.

Verlagshaus Würzburg produced an authentic two-volume work from my notes, pictures and documents and published the first edition in 2008. This translation into English is based on the sixth German edition of 2017.

I dedicate these two volumes to my Fallen and War-disabled comrades of the *Grossdeutschland* units.

Dr Hans Heinz Rehfeldt

Translator's Note

Throughout his military service in the Second World War, the author was a *Grossdeutschland* soldier serving one of the thousands of standard mortars of the Wehrmacht at battalion level. The Rheinmetall 8cm Granatwerfer 34 (GrW 34) weighed 64k (141lbs) and consisted of a smooth-bore barrel, bipod and baseplate dismantled into three parts for transportation. The mortar was a muzzle-loader, the bomb weighing 3.5kg: at a muzzle velocity of 172m/sec the maximum range was 2,400m. Rate of fire was fifteen to twenty-five rounds per minute. The barrel could be traversed between 10° to 23°, and elevated to between 45° and 90°. A panoramic sight was mounted on the traversing mechanism yoke. The spread at maximum range was 65m, therefore crew training was considered of the greatest importance for accuracy and rate of fire.

The mortar team consisted of the mortar captain, No. 1 and No. 2 gunners and two or three ammunition runners.

Geoffrey Brooks

Introduction

It was during 1978, at the latest, that I became obsessed with the history of the Second World War. That was the year I turned eight, and at some point around then I was left at home on a weekend afternoon, in the company of a babysitter I must not have cared for. Instead of socializing, I stayed in my bedroom, and started poking through the items my father had stored in the large walk-in closet. I found his copy of Cornelius Ryan's *The Longest Day*, and the photos and accounts quickly captivated me.

That was the era in which mass-market paperbacks about the war were widely published and easy to find. I started collecting any that looked interesting. The books included memoirs and campaign histories. The topics ranged from submarine warfare to fighting in desert and jungle terrain. Most concerned American and British-Commonwealth troops, but some translated German books were among them. These gradually came to interest me the most. I realized that what had happened on the Eastern Front was one of the most complex, intense, complicated and massive campaigns in military history.

Good works on the Eastern Front were hard to find in my early days of collecting and reading war books. It's been one of the pleasures of my life that English-language material on the subject, whether original works or in translation, has become increasingly common. I suspect that much of this is due to Western Front themes being thoroughly explored, but another factor is likely the growing momentum of readers discovering the mud and cold and little-known massive battles, and wanting to learn more.

The Eastern Front books have been joined along the way by a small flood of ones dealing with German elite units. I myself have contributed to the many works about the Waffen-SS. But the Luftwaffe pilots and airborne units have also been covered, as has the most elite unit of the German Army, the *Grossdeutschland*, which is the formation in which the author, Dr Hans Heinz Rehfeldt, served.

Infanterie Regiment *Grossdeutschland* was formed in the summer of 1939 from the former Wachregiment *Berlin*. This was the ceremonial unit that protected government buildings and provided honour guards for visiting foreign dignitaries. It carried on the traditions of previous Prussian and

Imperial German Guards regiments, as reflected in its 'Wach' (Watch) title. The Wachregiment wasn't trained for front-line combat, so it was combined with almost half of the Infanterie Lehr Regiment, from the Infantry School at Doberitz, to form the new *Grossdeutschland*. 'Lehr' refers to elite instructional and demonstration troops. In German tradition, these are the soldiers who test new weapons and tactics, and display them for the rest of the army. Thus, two elite branches were combined to form the new regiment.

Grossdeutschland was almost unique in the German Army of that time, being recruited from men from every part of Germany and Austria. Most other regiments and independent battalions were recruited from a specific region, and took on characteristics from that home area. The name *Grossdeutschland* means 'Greater Germany', to reflect its nationwide recruiting base. Enlistment was to be purely voluntary, but this changed during the war in the face of enormous casualties.

Grossdeutschland first saw action during the 1940 Western Campaign. It fought with distinction, particularly at Stonne, after the crossing of the Meuse River. Additional support elements were added, so that *Grossdeutschland* was almost twice the strength of a normal regiment. The relative ease of the Yugoslavian invasion was followed by extremely heavy fighting during the first four months of combat in the USSR. This is the point at which Rehfeldt joined the regiment, as a replacement.

During Rehfeldt's tenure, *Grossdeutschland* expanded from an infantry regiment into an armoured division, and eventually into an armored corps of two divisions, with three additional divisions fighting separately. The result paralleled what occurred with the Waffen-SS, as an elite core was watered down through expansion. In the conditions described in Volume II of Rehfeldt's memoir, an experienced cadre of men such as him were of extreme importance.

These books demonstrate that what Hans Rehfeldt had, more than any other quality, was good fortune. It's no accident that most memoirs are written by men with little combat experience. The authors are typically from supporting elements, or were only combat infantrymen for a matter of months. Front-line combat in the Second World War was so dangerous that most men became wounded or killed within a few weeks of serving. Rehfeldt himself was wounded several times, but always returned to duty. While in combat, as you'll read, he was constantly avoiding Red Airforce airstrikes, or hugging the earth during artillery barrages. Yet he survived these dangers, and was able to record months of combat in his diary. The survival of that diary is a minor miracle in itself. But it should also be mentioned that Rehfeldt always served with good intent, and his survival was never due to shirking.

The reader will note that Rehfeldt freely admits to having been in the Hitler Youth. This was compulsory for German boys during his childhood. In that organization, he would have received pre-military training of a sort that eased the transition to soldiering. Hitler Youth service also included political indoctrination, which made a generation of German boys more susceptible to participating in war crimes. *Grossdeutschland* is one of several units that murdered black French Army prisoners in France during 1940. It later executed civilian hostages in Yugoslavia. These atrocities were prior to Rehfeldt joining *Grossdeutschland*. During his service, he claims he never personally saw the Wehrmacht's Commissar Order for murdering Red Army political officers carried out. There's no reason not to take Rehfeldt at his word, especially since he shows empathy when discussing learning Russian, and then being able to communicate more easily with Red Army soldiers and Soviet civilians. It should be remembered, while reading Rehfeldt's diary entries, that his service was spent as an enlisted man and junior NCO. This means he wasn't in a position to order or be responsible for large-scale criminal acts. As it is, Rehfeldt records many horrific incidents, so his memoir can't be accused of holding back.

Mortar Gunner on the Eastern Front is not the only *Grossdeutschland* memoir to see print in English. *The Forgotten Soldier* is probably the best known. Franco-German Guy Sajer told his story in a dream-like, surreal manner. His book has won points as literature, but is criticized by readers seeking a more factual account. *The Good Soldier*, which I had the privilege of editing, was written by Austrian Alfred Novotny. It is based mostly on his memories, and is devoted equally to his service in Panzerfusilier Regiment *Grossdeutschland* and to his time in the Soviet Gulag. Some readers would have enjoyed more detail on his military service. Rehfeldt's diary fits well as a complement to these memoirs. It is lengthy, detailed and full of the combat action that is missing in more introspective accounts by the veterans of various armies. As published, the work also includes many photos not seen elsewhere, even in the several existing photo books about *Grossdeutschland*. Among those, *God, Honor, Fatherland*, titled after the unit's motto, is particularly recommended for readers seeking more details about the formation in which Rehfeldt served.

In closing, anyone interested in learning what the Second World War was really like for combat soldiers is likely to enjoy this two-volume set. Those new to the subject of the Eastern Front will be amazed by what Rehfeldt endured and survived, while those with experience in studying the war between Nazi Germany and the Soviet Union will find that this diary reads with great authenticity, confirming details read elsewhere while also adding new insight. Either way, get ready for a thrilling journey.

Marc Rikmenspoel
Denver, Colorado
7 March 2019

1941

Chapter 1

The Winter Offensive South of Moscow

---

26 October 1941: Neuruppin/Brandenburg

Upon completion of our basic training we were brought to the Reserve Battalion of 'Reinforced Infantry Regiment *Grossdeutschland*' for familiarization with infantry weapons. At the first inspection by the company commander, Hauptmann Dr Meyer, he had pointed to me and said, 'Mortar!' Now we could assemble and dismantle the heavy MG in our sleep; we had fired a rifle and 08 pistol; we had *run* cross-country with the heavy mortar until our every movement with the equipment was unerring. Our final inspection concluded, now we wanted to get to the Front and face the Russians.

On Sunday (then and later almost always known as '*Grossdeutschland* travel day') the order came to load up. We had slept in a proper bed for the last time: who knew how long it would be before we got to see another one. We began packing and loading up before noon. Then came the great farewells. It was all fairly light-hearted – I can probably be forgiven for saying that – for we could not imagine that war would be so cruel, exhausting and awful. We were enthusiastic – most of us, like myself, had come forward as volunteers. We thought that war would be a great experience! At 1300hrs we fell in with full pack and equipment and marched in a long column to the Friedrich-Franz barracks. Here we formed an open rectangle. The commanding officer of the Reserve Battalion 'Reinforced Infantry Regiment *Grossdeutschland*', Herr Major Tode, delivered a stirring speech in a hoarse voice. He spoke of fulfilment of duty, loyalty, preparedness to make the supreme sacrifice and of our oath of loyalty to the Führer. 'Whoever swears on the banner of Greater Germany has nothing left which belongs to himself! Germany – our beloved Fatherland, our glorious Führer, *Sieg Heil*!' Then the triple Hurrah! Hurrah! Hurrah! thundered across the barracks courtyard.

Led by the 'Jingling Johnny', we marched past the commanding officer and then through the town to the railway station. The population lined the street, people waved from their windows and many girls looked for 'their' soldiers and accompanied us. We were proud, terribly proud. *Achtung*! Now we're coming! That was probably what we were thinking. During this march I thought a lot about home. I suppose I realized that my parents and girlfriend would be thinking of it differently, their demeanour quiet and grave. However, we were young, self-confident soldiers full of courage.

At the station the order was given to break ranks and then we mixed in with the townspeople, joyfully accepting gifts of cigarettes, apples and even cakes. Wheels screeching, our transport – a goods train – trundled in. I boarded a truck with thirty companions and our '*Spiess*' [CSM, Warrant Officer II] Stabsfeldwebel Treptow. We fetched wood and coal for the iron stove. A goods truck is not a comfortable warm room. Apart from some benches and the rifle rack there was no furniture. The locomotive whistled and the train rolled slowly forward. Standing at the open door we waved and shouted '*Auf Wiedersehen!*' to colleagues who for one reason or another would not be coming with us just yet. The train picked up speed, clattering and shaking wildly; somebody shut the heavy door, it was the end of October and winter was approaching.

In our wagon chaos reigned. Belts with entrenching tools, gas masks, steel helmets, field packs, laundry bags and rifles hung on the rifle racks and clattered constantly against the walls throughout the entire journey. Our mood soared! The stove glowed, a stable lantern spread its meagre light and in a corner somebody was playing the harmonica. Some of us sang along; others had opened theirs travel rations and were chewing, cheeks bulging. We sat, collars up, hands in pockets. Here and there a cigarette glowed. So many questions remained to be answered: What would surprise us most about Russia? What did that country look like, which had kept itself hermetically sealed off from the rest of the world? Was it really 'the workers' paradise'? We would soon find out.

At about 2300hrs our goods train pulled into Berlin and halted briefly in the marshalling yards. This allowed us to 'organize' [Wehrmacht term for appropriating property without permission] firewood and coal from trains standing on adjacent lines. The rails gleamed in the dim light of our lamps, trains rattled past nearby. Shrill whistles resounded through the night. Berlin had a permanent blackout against air raids. The train pulled out: we were tired and everybody found his spot to sleep: on the benches, under the benches, in the gangway, on straw. Everybody slept well. The monotonous rattling and clattering was a wonderful soporific. Only the fire watch had to remain awake, this man's duty was to ensure that the straw in the wagon was not ignited by sparks.

27 October 1941

Everyone awoke at about 0800hrs. The first rays of the morning sun pierced through cracks in the doors and the small windows. I arose swiftly, folded my blanket, combed my hair, rubbed my eyes and had my morning cigarette. Our route was Küstrin–Schneidemühl into the border area of Poland. Here we could see the difference at once just by looking at the people and houses. Many seedy figures loitered along the railway embankment. Filthy children in rags begged us for bread. Then the typical craving for a cigarette. The terrain was partially under water, the rivers seemed to have been left to their own devices and silted up. 'Polish farming', we thought. Occasionally we saw traces of the campaign of autumn 1939. Shell and bomb craters, barbed-wire entanglements, infantry trenches, anti-tank obstacles, houses in ruins and blown bridges. We opened the wagon door a little and sat around the stove staring across the wide, flat landscape. The villages were small with the high draw-wells typical of the East. In the distance we saw the old German town of Bromberg and at the mention of its name recalled the pre-war Polish atrocity against its German inhabitants known as 'Bloody Sunday'. Here we made only a brief stop. It looked like a typical small German town. The locomotive whistled and took us next via Thorn and Alexandrov to Warsaw, passing through the Polish capital around midnight. In the moonlight the many ruined houses looked ghostly, eerie and gave us the creeps.

28 October 1941

On the journey through Siedlce–Brest-Litovsk there was not much of interest to see near the railway line. We noticed reconstruction work under way in villages and small towns. Our goods wagons had no toilet. Every time the train stopped, those wishing to answer the call of nature would jump down and crouch near the rails. Sometimes the whole gun battery would assemble in a row, keeping an eye on the signals or the locomotive. If the signal arm went up, or they saw a cloud of smoke rise from the locomotive, haste was required to pull one's trousers back up and jump aboard the wagon, for one cannot pursue a train comfortably with one's trousers around one's ankles!

29 October 1941

After a long run through the night we crossed the former Russian border at Brest. The train came under tracer fire. Partisans? We arrived at the ruined station buildings of Brest-Litovsk towards 0700hrs and stayed there until midday. After the usual weapon cleaning we drilled from 0900hrs until 1200hrs. To treat future warriors like ourselves as if we were raw recruits did nothing to foster our feelings of pride!

30 October 1941

We were happy to hear the order to get back on board. The next town was Zabinka. It was much colder there. On both sides of the railway the hedges were covered with snow. A line of fir trees acted as protection against snowdrifts but also obscured the view of the terrain beyond them. Here in the so-called central sector of the Eastern Front the railway line ran between huge woods with gigantic trees. The signs of battle were visible along this stretch. Large numbers of wrecked Russian tanks lay all around. The railway line had been bombed in many places, as evidenced by large craters very close to the permanent way. Onwards we went, ever eastwards, over repaired bridges and through stations, most of which seemed ruined, only a few of their buildings still standing, and on the tracks a confusion of bombed and shell-damaged transport trains.

31 October 1941

During the course of this day we reached Minsk, leaving there at 1800hrs, heading all night at a dawdle to Gomel, arriving at 0700hrs. Here we had to de-train, for this was the end of the German standard-gauge tracks and the beginning of the Russian broad gauge. We transferred to another transport train with large, broad Russian wagons but spent the night in our own wagon.

1 November 1941

We reloaded into the Russian wagons. They had much more space. Russian PoWs were at work around the railway. They looked uncouth types and gave us our first impression of our future opponents. We had to drill here for an hour and then settled comfortably into the spacious Russian wagons. We built a second tier at the corners with boards, and now we had a stove. The train pulled out during the night: it would only be a few more days.

2 November 1941

Russia, what an immeasurable land! The landscape was monotonous with its endless gigantic forests. Though distinctly colder, little snow was to be seen: swamps and woodlands, but rarely plains. There had been fighting here, the first German military graves. A wooden cross often with a steel helmet and a name. It fell quiet in the wagon. The bitter reality of war had caught up with us!

We passed through some smaller stations – Klinzy, Unetsha, and at night through Bryansk. Suddenly we heard the sound of shooting from the last wagon. We looked back and saw flames erupting from it. Horses were stabled there. Hand grenades were thrown and made a fine explosion. Great excitement! We opened fire too. Shots rang out wildly. We flashed a message to the locomotive driver with a hand lamp. The locomotive driver thought it was an attack by partisans and wouldn't stop. Finally he got the message and the fire in the last wagon was extinguished. What had caused it? A brake had jammed and heated up, and the sparks had ignited the straw. The driver had mistaken this for shooting. The journey continued.

3 November 1941

Orel was our final destination. After a railway journey of nine days the train pulled into the station at 1500hrs. Much destruction to the railway installations and in the town. The infantryman in each of us was now wide awake, and we sent out scouting parties to 'organize'. After a short while they returned with hens and pigeons. These were cooked or roasted on our stove. We spent that that night in our wagons, but for the first time we had to post two sentries.

4 November 1941

In the morning there was an air raid on the station. Had the Russians been tipped off? Our Flak drove off the aircraft, but three bombs fell near a bridge and killed a senior paymaster sergeant. A soldier's death!

5 November 1941

We left the train and went to a large church which had been taken over as quarters for the whole battalion. We made it as 'cosy' as possible. At night I was one of the two sentries. It was damned cold! We watched over 'our' church in the moonlight under a starry sky. Here I had time to think of home.

6 November 1941

After coffee and breakfast we set off at 0500hrs on the long march to the Front. Initially we walked into a cold wind along the Rollbahn.[1] Another 55km like this? An endless stream of traffic, mainly lorries, was heading to the Front along the Rollbahn with ammunition, provisions and other necessities: passing in the opposite direction came streams of empty lorries returning from the Front with 'the empties' and wounded. The first of our men seized the opportunity to steal a ride aboard lorries and towing vehicles. In the end I jumped on a lorry. I stretched out high up on top of hard ammunition boxes close under the tarpaulin. A bitter wind blew though it but better an uncomfortable ride than a long walk!

7 November 1941

In the evening we reached Mzensk and were billeted in a Russian house. The rest arrived later that evening. We finished off our rations and then each man stretched out, dead tired, wrapped in a blanket. In the morning we resumed our march to the small town of Tchern. During this march on the Rollbahn I kept an eye open from early on for the chance of a ride, but initially we had to 'march correctly'. Finally I grabbed the tailboard of a lorry and clung on for almost 30km. There were deep shell holes along this highway and I was often in danger of falling off. My hands grew ice cold and numb. I soon realized that the green issue gloves with fingers (as opposed to mittens) were pretty useless in the Russian winter. At Tchern we found a warm billet but had to wait for the field kitchen to catch up with us. As we stood in a line with our mess tin and implements, suddenly three or four Russian bombers came roaring at a right angle across the Rollbahn, dropping bombs and firing their MGs. We all got to cover in a flash, a few brave types fired at the bombers with their pistols. That was our first contact with the enemy!

8 November 1941

Today we were back on the road! As there were no lorries about, we loaded our packs on a horse-drawn cart and followed behind on foot. Gradually this endless plodding got on our nerves. Hadn't they promised us at Neuruppin: 'You will be fully motorized out there.' And from Orel we had not seen any vehicles from our regiment! The infantry grumbled but kept plodding. After 25km we made our quarters in a smouldering factory just off the Rollbahn. Some of the old senior privates returning to the Front from convalescence slaughtered a sheep. They had just finished cutting it up, and as I was going back to the factory with six full mess tins a Russian bomber came over and dropped a stick of bombs on the factory. I threw myself down flat and luckily the mess tins landed upright. The contents tasted all the better for the fright. Then we laid straw on the floor of a more-or-less intact room and slept. During the night Ivan flew over the Rollbahn several times and made a racket.

9 November 1941

Today was the last leg of the march: where it finished, vehicles from the regiment would take us the rest of the way. We marched for hours with full packs along the icy Rollbahn. At last we saw the large onion-shaped dome of a defunct Russian Orthodox church on the horizon. A rugged, partially ruined paved road led to the town of Plavsk, where a long queue of Opel-Blitz lorries bearing the tactical sign of our regiment – the steel helmet – stood waiting. When twenty of us were sitting up in a lorry it drove off. A hot meal was served by the field kitchen on a railway embankment in the cold wind. We noticed that night fell here at 1600hrs. We drove on until reaching a village for the night. The air was thick in our allotted Russian hut. It would serve no useful purpose to describe the misery in these dwellings. First one has to get used to it, but in any case we preferred a stink to high heaven to freezing in the open air and were soon asleep.

10 November 1941

Sunrise was at 0600hrs. We had to parade and were divided up into battalions and companies. We stood in a snow-covered field in an open rectangle. The officer leading the battalion this far made his report to the Regimental Commander, Oberst Hörnlein, who then walked along the front rank eyeing his new heroes before greeting us. As a mortar gunner I went to IV Platoon, 8 Company/II Battalion of the 'Reinforced Infantry Regiment *Grossdeutschland* (mot.)'. 8 Company was an MGK (Machine-Gun Company) with one platoon of 'heavy mortars' (four 8cm mortars).

We returned to our quarters in the village. The man of the house (the Pan or Opa) prepared tea for us in the samovar while 'Matka' his wife made us baked potatoes. I went to bed every evening in the 'hope' of having lice next morning to justify a change of billet but I remained lice-free. I hadn't yet learned the ropes.

11 November 1941

In our company lorries we rolled to the battalion command post where the Commanding Officer, Major Greim, received us. 'You should be glad and happy to have come to us here at II Battalion. Wherever we are, there's always something going on! I wish you tough days of heavy fighting and proud victories!' Then the loud triple 'Hurrah!' echoed across the parade ground. Suddenly we heard a buzzing in the air and an Ilyushin 2 ground-attack aircraft made a shaky turn above us. We could see the Soviet red star on the wings clearly! We dispersed rapidly to cover: a 2cm Flak let him have a few rounds as he turned away but unfortunately did not score a hit. Then the 8 Company lorries drove over snow-covered tracks to the Rollbahn, us newcomers reporting to our company commander Oberleutnant Schneider in a village called Vorobianka. II Battalion would have a few days' rest here to allow the replacements from Neuruppin to fit in. Then we were released to our platoons and groups.

Our platoon commander Oberfeldwebel Puls greeted us before giving us sound advice for our first mission. He made a very good impression on me, calmness personified.

IV Platoon was made up as follows:

	1 Group, 1 Mortars	**1 Group, 2 Mortars**
Group leader:	Unteroffizier Dittmann	
Troop leader:	Obergefreiter Bunge	Obergefreiter Mochen
Mortar leader:	Obergefreiter Wohner	Obergefreiter Weidner
Gunner 1:	Obergefreiter Johne	Gefreiter Barth
Gunner 2:	Gefreiter Leis	Gefreiter Rieger
Ammunition handlers:	Grenadier Keilhauer	Grenadier Portun
	Grenadier Schlossbauer	Grenadier Fischer
	Grenadier Rehfeldt	Grenadier Ladebeck
Messenger:	Gefreiter Monk	Gefreiter Monk[2]

The Group sat around a table and we newcomers had to introduce ourselves. One of our number, a baker by trade, made some pancakes for us on the Russian stove, later some schnapps arrived and we had a 'platoon evening'. I supplied the music on my mouth organ. The company commander also paid us a visit. When it ended we were all in the best of spirits! I had the 2300hrs–0100hrs sentry duty with the commander. The night was cold and dark, the wind sweeping icy cold across the Rollbahn. I wore a thick lambskin greatcoat. Ivan dropped a few bombs nearby. I was happy to be relieved at 0100hrs.

12 November 1941

This morning we had another talk with our platoon leader. In these short days resting close behind the Front we made contact with the experienced 'old hands', asking them everything which we thought would be of interest in the future. How to behave in battle? What kind of defences are there out there, infantry trenches or one-man foxholes? It was quickly made clear to us that in the front line it was quite different to what we had imagined previously.

In the evening the 'Platoon Chronicle' of the mortar platoon was read out to us. We were given the field post number and wrote our first lines home. Sender: Grenadier Hans Rehfeldt, field post number 03744. Now my people at home would know that I had arrived safely, but when would the letter arrive?

13 November 1941

'Make ready!' Was this it? We packed up swiftly, loaded our things and quickly reported ourselves 'ready to march!'. We were enthusiastic, everything good so far, but now we had to camouflage our steel helmets white. We had no paint, and made do with Matka's white cloths or curtains. While waiting for the order to leave, our motorcycle messenger Gefreiter Monk arrived with the order, 'Return to billets, we're staying here.' We reoccupied our previous billet, allocated the sentries and spent another 'peacetime' night. When I was on sentry duty I heard artillery fire rolling and thundering from Tula. I could even hear the chatter of MGs, the German and Russian types being distinguishable by their different rates of fire. The skies were often lit up brightly by star shell: the German illumination was very bright, the Russian lightly tinged.

14 November 1941

Today we again had to be ready to move out. Everything was loaded up and we prepared ourselves in battle order, which meant that only the absolute essentials were to be carried. Our waistbelts hung heavy with full cartridge pouches, sidearm, entrenching tool (important for survival), haversack with buckled-on eating utensils and field flask. Besides these we carried a carbine, two cases of mortar ammunition with three bombs each, a groundsheet and a woollen blanket. A nice load. At midday we had roll call wearing white-painted steel helmets.

15 November 1941

Still at Vorobianka we cleaned weapons and looked to the ammunition. Then we received instruction on how to proceed in winter, protect our weapons and bodies against the cold and so on. After spooning out our mess tins at midday came the order to march. We climbed aboard and after everybody had been reported present the engines were started up and lorry after lorry rolled out to the icy Rollbahn. We sat wrapped in our woollen blankets and stamped our feet to keep them warm. We were heading for Tula. Somewhere along the way we passed a large stuffed bear – a physical embodiment of the tactical sign of a Brandenburg panzer division. Towards evening we reached a small village, the column halted and we had to get out with our equipment and re-pack in readiness to proceed on foot in single file. To our right was a large ironworks destroyed by shellfire. We descended cautiously into a deep and flat gully not far from our position. Now came what I had feared: we novices, unaccustomed to the heavy load, were immediately weighed down. Teeth clenched and gasping for breath, we ran and stumbled forwards into the pitch-black night. We believed it impossible to go much farther like this, but there was no end to it. The NCOs had experience and followed close behind offering encouragement. I couldn't go on! The cases of ammunition, containing six shells with a total weight of 24.5kg, held me back like lead weights. My troop leader relieved me of one case for a while, enabling me to catch up the column. True comradeship! After a long forty-five minutes we reached the position, an isolated house in an orchard on a low hill. We stood outside in the cold bathed in sweat waiting to be ordered inside. To the left of the house was a rectangular pit where we installed our mortar. A second pit had to be dug for the second mortar. Except for two sentries everybody then went inside, made themselves as comfortable as possible, looked for somewhere to sleep and ate the cold rations. Some of our people set up heavy MGs in the rooms facing towards the enemy. When I had sentry duty with Sepp Leis during the night, suddenly I saw how far away Tula was from us. Some 'fireballs' came flying in our direction. 'Machine gun,' I thought and watched with interest. Then I said conversationally to Sepp, 'Look, that's an MG with tracer.' Before he could look round I heard a weird howling and Sepp shouted in horror, 'Man, Stalin organs!' and pulled me down with him into a slit trench. In reply to my astonished question of what he had meant he said merely, 'If they fall here, oh ha!' All of a sudden there rose up behind us a rumbling like a heavy storm. And I saw a sight I had never seen before! Cascades of fire, flashing glaring white, bright red and then glowing, spraying out sparks, next a whole 'wall' of these pyrotechnics pounded the ground. Something like forty-eight of them! Happily only a single broadside!

Sepp explained about the 'Stalin organ'. A lorry carried sixteen of these rockets on launch rails. The rockets were ignited electrically. The strange howl I heard was the rocket engine. We climbed out of the slit trench, looked at the time and woke our relief. We lay down dead tired. The small stone oven had to be kept lit all night, so somebody always had to be awake near it.

16 November 1941

Now for the first time I was a front-line soldier in the most forward outpost a few kilometres from the suburbs of Tula. Our location was Height 216 where we formed a battle group with 6 Company's infantry. Our mortars were to the left of the house, a few metres ahead of us was a nest of 6 Company's light MGs. We liaised on sentry duty. They protected Height 216 ahead and the flanks.

Behind our house was a zig-zag trench for shelter by a forest of fir trees. About 800m east was a railway embankment with the village of Gostevka behind it. The other 8 Company platoons were there. This railway line curved away to join up with another on the route north-east probably to Tula, the second set of tracks running about 600–800m beyond a flat depression to our north. Behind these second tracks lay a village ('A') in No Man's Land on a slight elevation. Flames and black smoke issuing from between its houses registered the occasional hit from enemy projectiles falling short. Our room faced south away from the enemy and in range of the aromas from our field kitchen.

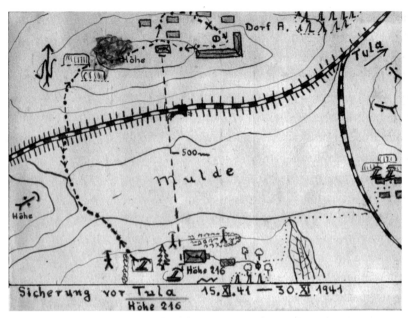

Sketch of the positions near Tula, 30 November 1941. Höhe = height, Dorf = village, Mulde = depression.

17 November 1941

During the night Ivan fired his Stalin organs into our area but we slept through it. Under a sunny clear sky on sentry duty I watched our artillery firing into Tula. The shells flew away above us making a strange sound, their arrival in the city being marked by explosions and mushroom clouds.

Some figures attempted to reach the Russian lines from Village 'A' in No Man's Land north of us. After warning shots they were mown down by our heavy MG and lay like black dots on and behind the railway embankment.

At 1700hrs our position came under heavy artillery and Stalin-organ bombardment, the nearest projectile falling only 3m from our house, shattering most of the windows. We made makeshift repairs with hay and straw but it was damned cold at night. Ivan persisted with nuisance fire throughout the hours of darkness.

18 November 1941

In the morning our artillery provided preparatory fire for an attack by two panzer divisions (each down to one-third of its required strength). Ivan replied and we had to spend two hours from 0600hrs in our trenches. Towards 0800hrs we set out carrying the mortar to scout Village 'A' to our north. We were wary of the stacks of straw on the approach but nothing stirred. The few local inhabitants were in their cellars or holes in the ground. We searched every house but found the village free of enemy troops. Our orders were to round up all men capable of work. While doing this we 'captured' some hens and other useful property. Soon I had five male villagers in tow. One of them spoke to me very heatedly. When I told him in phrasebook Russian that I didn't understand he raised his hand and removed his right eye, holding the glass eye under my nose. Not a reason to be excused labour. We assembled the men of the village and they boarded a number of our lorries which had driven up. The womenfolk appeared with their men's documents and papers, fearful that we were going to shoot them. We explained that they were only wanted for work although we had our suspicions about their choice of living between the front lines. The women could stay. They handed up cabbages, potatoes and bread into the lorries for the journey. We returned to Height 216, where all day 'normal' artillery activity persisted.

19 November 1941

During the night we saw many villages burning around Tula. Scorched earth? Fires set by Ivan to deny us shelter as we advanced? At midday a strong reconnaissance party went to Village 'A'. As we reached the first houses, we saw Russian troops running at the other end. We fired nine mortar bombs with good effect. The light MG also fired, forcing them to crawl through the snow. We searched the houses again thoroughly. When we requested kerosene for our lamps, the womenfolk began to sob pitifully, believing we were going to burn down their houses. We returned to Height 216 after occupying the village for three hours. In the afternoon I took two buckets to the draw-well, about 50m from the house in the orchard, drew the water using the long wooden arm, but then heard artillery fire coming from the north and almost at once the nearest shells exploded a bare 10m from where I lay, throwing up frozen clumps of earth while splinters whizzed over me. 'A soldier must be lucky' as the saying goes, and I rose unharmed from where I lay in the snow. 'Where the hell have you come from?' my comrades asked as they appeared from cover.

In the evening we had pancakes again. During the night Ivan fired in our direction with his Stalin organs but the rockets fell far to our rear as a warning that he had the range. To the north, the villages around Tula were still burning: Ivan's 'scorched earth'.

20 November 1941

The fiery glare of the burning villages lit up the whole foreground. The horizon glowed red. Artillery nuisance fire continued all day and night. Ivan sent a scouting party up to the railway embankment but they retreated under heavy fire. Our supply vehicles drove up to a point behind the woodland, from where ammunition and rations were brought to us in groundsheets. A minor artillery duel went on all day, but did not disturb us.

21 November 1941

This morning Ivan unleashed a heavy artillery bombardment on Village 'A' behind the railway embankment. Probably the villagers, mostly womenfolk, had made their presence too obvious and Ivan thought it was us. I was on sentry duty with the light MG gunner when the barrage began. The splinters actually whizzed back to our position! As quickly as it began it ended. The smoke cleared but some of the village houses were still in flames when night fell. Because the nights were very dark we decided to set fire to a large haystack to give us a better view over the front of our position. A small scouting party ventured to the collective farm and soon a stack flamed up. When the party returned, the Unteroffizier reported that he had seen Russians at the farm: we should take care. During the night both sides sent up flares. Towards midnight a weak enemy force reached the railway embankment, opening up on us with sub-machine guns and rifles. A flare went up but we already knew by the whistling and chirping of their bullets where they were. Once our heavy MGs got warmed up Ivan withdrew and the rest of the night passed peacefully. We needed to know if Village 'A' was occupied by the enemy and a strong patrol was sent to reconnoitre. We remained on our hill in readiness, waiting for the agreed flare, but all remained quiet. During the night only a small Russian scouting party had been in the village. After a house search our patrol returned, though not empty-handed, having 'organized' a whole sheep, hens, salt and, importantly, petroleum for our miserable lamps. At midday the sheep was ceremoniously slaughtered behind the house. I watched how it was done. After dinner, hunger appeased and satisfied, we slept soundly.

23 November 1941

Today was Sunday but no let-up from Ivan. A clear, bright day and standing watch I saw how the sun, low on the horizon, threw long shadows on the white glistening surface of snow. The last of its rays fell on the western edge of Tula, about 3–4km north-east of us. The small, miserable shacks in the suburbs, workers' settlements? Behind them tall buildings with many rows of windows, factories, the railway station with its large tanker compound – in good light everything could be seen clearly. I studied it all with binoculars. Some distance behind the city was a tall 'monument'. Three tall narrow 'towers', the central one higher than the other two. What that was exactly we never discovered. Often it disappeared into the mist, and then the 'tower' could be seen again clearly.[3]

Two Me 109s came from the west over the Rollbahn towards Tula, made a broad elegant turn before reaching the city and then roared off. The Russian anti-aircraft guns fired like crazy. At midday a powerful Luftwaffe bomber formation with fighter protection arrived. The growling thunder of bomb explosions, great plumes of smoke rising up, the city on fire at various locations. A fuel compound must have been hit on the city outskirts, with bright yellow flames, and thick black smoke came drifting towards us. The bombing raid lasted until late afternoon. Our sector of the Front here is very quiet but rumour has it that an attack by ourselves on Tula is in the offing. Right now? In midwinter? We sat cosily around our stove drinking schnapps and telling our life stories. We never laughed so much before!

24 November 1941

Two 6 Company men wanted to go over to Village 'A' – alone – in order to 'organize'. Ordered to wait for the next reconnaissance, they disobeyed and set off armed with sub-machine guns. If they got into difficulties, they would fire a red flare, and we would come to their aid at once. We watched them stamp through the snow and disappear up behind the collective farm. After a short while a red flare went up. The sentries reported hearing shots. A strong assault party consisting of a group from 6 Company led by Leutnant von Bruchhausen and my group with both mortars under Unteroffizier Dittmann set out and at the farm we found the bodies. They had had little chance, walking into an ambush, had time to fire the warning flare but then been shot dead immediately, one through the steel helmet, the other in the chest. The Russians took their weapons and also plundered the bodies, even the *Grossdeutschland* cuff title had been torn off the sleeve of their greatcoats. They were the first dead German soldiers I had seen.

We combed through the village: those left behind, old people, women and children, cowered in fear in their holes or cellars. They could tell us nothing. Our light MGs gave us cover as we took on a Russian heavy MG with the mortars. Our fire was accurate, and two of the enemy gunners ran for it through the snow. Firing at one or two fugitives with a mortar was not the done thing, however. Now, while changing our position, we came under fire from the Russians' own mortars. The rounds fell 20m to our rear. The situation was not in the least favourable and we decided to retire to our hill. Before reaching the railway embankment we received heavy artillery fire from the direction of Tula and were forced to seek cover in the depression. Here we endured long minutes with shells exploding all around us making black holes in the snow, also pinned down by a Russian MG in the woods to our right, its slow fire sending up sprays of snow. Finally I found a spot in the depression out of the line of direct fire. I was bleeding from a wound to my hand, Gottfried Fritsch was hit in the cheek. But we had been lucky! Scarcely had we regained the safety of our hill than a 7.62cm anti-tank gun raked us with fire, but after that things calmed down.

25 November 1941

A Russian light mortar began an accurate fire at our light MG post. They had probably seen it from the village. Soon their artillery joined in. Unteroffizier Stedtler's group bore the brunt, our mortar teams were training but remained on the alert. In the evening 6 Company group was relieved by new arrivals.

26 November 1941

While the mortar unit stayed put, a scouting party ventured forth again but encountered strong enemy opposition in Village 'A'. After a brief exchange of fire the scouting party came back in accordance with orders. The artillery of both sides maintained nuisance fire. We needed wood for our stove and felled several fir trees for the purpose in the woods behind our position. In the evening they provided a wonderful blaze in the squad-room stove. During the night a Russian scouting party which came up close to our position suffered heavy casualties, the survivors beating a rapid retreat. Greater watchfulness was ordered. These dark nights are very dangerous. It is essential to keep a first-class listening watch.

27 November 1941

Ivan has definitely occupied Village 'A' and seems to be keeping us under permanent observation. No sooner does a reconnaissance party set out for the depression than it comes under artillery fire. In the afternoon we went under cover to the Stedtler group for straw. The men there have burrowed deeply into the haystacks and are protected against the wind. From the observation post they have a telephone line to the fire direction post. A 5cm heavy Pak[4] is stationed there with its towing vehicle ready to go to wherever required. Both sides exchanged artillery fire all day long.

28 November 1941

In the early hours a scouting party went out, but scarcely had they reached the depression than they came under heavy artillery fire. The Russians spotted our every move. Village 'A' north of us between the lines is now infested with Russian troops. We were told this by a Ukrainian defector.

29 November 1941

This morning we were woken by our heavy artillery batteries bombarding Tula. In reply Ivan aimed his artillery at our position but most of his shelling hit the collective farm near Village 'A'. There are no German soldiers here. We hope he keeps it up and starts firing short into the village. Many of his projectiles landed in the depression, from where we heard the splinters whizzing.

30 November 1941

We were cleaning weapons while one mortar team stood at readiness. Suddenly the house shook, the last surviving windowpanes rattled, limestone and clods flew in our faces. 'Take full cover!' We sprinted to the slit trenches wearing our steel helmets. Quite a few of the shells were damned close. A few smashed some trees in the wood, from where splinters flew about our ears.

At midday officers of a unmotorized unit arrived for briefing prior to relieving us in the evening. Only the mortars remained combat-ready while the preparations were made to pull out. To mutual wishes of good luck we left in small groups with intervals between. Ivan noticed this, of course, and soon we came under fire from a rapid-fire 7.62cm anti-tank gun. Most of the shells failed to explode, probably being armour-piercing. The muzzle flash was followed shortly by the shell howling past with a strange sound like 'hoolooloolooo', coming to rest harmlessly somewhere in the terrain. But it was not a pleasant experience! Finally we got to the industrial plant on the Rollbahn, waited only a short time for our lorries, mounted up and off we went, wrapped in woollen blankets and stamping to keep our feet warm, shaken this way and that over rough roads until we came to a railway station and were given quarters.

1 December 1941

We awoke to heavy snow flurries. 'Make ready to leave!' Today we were to travel 80km north-east. The blizzard raging was the fiercest I ever saw. We huddled in our trusty Opel-Blitz. The snow swept in through the chinks and cuts in the tarpaulin, a wall of three or four blankets proving no defence against the cold, our feet ice-cold in the thin leather boots in which we had come from Neuruppin. The lorries struggled forward, then the whole column halted. 'Everybody out – push!' Wheels spinning despite the snow chains, engine howling and finally the vehicle would be in motion again and we would have to run behind to catch up, grasp the rear flap with frozen hands, haul ourselves aboard and hang up the curtain of blankets while wriggling our toes to keep them from freezing. All along the way we passed lorries from our convoy stuck fast, radiators boiling, and then it would be our turn again. We did not complain, for pushing kept us warm, particularly our feet. Finally we saw a village on a ridge but the slope was steep. After much slipping, sliding and pushing, the first lorries proved the ascent was possible. In the dark we searched for quarters, finally discovering an undamaged house with a room large enough to accommodate the passengers of our lorry. After a quick supper, we put straw down and were soon asleep. The family in the upper floor had two small children. They began crying and despite pleas the Matka could not quieten them. Bubi Weidner fired a round from his small pistol into the roof, the plaster flew, silence fell and we all got off to sleep.

2 December 1941

Today we slaughtered a pig. Opa, Matka and the two children got portions: after all, it was their pig. The rest of the day passed cleaning weapons, polishing and washing.

3 December 1941

At 0400hrs we were ordered to move out. Our destination was Dorovyeva, as 'assault reserve'.

4 December 1941

Back on the Rollbahn to Tula we travelled 25km, more time spent pushing than riding. The snow had drifted into great dunes. Suddenly: 'Halt. Everybody out with equipment, prepare for action!' As the ammunition runner I took my two metal cases, bound together tight with a leather strap, each containing three mortar bombs, hung them over my shoulder, grabbed my carbine and left the vehicle. It was already late afternoon as we advanced slowly through knee-high snow towards a wood. The pioneers led, followed by the 2cm Flak guns then our group attached to the infantry company with heavy MGs and two mortars. The terrain ahead was dense woodland and difficult to survey. The Russians had laid mines. Our orders were to tread carefully into the deep footprints of the man ahead, and not step outside the yellow tape our pioneers had laid. Beyond the wood was the village of Kolodesnaya where our motorcycle company had been surprised a few days before and suffered heavy losses. We advanced with mixed feelings, eyes watchful. On our flanks we could hear the infantry company moving forward through the undergrowth. Otherwise it was dead quiet. Suddenly from where the village lay came crazy MG and sub-machine gun fire, tracer rounds flitted through the trees close to us and our infantry returned fire. The woods and deep snow absorbed much of the sound. We crawled forward, noses in the snow, looking ahead and to the left. We had no winter uniforms, only our steel helmets were white. In the snow we made a nice target in our green greatcoats. Carbine at the ready, I stretched out on a narrow path. I could hear Ivan firing but could see nothing and so lifted my head to observe. A burst of sub-machine gun fire whistled past my ears. I noticed its direction of origin before returning my nose to the snow. When our 2cm Flak sprayed the wood with explosive rounds I fired a few times with my carbine wildly: Ivan saw me. In order to lie lower, I shovelled the snow away from beneath me with my hands as his bullets splashed into the snow close by. I had placed my two ammunition cases in front of my head as protection: I heard a metallic sound as a bullet went through one of the cases. This was too close for comfort and after hanging my carbine around my neck I took both cases and crawled to my right into a depression for better cover. Ivan now resorted to his mortars and wounded our company leader Oberleutnant Schneider, who had come out with us from Neuruppin, and Feldwebel Ruder fairly seriously. Obergefreiter Zippel was killed. Leutnant Hoffmann took over the company. House-to-house fighting and skirmishes in woodlands by night are always dangerous and unfavourable activities. Now our 15cm heavy infantry gun joined the battle not far to our rear. A round roared over our heads, we heard the impact, the first houses blazed yellowish-red! Kolodesnaya village lay between 150 and 200m beyond the wood. This would warm up Ivan. We were still on our stomachs, and this was damned cold at minus 20°C. The Russians were firing less regularly and after ninety minutes we occupied the village, eerily and suspiciously quiet. We set up a mortar behind a haystack. Ivan was still firing from the outskirts, however, so it was difficult to know which side of the stack was the safer. There was a pond in the village, frozen over, and upon the ice was positioned a sledge to which an almost naked body had been bound. The soldier had been most cruelly mutilated and was identified as a *Grossdeutschland* comrade of the motorcycle company. Seven Russian soldiers were discovered in hiding. These men were shot dead immediately for complicity in the atrocity. Later, on sentry duty near our heavy MG and staring into the darkness, I saw two Russians crawling away. The MG jammed after the first round and both Russians made it to the woods but ran into a 6 Company patrol who shot them dead. *C'est la guerre.*

Some of our infantry had excavated deep hollows into the haystacks for protection against wind and cold. I made my own nest in a trench protected against the wind with a floor of hay and straw. I pulled the woollen blanket over my head, placed one hand between my legs and the other under an armpit. Warm hands could mean the difference between life and death when suddenly called upon to handle a carbine, MG or mortar. Because of the intense cold, sentry duty was limited to thirty minutes or an hour. Every half hour off-duty men sleeping were awoken so as not to freeze to death, and then we had to mark time swinging our arms before being allowed to return to a now freezing-cold bed in the ground. The moment came when I had no feeling in my feet after the kindly half-hourly boot in the ribs woke me, and marking time was very painful. Finally I got the feeling back in my toes but I was frozen through and went into a burning house to warm up. I realized how serious it could be for a person if the sentry forgot to wake him. Gottfried Fritsch had not been woken once or twice because it wasn't known where he had his spot. He had first-degree frostbite of the feet. Russians wore quilted flock-wool jackets and similar trousers, fur boots made watertight with galoshes while we had mostly narrow metal-studded boots. We had no winter uniforms because the war in the East was supposed to be over by Christmas. The Wehrmacht was not prepared for a winter war in Russia! Yet it still was not winter even though night fell at 1600hrs and lasted until 0700hrs, and the temperature was minus 30°C with an icy easterly wind often accompanied by a blizzard. Even panzer crews had no heating and used a blowlamp to warm their steel boxes. Poor Germany! To keep panzers and assault guns mobile, they often kept the motors running for long periods in the night.

At night time four SP assault guns came up with some 3.7cm Pak known as 'door knockers' because they couldn't penetrate the T-34 armour. Two more Flak guns and two armoured reconnaissance vehicles reinforced our unit. At daylight the order came to prepare to move. Tula had to be taken. Our first attempt to capture the town had failed, now we were going to try an encirclement. To do this, our 5 Company had to reach Kashira and Ryasa, south of Moscow and east of Tula.

5 December 1941

Our assault guns rolled out, Flak and tractors towing Pak following, all ploughing through the snow. Our battalion commander Major Greim led the way in his personal motor car. Only 100m after leaving Kolodesnaya the leading assault gun slipped off the icy Rollbahn. The panzers' tracks were unsuitable for winter. Our column passed by while the other two assault guns attempted to drag the leader back on the road. Veering into woodland, we followed a narrow track northwards. The order came down from above, 'Take no prisoners!' This was against international law, but the Russians were not signatories to the Hague Conventions, and so their troops were outlaws. The reason was the body of the *Grossdeutschland* comrade found on the village pond at Kolodesnaya, tied to a sledge, his tongue cut out and his skull smashed in. Who knows what other excesses he had to suffer at their hands before dying? And he was not by any means the first German soldier to have been found cruelly mutilated. Nobody knew who had issued the order.

In the woods, we came across burned-out Russian lorries, mangled guns and abandoned equipment. In the driver's compartment of one lorry the charred body of the driver, consumed by flames, remained upright at the steering column. Inwardly we wished all Bolshevists the same fate. That is what war does to people. Suddenly our spearhead halted and we tumbled out into the trees for cover. Our heavy MGs were set up: white-clad soldiers on sleds were coming towards us. They revealed themselves as German soldiers mopping

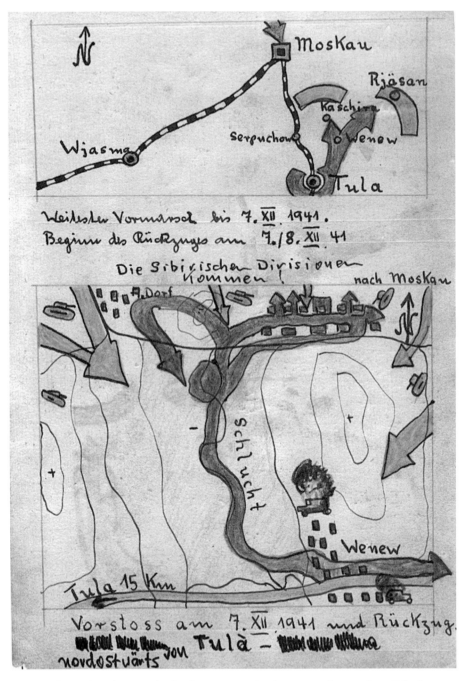

Map by the author showing the farthest points of advance north-west from Tula for Kashira-Ryasa towards Moscow up to 7 December 1941.

up Russian stragglers. From them we learned that the encirclement of Tula was complete except for the railway line and the Rollbahn to Moscow. Our convoy resumed and after a dozen kilometres arrived at a village occupied by 3 or 4 Panzer Division with very few tanks. The panzer men warned us that Ivan often bombarded the village ahead with artillery and anti-tank fire. We crossed a flat elevation to avoid it, our lorries clearly visible despite the white camouflage, and saw the village to our left; we entered it. By the map we were north-east of Tula. From here we could see the strange monument with one tall and two short towers first noticed from our Height 216 south of Tula. Now it was distinct and large, about 8km away. As warned, now we received anti-tank rounds, mortar and rifle fire which convinced us to go through a gorge to the small town of Venev. Here we continued to receive random aimless fire, so we only bothered to take cover if an aircraft flew over. Our task now was to secure the Tula–Venev road.

6 December 1941

To conserve effort and energy, this morning we built a sled big enough for eight cases each containing three mortar bombs (twenty-four rounds in all). Russian tanks had attacked a village named Dedilov. We reached it through a long, deep gorge. Dedilov was the farthest we penetrated towards Kashira and Ryasa, our target. Once our mortars were set up they fired at everything that looked like the enemy. Returning to the mortar towing a full sled, I was lucky to escape harm when a Russian shell exploded a few metres behind me in the tortuous gorge. Towards evening it grew quieter. We had quarters behind a high brick-built storage building. Our artillery spotter was in the roof. As a result of raiding to make up for no rations arriving, we feasted on local chicken and jacket potatoes.

Notes

1. A Rollbahn bore no resemblance to a German Autobahn. It could be anything from an unconsolidated track, created cross-country by frequent use by motor vehicles, to a proper asphalted highway. Depending on their condition, the officially recognized large Rollbahns were designated from I to V and higher. (TN)

2. Upon entry into the British Army, a soldier is at once a 'Private'. The German equivalent was or is 'Grenadier' or 'Gunner' etc. The rank of 'Gefreiter' indicated a trained private soldier with some time served who had shown himself worthy to be entrusted with some authority although not having the status of NCO which attaches to the rank of a British Lance Corporal. The next rank up was 'Obergefreiter', on a par with Lance Corporal as evidenced by lace on the jacket collar, but still not of NCO status. The lowest NCO rank in the German Army was 'Unteroffizier' (Corporal) for which the candidate had to successfully pass the appropriate training. The next *Grossdeutschland* NCO ranks up were 'Feldwebel' (Sergeant), 'Oberfeldwebel' (Staff Sergeant), 'Stabsfeldwebel' (Warrant Officer II) and 'Hauptfeldwebel' (CSM, Warrant Officer I, also known as *Spiess*). (TN)

3. The monument seen by the author here, and again on 5 December, was possibly, though not necessarily, part of the Tula Kremlin, a stone fortress built to protect the two cathedrals it surrounds, now a major tourist attraction. (TN)

4. Pak = Panzerabwehrkanone, German anti-tank gun. Flak = Flugzeugabwehr-kanone, German anti-aircraft gun. (TN)

Back and front of the author's Deutsche Jungvolk membership card.

Inside pages of the author's Deutsche Jungvolk membership card.

Inside pages of the author's Deutsche Jungvolk membership card.

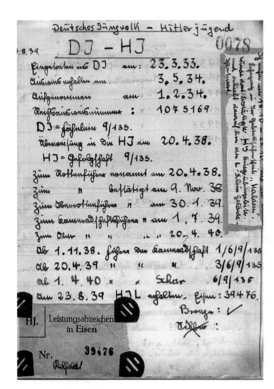

The author's Hitler Youth membership periods neatly listed.

Hans Rehfeldt as a 17-year-old schoolboy in 1940.

The provincial Waldmannshausen boarding school attended by the author.

Lessons were held in the open air as often as possible.

A biology lesson in the meadow.

Roll call in the courtyard of the boarding school before returning home.

The Deutsche Jungvolk area leader school at Haldem, October 1939.

Dr Reinert, one of the author's teachers at Jahn secondary school, in 1940. On the wall instructions to be followed in case of an air raid.

The famous Möhne Dam destroyed in the Dambusters Raid, 1943.

NSDAP. / Hitler-Jugend
Gebiet Westfalen (9)

Münster i. Westf., am .....25.10.1939..... 194......
Diepenbrockstraße 30

K-Übungsleiter-Ausweis Nr. .....50..... /9

Der   Jg. ~~Kurt~~ **Hans** Heinz R e h f e l d t

hat vom .....15.10..... bis .....25.10.1939..... am K-Übungsleiter-Lehrgang

in ..... H a l d e m ..... teilgenommen, die Prüfung als K-Übungsleiter

mit .....gut..... bestanden und kann in der Kriegsausbildung der

Hitler-Jugend im Schieß- und Geländedienst eingesetzt werden. Er ist abnahmeberechtigt für die

Bedingungen im Schießen und Geländedienst zum HJ.-Leistungsabzeichen innerhalb der K-Ausbildung.

Der Lehrgangsleiter: Der K-Gebietsführer:

D 8 / 119 5. 40 Idein

Certificate awarded to Hans Rehfeldt as Exercise Leader authorizing him to instruct
Hitler Youth members in shooting and fieldcraft.

Nationalsozialistische Deutsche Arbeiterpartei
Hitler-Jugend, Bann Mark (135)

Briefanschrift:
Hagen / Hochstraße 33
Fernsprechnummer 255 15

Bankkonto:
Nr. 4921 Sparkasse der Stadt Hagen

An den

Jg. Hans Rehfeldt

H a g e n.
Mackensenstr. 8

Betr.: Lehrgang an der Gebietsführerschule.

In der Anlage erhälst Du Deinen Stellungsbefehl.

Heil Hitler!

Der Leiter der Personalstelle
des Bannes und Jungbannes 135

(Wolff)
Gefolgschaftsführer.

Anlage:

The NSDAP had ultimate control of the Hitler Youth.

Hans Rehfeldt found this leaflet providing information regarding the *Grossdeutschland* Regiment very interesting. Subtitled 'The Regiment of Lifeguards of the German People', the text reads: 'No doubt you have seen the soldiers, NCOs and officers who wear on their shoulder straps the entwined initials "GD" and on the sleeve of the field-grey uniform jacket the black cuff title with the word *Grossdeutschland* embroidered on it in silver lettering. They belong to the "Leibregiment des deutschen Volkes", the Infantry Regiment *Grossdeutschland*. This fully motorized regiment is composed purely of volunteers, and besides heavy and the heaviest infantry weapons has its own artillery, its own pioneers and all other weaponry normally found at divisional level. It is a special

honour and distinction to be able to serve with this regiment. The Führer has stipulated that the peacetime garrison will be the Reich capital, where the regiment will carry out honour guard and security duties, and represent the German Wehrmacht and Army on ceremonial occasions at special locations. The soldiers of this regiment, which distinguished itself particularly on the field of battle during the campaign in the West and in the heavy and successful struggles against the Bolshevists in the campaign in the East, are called "grenadiers". The grenadiers of the Leibregiment are all of German stock and originate from all political districts, and thus the regiment is quintessentially a symbol of the concentrated soldierly might of the Greater German Reich forged by the Führer. The man who wishes to become a grenadier, pioneer, panzer gunner or artilleryman with the Leibregiment must be especially keen and spirited, aged 17 to 22, at least 1.7m tall [5ft 6in] and willing to sign on for a twelve-year term as an applicant for the career of NCO. What German young man would not want to serve in this regiment and in its ranks face the enemy? It is open to everybody who joins the Army as a volunteer and can meet the above-stated conditions!'

19. VIII. 1940.

Mein freund Hans.

"Einjähriger" d.h. er blieb nicht bis zum Abitur.

Zuerst Arbeitsdienst, dann Wehrmacht

Caumont - Nordfrankreich 18. VII. 40.

A schoolfriend, Hans Salzmann, volunteered for a one-year term with the Reich Work Service (RAD), leaving school before the final exams (Abitur), then joined the Wehrmacht and fell in France, 1940.

Hans Salzmann, indicated by an 'x', with motorcycle messenger colleagues, 1940.

Hans Salzmann on a BMW R-12 combination of a motorcycle platoon.

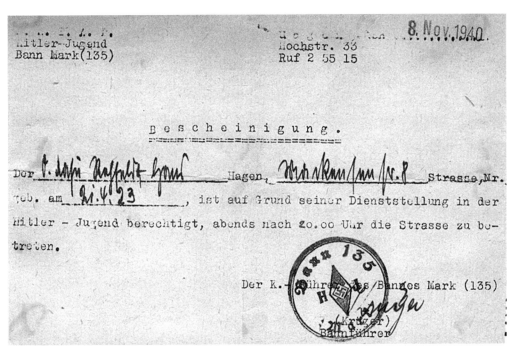

Hitler-Jugend
Bann Mark (135)

Hochstr. 33
Ruf 2 55 15

B e s c h e i n i g u n g.

Der .... Hagen, ... Strasse,Nr.
geb. am .... , ist auf Grund seiner Dienststellung in der
Hitler - Jugend berechtigt, abends nach 20.oo Uhr die Strasse zu be-
treten.

Der K.-Führer des Bannes Mark (135)

(Krüger)
Bannführer

In 1940 a nightly curfew was imposed from 2000 hrs. This pass authorized the author to be on the streets after that hour by virtue of his service in the Hitler Youth.

The author with his schoolfriend Günther Liedtke in 1940.

Gültig vom 12. 2. — 10. 3. 1940

Reichsbrotkarte

EA: Hagen

Name: Hans Rehfeldt
Wohnort: Hagen
Straße: Mackensen 8
Nicht übertragbar! Sorgfältig aufbewahren!
Ohne Namenseintragung ungültig!

Part of a bread ration card issued to the author at Hagen in 1940.

Volksgenossen!

Macht die Straßen frei, wenn feindliche Flugzeuge in der Luft sind. Jede Neugier rächt sich bitter!

Um Euch vor dem Abwurf feindlicher Bomben zu schützen, muß die Flak schießen. Dabei können stets Geschoßsplitter und auch größere Teile herunterfallen und Euch auf den Straßen gefährden.

Also: Herunter von den Straßen und hinein in die Luftschutzräume!

Der Oberbürgermeister
als Ortspolizeibehörde.
Vetter.

From 1940 British bomber formations carried out occasional attacks on Germany. This interesting leaflet issued by Oberbürgermeister Vetter acting for the local police authority reads: 'German Citizens! Clear the streets when enemy aircraft are around. Curiosity can have a bitter outcome! In order to protect you against bombs being dropped, the Flak artillery has to fire. This can result in shell splinters and other large fragments falling and putting you in danger on the streets. Therefore: Get off the streets and into the air-raid shelters!'

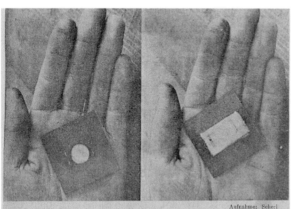

Aufnahme: Scherl

Ein besonders gemeines Kampfmittel der britischen Luftpiraten

Seit dem 11. August wurden zunächst vereinzelt und dann in ungeheuren Mengen von den britischen Luftpiraten sogenannte Brandplättchen während ihrer feigen Nachtflüge über Deutschland über weite Strecken unseres Landes verstreut. Die Plättchen, die in unser Bild zeigt, bestehen aus Zelluloid und tragen in der Mitte eine Brandpille, die in Brandwatte eingepackt ist. Die Plättchen fangen unter der Einwirkung des Sauerstoffs der Luft, auch unter Einwirkung der Sonnenbestrahlung Feuer und geben eine Stichflamme von etwa 1 m Höhe. Hier handelt es sich um ein besonders gemeines Kampfmittel, denn zur Schädigung militärischer Ziele sind diese Brandplättchen völlig ungeeignet. Sie haben lediglich den Zweck, Bauernhäuser, Scheunen, erntereife Felder und Forsten in Brand zu setzen. — Unser Bild zeigt, Brandplättchen, die die britischen Luftpiraten abwarfen.

All kinds of weird weaponry was used early on to cause harm to German non-military personnel. This newspaper article headlined 'A dirty lowdown weapon dropped by the English air pirates' reads: 'Since 11 August, during their cowardly night flights over Germany over long stretches of our country, at first isolated and then large formations of British air pirates scattered so-called fire tablets. The tablets, shown in our pictures, are of celluloid with a fire pill at their centre in cotton packing. The devices catch fire on contact with oxygen in the air or in the rays of the sun and give off a stab of flame about 1m long. This is a dirty lowdown weapon because it is unsuitable for causing damage to military targets. Their only purpose is to set fire to farmhouses, barns, fields ready for harvest and forests. Our picture shows the fire-pills dropped by the British air pirates.'

Der Oberbürgermeister
als Ortspolizeibehörde

Hagen, den 20. 9. 1940.

Anmeldebescheinigung

Der Dienstpflichtige **Hans-Heinz R e h f e l d t .**
(Vor- u. Familienname)

geboren am **21.4.23** zu **H a g e n**
(Tag, Monat, Jahr) (Ort, Kreis, Regierungsbezirk)

wohnhaft zu **Hagen,Mackensenstrasse 8 bei den Eltern.**
(Ort, Straße, Hausnummer, Untermieter bei)

hat sich heute zur Anlegung des Wehrstammblattes angemeldet.

Hagen, den 20. 9. 1940.

(Stempel)

Die polizeiliche Meldebehörde
(Meldestelle)
5.Polizei-Revier.
I.A.

Bestimmungen auf der Rückseite beachten !

Polizei-Meister.

Certificate confirming that the author reported to the police authority on 20 September 1940 to register his basic military record sheet.

Muster 4

Wehrbezirkskommando Hagen
(Einberufende Dienststelle)

Hagen 7. 10. 1940
(Ort) (Tag)

Aufforderung

Sie werden hiermit aufgefordert, sich am **9. Okt.** 1940 um **7 45** Uhr
(Tag, Monat, Jahr)

bei **Wehrbezirkskommando Hagen** in **Lattow=Vorbenkstr. 9**
(Dienststelle) (Ort, Straße, Gebäude)

zur **ärztl. Untersuchung** einzufinden.
(Zweck der Aufforderung)

Diese Aufforderung ist mitzubringen und bei der (de **Wehrbezirkskommando Hagen** (Dienststelle)
abzugeben. Den Ausweis zur Erlangung von Wehrmachtfahrkarten für die Rückfahrt erhalten Sie nach Ausstellung wieder zurück *).
Die Kosten für die Wehrmachtfahrkarte(n) — werden Ihnen gegen Vorlage der Fahrkarte für die Hinfahrt erstattet *) — haben Sie selbst zu tragen *).

(Dienststempel)

*) Nichtzutreffendes ist zu streichen. (Unterschrift des Kommandeurs der einberufenden Dienststelle)

Order to report to military district centre (WBK) at Hagen on 9 October 1940 for a medical.

Der Rekrut von 1944

Die vormilitärische Ausbildung der westfälischen Hitler-Jugend, ihr Sinn und ihr praktischer Wert

(Von unserem Schriftleiter, Gefolgschaftsführer Werner J. Bayer)

Eine so gut getarnte Stellung würde se...

Die Kirche, die südlich zum Hannoverschen Berg führenden Feldwege. Hoet ist auf der...

A newspaper article from 1940 imagining the future of the recruit of 1944. Events did not unfold as predicted.

Wehrbezirkskommando

Hagen Nr./Bez.   Hagen 16. April 1941

(Einberufende Dienststelle)   (Ort)   (Tag)

Aufforderung

Sie werden hiermit aufgefordert, sich am 18. 4. 1941 um 8–12 Uhr

(Tag, Monat, Jahr)

bei **Wehrbezirkskommando Hagen** in **Hagen**

(Dienststelle)   (Ort, Straße, Gebäude)

zur _Besprechung_ einzufinden.

(Zweck der Aufforderung)

Diese Aufforderung ist mitzubringen und bei der (dem) _mit Nachgab_

(Dienststelle)

abzugeben. Den Ausweis zur Erlangung von Wehrmachtfahrkarten für die Rückfahrt erhalten Sie nach Ausstellung wieder zurück *). Die Kosten für die Wehrmachtfahrkarte(n) — werden Ihnen gegen Vorlage der Fahrkarte für die Hinfahrt erstattet *) — haben Sie selbst zu tragen *).

(Dienststelle)

*) Nichtzutreffendes ist zu streichen.

(Unterschrift des Kommandeurs der einberufenden Dienststelle)

Oberstleutnant

Order to report to military district centre (WBK) at Hagen on 18 April 1941 (documents required illegible).

A covering letter advising of an enclosed acceptance docket to be taken within four days, together with two photographs signed on the back, to the author's competent military district centre at Hagen, call-up date expected by or before 15 July 1941.

Mounting the guard at the War Memorial in Berlin.

A march through the Brandenburg Gate

One of the entrances to the infantry regiment *Grossdeutschland*'s Berlin-Moabit barracks.

Grenadier Hans Rehfeldt in walking-out uniform with steel helmet.

The walking-out uniform with peaked cap mockingly called the 'Sarasani uniform' (after the Sarasani circus of the time).

The fully motorized regiment *Grossdeutschland* rolling through Berlin.

Berlin 1941: the street lighting has blackout covers, and the Victory Column is protected against bomb damage at its base.

Chapter 2

Retreat in the Bitterest Cold

---

7 December 1941 Dedilov

The Red Army had apparently brought up reinforcements. During the night I heard tanks rolling and shooting for hours. Left of us an anti-tank gun fired, to our right tanks rumbled and fired. Ours or theirs? We assumed wrongly: they were T-34s and 52-ton KVs transferred from Siberia to help defend Tula.

Ivan could see into Dedilov and the descent into the long gorge. He maintained constant mortar fire into it, our safe connection to Venev. During the day horse-drawn sleds brought up ammunition, but since the gorge was not accessible to them they had to proceed along its upper edge where naturally they attracted Russian fire. Therefore the sleds arrived at the gallop, as did a 3.7cm Pak, our only gun able to penetrate armour.

We ammunition carriers had to tow our sled from cover to cover through the gorge. Pausing for breath, Franz Schlossbauer said he had seen Russians looking down into it from above. We glanced up but saw nothing, fetched the ammunition from Venev and raced back to our mortars at Dedilov. Then on a rise we saw a Russian scout car and two lorries. Our heavy infantry gun at Venev fired at them at once and destroyed all three. Ivan tried to get a fourth lorry away but this too was hit. The troops it was carrying jumped out and ran for it. Our situation was none too rosy. We had no protection on our flanks, too much was being asked of the whole unit, our vehicles were not in the best condition and the panzer division was down to a third of its authorized strength. We also had supply difficulties due to ice and snow on the Rollbahns.

Four of us had to go through the long gorge to Venev for rations. Every hand carried eight mess tins in a wind so icy that pea soup froze solid in them. Our green woollen cap comforters worn round the neck and over the face froze solid over our mouths. Coming out of the gorge into the village street at Dedilov, we heard some shots and cries but after a pause continued to our quarters. The pea soup had to be thawed out: the bread was frozen through. Our messenger arrived. Two signallers who had gone into the gorge to check the telephone line had been bayoneted and then shot dead when they cried out. We four ration-carriers had passed through the same spot only minutes before. Another lucky escape.

In the evening the order came to evacuate Dedilov. The encirclement of Tula, which was almost complete, was being abandoned and we were to embark on a retreat of whose horrors we had no inkling, and which would last until Christmas.

8 December 1941

In silence, the retreat began at 0500hrs. Leaving behind a token security squad, we looked like mountain troops, our gear strapped to six horses, the dismantled mortars and ammunition on sleds. Hands deep in pockets, carbines slung across our backs, cursing the bitter cold ('Fully motorized, ha ha!'), we plodded along the gorge. At Venev we had to wait for our lorries. Some of the drivers were making desperate efforts with petrol and rags ablaze in tin cans placed beneath the chassis to warm the engine and the oil. Regimental commander Oberst Hörnlein and battalion commander Major Greim issued their orders. Everything must proceed with great haste. Vehicles which refused to start and could not be towed must be blown up by placing a hand grenade behind the radiator. Many drivers were close to tears as their vehicles were sacrificed in this manner and left burning by the roadside. Hörnlein was everywhere, trying to drum up as many lorries as possible. I considered this to be an 'historic moment' for my camera, got up close behind him, he turned and gave me a hard stare. I clicked the button, saluted with my right hand touching the rim of my steel helmet, and then photographed Major Greim as well. Hörnlein growled something and threatened me with his walking stick. My group leader, Unteroffizier Dittmann, grinned: 'Just perfect!' – his catchphrase. Hörnlein did not like being photographed. Probably I should have asked his permission first. Frantic activity reigned. Finally every vehicle capable of being made mobile got away. Those drivers and soldiers made 'homeless' were shared out among the other vehicles. Thus there were twenty of us in our good old Opel-Blitz. A long convoy of grey lorries whitened with chalk, Flak guns and fully tracked assault guns made its way through the snow. Every village through which we passed we burned to the ground to deny the Russians warm shelter. Often whole houses were blown up. Black clouds of smoke drifted across the grey-white steppe. We demolished large collective farms, the debris from the explosions sometimes flying about our ears as we cursed our way through the villages. Scorched earth! The Russians themselves had invented the term! Burning villages, abandoned vehicles, other remnants and wreckage littered the route of the retreat. We saw dead Russians lying in the snow, the hard-frozen earth making burial impossible. A hero's death? The icy wind would soon cover them with snow. What do people count for in Russia? That was the question in the past and now – will it still be so in 100 years' time? We rolled on all day and night. Huddled tightly together in woollen blankets in the back of the rattling lorry, we listened with eyes closed to the harmonious working of the engine. It was always an anxious time when the lorry got bogged down and the engine was run furiously fast. If that failed we had to get out and push with the last of our strength. An unbridled blizzard swept the terrain, snow hard as ice lashed the Rollbahn. In the cone of light from the headlamps the driver's visibility was only 5m. The thermometer read minus 48°C, the cold crept slowly but surely through one's clothing and leather boots. First feeling would be lost in the feet: here frostbite would have its beginnings.

The assault guns and a few panzers covered the retreat, Generaloberst Guderian, commanding Panzergruppe II at Tula, had taken the decision personally, fearing that his men would go under. Ivan was hot on our heels. At midday we reached the industrial town of Bolchov with its factories and mineworkings. After preparing quarters, in the late afternoon we went out to reconnoitre. A wrecked T-34 was found on the arterial road, we surveyed the open country and called it a day when darkness fell. At night Ivan's artillery bombarded the town but missed us.

10 December 1941

Though ready to pull out at 0500hrs, we were sent instead to the outskirts to dig in. After spending half an hour with the lorry's pickaxe excavating a hole 15cm deep in the frozen soil the pioneers came with explosives. Below the top metre the ground was softer and steamed in the cold. While enlarging these holes for the mortar position, we heard Ivan's mortars exploding in the distance and also his shrapnel shells, which had an effect like 8.8cm Flak rounds. Later the idea of having this position was given up and we returned to quarters. I had forgotten a pickaxe and had to return alone, head bent low on account of the icy wind. I passed two sentries staring into the night. After some searching I found the tool buried in a snowdrift.

11 December 1941

We pulled out at 1000hrs and drove for nineteen hours through great stretches of woodland, jumping out to push as the occasion demanded. The old routine. The cravings had to be desperate before one would set about smoking. To find the pack of cigarettes inside one's greatcoat, breathe into one's cupped hands as often as possible to keep the circulation going, take a cigarette out and then light it was asking a lot of one's fingers. After a long and unpleasant ride we arrived at our destination, Upkaya Gatiji.

12 December 1941: Upkaya Gatiji

The official bulletin stated that 'German troops in the front sector between Moscow and Tula are pulling back to their prepared winter positions'. Where these were nobody had a clue. Apparently our job here was to cover the withdrawal of 3 and 4 Panzer Divisions. We were billeted in an old hut abandoned by its former occupants. It had a stove for heating. The locality seemed blessedly quiet, no sign of the Red Army.

13 December 1941

That night we stood watch by a high embankment, our 15cm infantry gun behind us. Soon we heard shooting and at daybreak we watched Russian soldiers entering a village about 800m away. Our position was pretty unfavourable. Their village was higher up than ours, enabling them to see down into our position. Separating the two warring groups was the frozen river Upa, across which the Rollbahn went over a large bridge. It was not long before we were exchanging fire: we had to abandon our hut because Ivan could fire into it through the windows and anyway the thatched roof was soon ablaze. Our mortars were in position but being low on ammunition fired only sparingly. Our 7.5cm light infantry gun fought a duel against their light artillery, mortars and anti-tank guns. I was liaison man in the shouting chain from the observation post to the fire-direction post, and from there I relayed orders to the mortars. I was ordered to fetch more ammunition. This meant crossing the Rollbahn to the ammunition lorry. Every time one of us made this run he would come under MG and mortar fire. One had to ignore the firing and sprint back with the ammunition cases and then, gasping for breath, throw oneself down and pass them to the mortar team.

Ivan fired all day long but eased off towards evening. We had to remain alert for he would probably have realized that our village was unprotected on the flanks and he could try to get behind us by going around. Almost all the houses had been totally gutted by fire and our twenty men were accommodated in an underground potato cellar. The light MG guarded the entrance. During the night the pioneers blew up the bridge over the Upa to make it more difficult for heavier Russian units to reach our side.

14 December 1941

At 0500hrs we pulled out without the Russians noticing but stopped 8km farther back in the direction of the retreat. At midday we turned about and drove into a forest along its only road. Behind us our pioneers laid landmines and prepared to blow up trees at the edge of the track to hold up any pursuit. Once out of the woods we masked our faces with the cap comforter and rags to prevent mouths and nostrils freezing. Shortly we came upon a district of burning villages, and headed for the wholesome welcoming warmth of a scorching firestorm hot enough to singe the hair, sparks flying everywhere, houses collapsing. The villagers ran between their burning huts attempting to salvage what they could from the disaster. Their thatched wooden houses burned like tinder. Behind us lay the remains of other smouldering villages. Scorched earth. Loaded down by their sacks and bags, the Opas, Matkas and children set off in despair – to where? Probably they did not know that themselves. They had had their fill of Bolshevism, but neither did they want to be with these invaders who had burned down their villages. The worst thing was this persistent, bitterly cold autumn weather. On a low ridge about 1km behind the wood we dug holes in the snow and built chest-high walls with blocks of ice. They would protect us against the icy wind but not bullets. We remained here with our No. 1 mortar while Unteroffizier Dittmann went to a village a couple of kilometres behind us to our right. In the dark we couldn't see it.

We dug a large hole in the snow and lined it with straw. The mortar was assembled, the ammunition nearby in groundsheets. The temperature was minus 48°C. We huddled together for warmth. After midnight a fierce snowstorm set in. We covered ourselves over with snow but had to get out every thirty minutes so as not to freeze to death. The storm howled, the snow getting through all cracks and inside collars. The sentry could see nothing. At 0030hrs our relief arrived, totally exhausted, and said they had been lucky to find us: everything was grey-white and unrecognizable. Gladly we packed our things and then listened to the description of the way to Dittmann's village. All we had to go by was a telegraph pole which we couldn't find. Instead we came to a depression with a frozen brook. This hadn't been mentioned. We stopped to discuss our situation. Flying snow stung our eyes, the flakes melted on warm eyelids but froze again at once so that the eyes stuck shut. The whole face was covered by a thin layer of ice. I set off alone across the frozen brook and with trembling knees struggled towards some dark shadows which I hoped might be the houses of Dittmann's village. They turned out to be three haystacks: no sign of the village. Returning to the depression I noticed three red points of light. They marked an abandoned car stuck in the snow but beyond it by pure chance we glimpsed the first houses at the edge of the village. Having lugged the mortar along with us we were totally exhausted. The cold had penetrated to the very marrow of our bones! Our boots and feet had become lumps of ice! Patches of frostbite on my legs were suppurating and very painful.

15 December 1941: Village Near Lominzev

It had taken us three hours to cover a couple of kilometres, leaving us only two hours for sleep before we had to return to duty. We took with us a Russian pot and some firewood. By now the storm had cleared and we reached the snow bunker in an hour. The village was visible from there at last. The mortar was assembled, we drew up a sentry roster, rebuilt the wall of ice surrounding the snowhole and then, beneath a roof made of every available blanket and supported by a rifle and bayonet in the centre, made ourselves as cosy as we could. Thin shavings of wood alight in the pot gave more smoke than fire, however, and so with watering eyes we tried to grab what little warmth it provided.

At midday we saw a troop of Russians emerge from the woods a kilometre away and enter a small village near Lominzev where houses were still burning. Later more Russians arrived there in battalion strength. The Red Army was still snapping at our heels. In the afternoon, after being relieved, we reconnoitred the depressions to a triangulated point. When we got back from this rest period, we had to return to the snow bunker. By then it was night and icy cold. When would we be relieved at last? Or, where were the reported 'prepared winter positions'?

When would we finally have some kind of base to get properly warm? The 99 per cent of men who asked, 'When do we get back to the Reich?' were told, 'The only way home is by ambulance.' Relief? Yes, that was talked about. But the events since the last German attacks, the harsh autumn, the difficulties of supply, the failing strength of the attackers, the arrival of the Russian reserves from Siberia: there could be no question of relief.

We had not received rations for three days. We had eaten snow, frozen potatoes from underground stores and apples and gherkins preserved in vinegar. The result was very runny diarrhoea. And who likes to drop his trousers in minus 45°C? The patches of frostbite on my legs grew larger daily and the pus stuck to my underpants. Nothing healed in this cold! Moreover, the sudden appearance of masses of Russians joining the hunt for us, and us too weak to hold them off for long: proud, battle-hardened, victorious *Grossdeutschland* regiment – are we to go to the dogs right here? Of course, we had no knowledge of the situation on the whole front between Moscow and Tula, we saw only a small section of it. Naturally we received no post; ammunition and provisions took priority in transportation!

16–17 December 1941: The Black Day

Unteroffizier Dittmann, bearer of the Iron Cross First Class, was my No. 1 Group Leader in Mortar Platoon, 8 Company/II Battalion/(reinforced) Inf Reg *Grossdeutschland*. He always made a great impression on me by his admirable calm in difficult situations. He predicted once, 'But that black day will come when everything goes wrong and then I shall be done for.' Our squad was still on that low ridge, our only shelter a bitterly cold snow bunker. In recent days the average temperature ranged from minus 30°C to minus 40°C, once even falling to minus 52°C. We put on whatever clothing we could find to maintain body heat, the officers did the same, and we remained a sight to behold until the snow shirts arrived what seemed years later. The outside sentry said to me, 'It's too quiet. I've just got this feeling that tonight it will stink here.' I had scarcely returned to the bunker when I heard shooting, loud cries and the shout 'Mortar! Mortar!' We turned out and replied but were met by silence. Suddenly came the noise of firing from Dittmann's village: tracer flitted here and there, sub-machine guns chattered, flares briefly lit the sky. Then a messenger stumbled up through the snow and gasped the bad news: 'Ivan got around us and attacked the village. You must leave immediately and fall

back to another.' No sooner had he said it than we came under enemy fire
and our MG gunners pulled back swearing: their weapons had literally frozen.
We left behind our blankets, the warm 'fire pot' and other equipment, ran as
fast as the snow allowed to our mortar and, under fire from enemy infantry,
dismantled it. In the dark I couldn't find the carrier for the bipod and grabbed
the barrel instead. In Dittmann's village the houses were burning and we could
hear wild shooting. We were eight mortar crew and about the same number
of MG gunners: we decided to head for III Battalion, which appeared quiet.
Pistols and rifles at the ready, the mortar crew with the heavy equipment on
their backs or the barrel on the shoulder, we trudged forwards over frozen, icy
snow, encouraged by Ivan's vengeful shooting behind us. We could hear it very
distinctly, and the rounds whistling overhead: the Russians nearly always fired
too high from the hip when using the sub-machine gun during an attack. Soon
we were out of range and could proceed somewhat slower. Ahead was a frozen
brook to cross and a slope to ascend before finally we saw the first houses of the
III Battalion village. Our joy was short-lived! Now it was coming under attack.
Flares lit the sky, shells were exploding in the village. If the defenders thought
we were Russians, they might fire first and ask questions afterwards! 'Password?'

In case of doubt it was always '*Grossdeutschland*!'

'OK, come quickly and report yourselves.'

The village was like a beehive with men running in all directions to their battle
positions. The Russians had fired into some houses and haystacks, setting them
on fire. We reported ourselves and were told to assemble in the woods which lay
on a slope beyond the burning houses. While we were at the edge of the village
with weapons at the ready, we saw the Russians coming, suddenly bursting into
their loud, almost animal-like shouts of 'Huuurra!', emboldened by vodka. They
simply ran into our defensive fire from three sides and were mown down by our
MGs. Undeterred, the survivors kept coming! On a damaged bridge an artillery
tractor had stuck fast with a Pak gun in tow. Our infantry was trying to shift
it, but it refused to budge. Near the burning houses the flames were very hot.
Sparks flew, the smoke stung the eyes. We made our way house-to-house to the
end of the village. We learned it was to be abandoned. Meanwhile heavy MGs
were protecting it on all sides. Behind us the village burned, while ahead lay the
slope up to the woods where we were to assemble.

The sight of a dozen of our infantry struggling and panting up to the crest
showed us that it would be a demanding climb. I was just debating with myself

whether to go up with the group since they would be more likely to attract fire than an individual alone when the infantry on the slope came under anti-tank fire. I dived to the left; another shell passed over my head and exploded on the slope. I got up and waded through the snow towards the wood. Our group was now reduced to twelve stragglers: no NCO, no officer, nobody knew where we should go. After a brief discussion we decided to act on our own initiative. I had been stricken with diarrhoea and my underclothes had frozen stiff as a board. My inner thighs burned with the friction. I could not feel my feet. After two hours moving through gorges and cross-country we saw a light and beyond it a Rollbahn. Not all Rollbahns had ever been proper roads. The light came from a wrecked car. 'No villages here!' After several more hours we came to a small village. Papka and Mamka were at home. We needed to rest a little. We posted sentries all round, then I explained my problem to the Mamka whose name was Marusya. My clothing and lower body were indescribably filthy but Marusya was not shy. She grasped my shoulders and said, 'Fritz, war not good, peace is good. At home, Mama and Papa, and girl? Stalin not good nor Hitler.' She had real sympathy for me. Perhaps she had a son at the Front? Once I was clean and dry with her help we decided to pull out at once. We asked the way but could not understand the answer. So we needed to take one of the old men as 'pathfinder'. Now they were all up in arms! Matka thought we would shoot her Pan once we got to where we wanted. We assured her that we would definitely send her Pan home. But Opa must come!

Towards 0600hrs it grew light and we saw a village. Great uncertainty! Who would be in it? We approached with weapons at the ready. Suddenly a figure appeared in a doorway wearing a snow shirt. He was a straggler from our regiment. After a quick search of the village we established that no Russians were here. We were tired and worn out: the insides of my thighs had open wounds and burned like hell. We set sentries on a half-hourly roster. The rest of us went to sleep. Shortly a sentry woke us. Engine noises had been heard in the woods. We took cover, ready to fight to the last. The sounds grew louder, the first vehicle became visible – a Wehrmacht artillery tractor, then a private car, and then our Opel-Blitz lorries! Many other vehicles were in tow either to save fuel or because the motor wouldn't start. And in the lorries, exhausted infantry, their heads sunk low. What unit were they? On the village street we recognized the tactical signs of our regiment on the mudguards of the lorries: the white steel helmet inside a blue circle. It was our II Battalion! 'We're saved.'

18 December 1941

Hauptmann Samson was apparently now battalion commander. A civilian car drew up with our heavy mortar platoon leader, Oberfeldwebel Otto Puls. Two dead bodies covered in blood, those of Unteroffizier Dittmann and Grenadier Keilhauer, were lashed over the bonnet. I was deeply distressed. So it had come, that Black Day which Dittmann had prophesied for himself. More of our fallen comrades were bound by ropes and straps to other vehicles. On the journey their arms or even their heads moved due to the jolting and bumping. Shooting broke out ahead: Hauptmann Samson was wounded. Our infantry companies, often only twenty to fifty men each, repelled the enemy force. Here for the first time I had a close look at our 'Do-Gerät' rocket launcher. It made a strange howl at firing, said to make Russians go 'weak at the knees when they heard it', and the rockets left a smoke trail in the sky to mark their passage. Unfortunately this tended to betray the launch position, which then received fire in return. Only later did smokeless powder arrive at the Front, long after the Stalin organs had it. We were just setting up our mortar position in the village to the right of the Rollbahn when the order came to relocate instead below a railway bridge. During the transfer we received fire from a T-34 tank but arrived at the bridge unharmed. When our 3.7cm Pak opened fire at the T-34, we saw the shells bounce off the hull with a spray of sparks. That was why we called the gun the 'door knocker'. Finally it grew quiet and we warmed ourselves in the houses. We found food under the floorboards: potatoes, sour gherkins and apples in vinegar. At about 0300hrs the order came to make ready, dismantle the mortar quietly and then assemble for departure. We 'liberated' a sled and packed it with our mortar and ammunition. The small steppe horses pulled tirelessly through the snow. To reach the Rollbahn we had to go down a steep slope to a frozen brook and then go up the other side. The retreat was a tiring ordeal, everybody depressed and cursing this 'shit war'.

Chapter 3

Cold, Retreat, Hunger

---

20 December 1941: Vassiliyevski

After a difficult night march, feet burning and painful, totally frozen through, we arrived at a village in a new 'security line' and relieved Infantry Regiment 33. Once assigned quarters we searched for a place to install our mortar. Unteroffizier Stedtler had taken over as group leader following the death of Unteroffizier Dittmann. 'Shit position here,' he said, and set off to find a better one. The choice fell on a deep gully forward of the village from where our fire would be indirect with a limited field. We cast a baleful eye over our line of retreat. If Ivan attacked and reached the heights first, we would have to pull back into the village under his fire.

At midday Ivan attacked with four tanks and a horde of infantry. Our small 3.7cm Pak hit a T-34 and left it immobile and burning! Because of the other three tanks, we decided to abandon the gully and set up a new firing position behind the first houses in the village, our spotter watching from inside the roof of the neighbouring house. The Russians seemed subdued after the loss of their T-34 and towards evening the shooting died down. We stood the usual thirty-minute sentry roster in the bitter cold, the edge of the village being protected by our MGs and some infantry. Our company had not received rations for several days and we were condemned to the cold buffet again. Whilst we stood around the table watching the sharing-out, wild shooting started outside, and very near. One of our light MGs responded and suddenly Obergefreiter Herbert Johne crashed the party shouting, 'Out! Out! The Russians are in the village! One of them was almost at the door of your house, I gave him an uppercut or I wouldn't be here now!' The nine of us, including the *Spiess*, seized our weapons and steel helmets and crowded in the porch. When one man peered out cautiously, sub-machine gun fire thudded into the door frame in reply. We stood closely pressed together calling for help, but none came. The shooting in the village grew ever more infernal. Next Obergefreiter Bunge pushed a rifle around the door frame and fired 'around the corner', but the Russians were content to stand in the cover of the house corners waiting for us to come out and be shot down. 'Who has hand grenades?' I always carried at least five blue egg-type grenades in my greatcoat pockets and haversack, and passed two forward. It was our plan that immediately after throwing them, three men would sprint across the street and disappear into the darkness on the other side. Two were thrown and exploded left and right of the house: Obergefreiters Johne and Bunge, and Grenadier Franz Schlossbauer made a run for it across the street, brightly lit up by the burning houses. Barely had they covered a few metres before sub-machine gun fire chattered from the house corners. I heard a cry but all three kept on running. Thinking 'Devil take the hindmost', I pushed my way forward to join the second group. Great haste was now needed for our own artillery had begun firing on the village and from the room at the rear where we had been sharing out the rations came the clink of breaking windows. Obergefreiter Erwin Rieger said he wanted to 'assess the situation' first. He peered out, and the split-second Ivan saw him a sub-machine gun chattered and we heard peng-peng-peng on his steel helmet. He recoiled back inside and said calmly, 'That was crazy. The swine dented my helmet!' It sat at a slight angle on his head and I could see the long, shallow track above the front edge. 'Man, you were lucky!' The next couple of hand grenades were tossed out but rolled back and exploded 2m short. The Russians unleashed a burst of fire but by now we had given the matter more careful thought and after removing the pins began counting to twenty-five before lobbing. They hit the ground close beyond the house corners, exploding immediately, I heard windowpanes shattering and then Obergefreiter Rieger, Gefreiter Fritze Barth and I made a hasty exit and sprinted across the street towards the haven of the nearest dark spot. Almost there, Ivan opened fire and the bursts whistled past our ears. Grasping my carbine, while running for a small earth bunker such as many Russian villages have, I looked back instinctively and saw three figures in their dark-green uniforms sprint into the street from the house. The Russian sub-machine guns chattered and all three fell, uttering cries of pain, then silence. They hadn't thrown hand grenades before making their attempt and that was their fatal error. Suddenly I fell, tumbling almost head over heels into the deep snow of a steep slope. The snow got into my clothing through my collar and sleeves. Upon reaching the bottom I could no longer see the burning village, only its bright reflection on the snow. Rieger and Barth had both struggled to their feet. 'Where are the last three?' I reported what I had seen. It would be almost impossible to climb back up that slope, and when we came under fire down here too, we made our way through chest-high snow to the other slope beyond which lay the Rollbahn, calling out several times the names of the last three men: 'Fischer! Ladebeck! Portun!' but there was no reply. The village was in any case now under very effective German artillery fire, the shells roaring overhead to explode like thunder between the houses and in the streets. Finally we got to the Rollbahn where Flak guns and SPWs[1] stood waiting to cover the retreat. Officers were running around, sending everybody with a rifle to join the infantry in the trenches, We three 'stragglers' had no desire to end our days here. As mortar gunners, Rieger and Barth were armed only with pistols, I was still holding my carbine. Rieger said, 'Stuff that out of sight under your greatcoat.' I did as he said so that when an officer appeared and wanted to send us to the trenches, we informed him that we were a mortar crew armed only with pistols and he let us go. Infantry were running here and there on the Rollbahn in great confusion. After a couple of kilometres we reached the village from where our artillery was firing. We found 8 Company command post and reported to Leutnant Hoffmann. When we told him that we had had to abandon our mortar ('Shame on you!'), he ordered us to return to the village with other stragglers and take it back from Ivan. We found Bunge and Johne sitting on the tailboard of a lorry. They had both been wounded in the foot, and Schlossbauer had a chest wound. As I watched their lorry drive off, I was overcome by a peculiar feeling. Was it envy? They were on their way to safety, perhaps even a military hospital in Germany. 'My greetings to the Homeland,' I called out after them. The three of them waved – then the lorry was gone. Now we had to retrieve our mortar from Ivan. We plodded back, always watchful to our right where the Russians were strongest. Arriving at the last Flak gun an officer called out, 'Halt! Are you tired of life? Get back in the village!' We turned about happily and did as he said.

The retreat continued in pitch darkness with a biting easterly wind. Troops accustomed to victories had been pulling back for fourteen days already, with no end to it in sight, and in an exceptionally cold autumn. Our MGs, motors and even panzers had their problems. The anti-freeze in the artillery recoil brakes was inadequate. The gears of lorries froze. MGs couldn't fire bursts, one had to be happy with a couple of rounds, and often it was a hard job to fire off a single one. Only the mortars had next to no problems with the cold. A muzzle-loader without complicated technology, the firing bolt at the foot of the barrel discharged the 8cm bomb through the smooth barrel – no rifling – in high-trajectory flight to Ivan. We could almost always be relied upon! Our only complaint was lack of ammunition. Now we were pulling back before a numerically superior enemy, far stronger in men and materials. The German Army had advanced too far east beyond Tula (we never captured that city) and south-east of Moscow in the belief that the capital would fall before 1941 was out. In addition our lines of supply were too long. The railway stopped at Orel. From there, weapons, provisions, ammunition and other necessities had to be brought up to the fighting troops by lorry or horse-drawn sledge, 300km from Orel to Kashira-Ryasa in the most extreme winter conditions. The front-line troops lacked men and materials. The panzer divisions were well below authorized strength. In the last weeks of the advance, too much had been asked of the 'rolling vehicles' – lorries, panzers, towing machines, assault guns. Then came the surprise of the Siberians brought to the West, fresh troops well-equipped for winter warfare in special uniforms with padded jackets and fur boots, white camouflage suits – whole ski battalions – and T-34 tanks. Along with the Siberians, in and around Moscow any man able to hold a rifle had been mobilized. And us? We stood at the brink of an abyss. Where was a coherent German front line between the Waldai Heights and Jefremov in the second half of December 1941? In temperatures of minus 40°C to minus 50°C,[2] the record low being minus 52°C on 7 December, we stood in the snow in our tight leather boots with studded soles, in thin cloth uniforms, our only 'winter wear' being the thin woollen cap comforter, to which the breath froze if pulled up too high near the nose, and thin woollen gloves which were easily torn. As an emergency measure we infantry each received a lorry driver's greatcoat. Sweat forming under the steel helmet trickled down the forehead and cheeks where it froze solid. Often we lay all day in the snow on the edge of a wood unsuccessfully trying to dislodge Ivan from a warm village. If there was no 'cold fare', we had to scour abandoned houses for whatever was edible. Even when rations did arrive, they would be in the form of deep-frozen soup, bread, sausage and cheese in tubes. This diet was the prime cause of the diarrhoea from which we all suffered. Apart from the climate, our worst enemies were the 'small partisans' – lice, which caused us unimaginable discomfort, worse if one had an injury, for then they would get under the bandage to feast on it. Then even the poorest Russian house would become the finest convalescent home, a chance to get warmed through and sleep after days or weeks in the snow. The gigantic haystacks outside villages made the most glorious hostels. Ivan was affected by the cold as much as ourselves and it sometimes happened that he would burrow in at one end of a 60m-long haystack, ourselves at the other. By tacit agreement the sentries posted by both sides ignored each other until morning came. That was how things were with us. How things stood with neighbouring divisions and on the other sectors of the front remained a mystery: we had no news. Some of the villages during our retreat in December 1941 were: 16th Ssulava, 17th Ssury Nishniye, 18th Lapokov, 20th Vassiliyevski. Always bitterly cold, fighting defensively, frozen through and hungry.

21 December 1941

First day of winter. After a night march which seemed to last forever we were told that our lorries were waiting for us in the next village, maybe with a field kitchen, only 2km farther on. We dragged ourselves through burning villages with that single thought in mind. The village appeared: we saw the long row of lorries. We ran towards 8 Company joyfully. Our drivers clasped our hands in welcome. 'Where are the others then?' We gave them a look and fell silent. Of our seventeen men, three were dead, four missing, six wounded. We four – Obergefreiters Mochen, Barth, Rieger and Grenadier Rehfeldt – were the survivors. 'Climb up!' We sprang aboard our 'home'. Here we had a change of underwear, field pack and ancient iron rations. My God, what a glorious feeling! No more running on half-frozen feet, no more carrying heavy mortar components or ammunition cases. After a stormy night drive we were given quarters in a village north of Mzensk.

Notes

1. SPW= Schützenpanzerwagen, armoured personnel carrier. A half-track vehicle from around 6–9 tonnes in weight, often fitted with a 7.5cm Pak gun, armour up to about 15mm, of numerous sub-types from light to medium. Alexander Lüdeke, *Panzer der Wehrmacht Band 2, Rad- und Halbkettenfahrzeuge, 1939–1945*, Motorbuch, 2012, pp. 70–112. (TN)
2. The climate of Tula is classified as 'humid continental with warm summers and cold but not severe winters by Russian standards'. The official Russian record

lowest temperature is stated as minus 36.1°C. The German Army entered the local meteorological readings into their War Diaries every day: their records show that the degree of frost at Tula ranged generally between minus 40°C and minus 50°C during November and December 1941, the coldest day as recorded by the German forces being minus 52°C on 7 December 1941. What would it benefit the Russians to falsify their meteorological records as to the degree of cold at Tula in the late autumn of 1941? (TN)

Chapter 4

The Retreat of *Wackernagel* Company from Tula

---

21 December 1941

The remnants of the 'Reinforced Infantry Regiment *Grossdeutschland*' were amalgamated into 'Company *Wackernagel*' due to our enormous losses over the last three weeks. Without hope of relief, our lorries brought us far enough back to make us think we might remain undiscovered for a while. A thick layer of cloud hung low above the houses: soon we heard the sound of Russian aircraft. Recently these had been small Ilyushin 2 ground-attack aircraft to which we referred disparagingly as 'sewing machines', but even so they could inflict serious harm on the village in a bombing raid. I was at the field kitchen when I heard a noise almost directly overhead and saw a 'lame Ivan' biplane through a gap in the cloud. He was so low I could have shot him down with my carbine. I even saw the pilot looking down at us directly over the side of the cockpit. His engine noise diminished, and then six to eight bombs dropped from nowhere, four of them exploding immediately. After he had been forgotten, there were four more blasts which shook our hut and rattled the windowpanes. Delayed-action fuses! In the afternoon we sat up combat-ready in the lorries to be driven with the remainder of II Battalion into open country about 3km away where our artillery, Pak and the light infantry gun were parked. After unloading equipment and ammunition on a back slope the order came to move out in single file, 5m between each man. From the crest of the slope we saw a village about 800m away and a dense black wood 200m beyond it. In the foreground stood some large haystacks for cover. Initially it was quiet, but then from the village the first rifle rounds whipped out, a Maxim MG babbled and the snow sprayed up around us in small clouds. It was possible to see the line of MG bursts coming ever nearer. At last our guns replied to this heavy defensive activity with a short impressive concentration of fire. We had to economize on ammunition, however. Our heavy MGs set up behind an undulation from where they fired into the village, setting some houses afire. The black smoke interfered with our observation. My mortar was located behind a large haystack, the No. 2 mortar placed a little back to our left. We considered this good cover, untouched while rounds whistled past either side and shells overhead. The Russians on the edge of the village were running in all directions; these were taken under mortar fire, as were the spotted MG positions in the village. The 'pitiful remnants' of our company of infantry now attacked as per the manual, but Russian mortars had calculated our mortar position behind the haystack, dropped their bombs very close to it and set the haystack afire with incendiaries. The wind drifted the smoke into our eyes. Soon several haystacks were blazing; as the MG ammunition runners came through the snow they were fired on by enemy riflemen with aimed single rounds, but all made it into the woods. Soon they reappeared with empty cases and came under fire again. We watched them lie low in the snow, then make a run for it. One fell while running and lay still. The enemy fire was so fierce that one of our armoured cars had to be sent for him, but they found him dead. After that the armoured car brought up the ammunition. The wind had fanned the flames of our haystack, the acrid fumes and smoke made us cough and our eyes water: this prevented us from spotting our fall of shot and we needed to change our location urgently. However, the only way to run the 100m safely to the next haystack was for the armoured car to feign an attack on their village. Once our mortars were dismantled, the armoured car set off, all barrels blazing from its 2cm cannon and MGs, scattering snow in all directions. Ivan went to ground at once, concentrating his MG and rifle fire on the armoured car, the bullets bouncing off it. I set off with two ammunition cases, carbine in hand, accompanied nearby by the other mortar crew. Ivan saw us shortly before we arrived at the next haystack, forgot the armoured car and fired at us. A messenger came trudging through the snow from our rear and ran directly into the Russian fire. We shouted to him: 'Go to ground, they're firing at everything that moves!' He heard us but stopped in his tracks, knelt in the snow, propped upright grasping his rifle. At our encouragement he rose and laboured towards us. Ivan fired: the messenger dragged himself slowly forwards, then collapsed with a cry. He was hit, barely 20m from us, calling for help. 'Come for me, don't let me lie here!' We had just set up the mortar in position, the gunlayers were cranking the elevation and traversing gear, I was making the first bomb ready with an additional charge: we couldn't leave. We saw a medical corps man and three others running up, and they carried the wounded man into cover behind the haystack. He was groaning quietly, glad to have been rescued. He had a through-and-through wound in the upper thigh and was losing a lot of blood. After being bandaged up they laid him in the straw covered with a blanket. When he begged for water we reached for our field flasks but the tea inside was frozen. At dusk the village was lost to sight beyond the smoke and flames of the burning haystacks. Being unable to eject Ivan from the village he was occupying, we had to return to 'our village' to set up a defensive line: in the meantime we maintained a rearguard action. Under cover of darkness the wounded man was carried back in a groundsheet, followed by all our force, save a couple of sentries left 'at the enemy'. It was all done very quietly to make Ivan think we were withdrawing, but at the first haystacks ahead of our village we stopped and set up the mortars. The infantry company, amongst them our heavy MGs, formed a broad semi-circle in the middle of which the path ran from village to village. In the dark we could hear and see nothing until some infantry came up for straw to line their freezing holes in the snow. It was better for us, for we could burrow into the haystack. In a blizzard our sentries were changed every half hour, off-duty men huddled together for warmth in the stack. Our sentries 'at the enemy' came back reporting that the Russians were hot on their heels with horse-drawn sledges and long columns of infantry. At the order: 'Highest watchfulness. Flare pistols ready!', we climbed to the top of our stack and kept a listening watch. Soon we heard strange sliding noises in the snow and horses snorting: Ivan with his sledges. Soon we could hear the Russians speaking softly. Suddenly the flares rose up from our semi-circle and lit the foreground almost as light as day: before us we saw the long dark shadows of horses, sleds, men, carrying on their backs long rifles with the sharp three-edged bayonet and then, before they grasped what was happening, a fearsome rifle and MG fire swept across them, bringing death and destruction. They threw themselves down in the snow but MG bursts and rifle fire sought them out. Each time our mortars fired, a stab of flame rose from the barrel into the night sky: fired at almost exact intervals the bombs whined on their short trajectory to fall like Stalin-organ fire amongst the surprised Ivans. Flares continued to rise up: the fire from our semi-circle was concentrated on the approaching infantry column like the beams from a concave mirror. The Russians had little answer to offer. Since the two ends of our semi-circle had no cover on the flanks – only snow for kilometres – there was now a danger that after they had recovered from the initial surprise, the Russians would attempt to get behind us. I was sent forward to report to Hauptmann Wackernagel as a messenger. My orders were: 'Go immediately to the end of the right wing and report to Oberfeldwebel B. that he should wheel inwards to avoid being outflanked. After sixty minutes if unnoticed by the enemy he is to disengage and assemble on the Rollbahn behind the village.' I repeated the order and then tramped off through the snow as quickly as I could, from one infantry foxhole to the next to the end of the semi-circle to find Oberfeldwebel B. In the glare of the flares, very visible in my green uniform, I came under fire, but our MGs held Ivan down and I got through unscathed. Suddenly I could not find the next infantry hole: I had lost our front line, which meant I could go astray and finish up with Ivan! Therefore I went back from hole to hole until regaining the route by the straw lying in the snow brought from our village. The infantry was widely spaced but finally I found Oberfeldwebel B. on a haystack 50m on and made my report. He asked what it looked like and I told him 'The best!' before disappearing into the darkness. The Russians were now discharging some rather greenish flares: by their light I was unable to find my mortar position and so reported the completion of my mission to Hauptmann Wackernagel, who directed me to join my troop on the road behind the village. When I got there I saw the telephone lines being taken down, the village itself was under desultory fire from distant Russians, the forward sentries watched out for Russian ski troops. Gradually individual II Battalion groups and units gathered behind the village: finally the count was right and we could pull out. Our weapons at the ready, we had moved forward barely 5m before an MG released a burst of fire with tracer. I heard a cry behind me and threw myself down, but no Russians were near. One of our number lay dead, shot through the back of the head and neck. The No. 1 gunner of an MG had slipped and fallen, activating the trigger of his weapon, which had been cocked. The man stood there white as a sheet. The order had been to keep weapons ready to fire. Who could blame him? The body was laid on a sled and we trudged off into the icy-cold night. Somewhere in a village our lorries would be waiting to give us fresh courage and hope. They would find our force had grown smaller again. This unplanned retreat had been ordered by Army leader Guderian. Siberians, superior to us in numbers and material (for winter warfare) had come as an unforeseeable, nasty surprise. To survive, one had to have the will to pull through at all costs. It sometimes happened that totally exhausted men simply lay down to sleep in the snow. 'I can't go on!' But we would drag them to their feet, for sleeping in the snow meant certain death. We found soldiers of another unit, dead, frozen stiff, not wounded. Occasionally two together, clinging to each other, under a light covering of snow. It was a job to get the ID discs off them, for the uniforms would be frozen hard as a board. Whenever possible we would load the bodies on a sled or another vehicle for burial later in a village with others or in waiting empty graves. Certainly many would not be found.

Chapter 5

The Defensive Struggle at the Oka Bridgehead

---

22 December 1941

During the morning we headed via Mzenk to Bolchov, a small town west of the Oka river. Here we were supposedly going to spend Christmas. At 0030hrs Alarm! Prepare for action! We set off for another location. A blizzard raged through the icy night. Towards first light we reached the hamlet of Yamskoiye.

23 December 1941

There we stayed only a short while to warm up before continuing to Voronezh on the west bank of the Oka. We crossed the river by an 'ice bridge', climbed the steep eastern bank and found a street with a village straggling along it. Our orders were to establish a bridgehead beyond the village. After our reconnaissance it was decided that positions should be set up about 100–150m east of the village after explosives had been used to break up the ground. Our mortars were placed provisionally in a ruin and then we looked for quarters. The night was quiet: the terrain was an open plain beyond which lay a distant wood. In daylight it would be difficult to attack it, only ski troops could get here reasonably quickly.

24 December 1941

During the day we chose our positions for the pioneers to begin dynamiting tomorrow. In the evening we sat around our table and celebrated Christmas Eve. On the table stood a small 'Christmas tree' in a large can wrapped in silver paper. Post was distributed but I came away empty-handed. Nothing since 26 October! Our platoon leader Oberfeldwebel Puls arrived in the car with some schnapps and handed out two parcels to each man before making a short but stirring speech. He mentioned the last few evil weeks and expressed the hope that here we could hold the Front. 'Germany must live even if we must die.' So, we had to hold the Front here, no more pulling back. The men who received mail read their letters over and over. The petrol lamp supplied just enough light for us to see the table and who was sitting at it but gave off a dreadful amount of smoke. My parents must be very concerned for me. The post often takes weeks because ammunition and supplies are more important. At midnight we broke up and went to what would become our 'bunker'. Standing in a foxhole free of snow, greatcoat collar up, field cap deep over my face, cap comforter around my neck and pulled up over my nose, hands wearing thin gloves thrust deep into my pockets, I walked up and down to keep my feet alive. The leather boots are hard and my feet ice cold. The nights are dark and the biting frost covers everything. So far, Ivan hasn't tried to attack us here.

25 December 1941

We two groups of 8 Company/II Battalion – one group mortars and the other the heavy MGs – share a house. Our battle positions lie 100m apart. We work a six-hour roster. The mortars stand watch from 0900hrs until 1500hrs, then we are relieved and return to the village where hot food and cold fare will have arrived. The post came but for me still nothing. *Volksdeutsche* in Yugoslavia sent so many parcels to our regiment in gratitude for their liberation by the *Grossdeutschland* Regiment (earlier in 1941, before my time) that those of us who received no mail got two and a half parcels – cakes, biscuits, clear honey, bacon, nuts, sweets, chocolate, marzipan and dried fruit! Every parcel has a letter in broken German sending us Christmas greetings and especially *Soldatenglück* [Soldier's Luck] for 1942. We enjoy reading the letters from the grateful people of the Banat. Now we can tuck in like we do at home, the men say jokingly. We go to bed early, for we have to relieve the other shift at 2100hrs.

26 December 1941

It has got colder and we have to fetch wood for heating. I couldn't find a supply and so took it wherever I could. We started with 'our' own house. Axe in hand, I looked around. 'Why does this house need a porch?' Soon we had wood enough for two days. Next time we'll take the cowshed. The lattice fence had long since gone up in smoke. We found that even fresh birch wood burned excellently. When we come back off sentry duty, first we get thoroughly warmed up, then we eat, write our letters and most important of all, crack lice. Finally we have time for it. They drive us almost crazy. Our underclothes are black with them. We find them in masses in our pullovers and uniform coats. The disgusting feeling and the itching can drive even the most peaceful man mad. I have scratched myself on the legs and body until I bled. My frostbite is deep and suppurating, especially at the heels, where my boots froze during the retreat. In order to be on time to relieve the other shift I have to leave ten minutes early. To keep out the cold we have bound skins and furs to our boots with telephone cable. This makes it difficult to walk, however. When we are relieved I get back twenty minutes after the others, groaning with pain. It takes two men to pull my boots off, and even then I am in agony. I reported sick, went down the slope, crossed the ice of the Ola and saw a doctor in the village of Voronezh.

27 December 1941

After examining me the doctor smeared 'Peruvian balsam' on my frostbite and sent me back. Today the pioneers are going to dynamite the foundations. The bunker will have space for ten men. Some will do the spadework after the explosions while the others fetch beams, boards and nails. The building material is to be brought up by horse and sled. I was working with my group in the bunker excavation when we saw some black figures at the edge of the distant wood. They made no attempt to encroach. 'Peng!' and the first rifle rounds came whizzing over. We raged as we took cover and returned the Bolshevists' fire. Plenty of ammunition was available, the barrels soon ran hot but we were free to fire at will! The Ivans soon disappeared. Four of us drove them off. We were really angry because they had turned up before our bunker was ready.

28 December 1941

At night the sentries have to be especially alert since Ivan 'contacted' us. We relieved the other shift in a wild blizzard. The wind drives the snow into our faces, and we have to keep our eyes closed or otherwise the snow thaws around the lashes, freezes to ice and sticks. That is very painful. The thin woollen cap comforter is soon wet and then frozen. We found a grandfather's thick fur coat in the house and sling it across our shoulders as protection against the blizzard while heading for the bunker. Our bunker has been given a temporary roof but no stove and so is as cold inside as out. It is almost impossible to see anything in the conditions. Now and again flares sent up by the nearby MG sentry illuminate the terrain briefly. He fires them high into the wind which then carries them away to burn out in the far distance. What use will they be on the night when the Bolshevists decide to come?

29 December 1941

Our bunker is now ready. To make it waterproof we took the metal roof off a house and laid it over the roof of boards, camouflaging it with snow. We have boarded off a corner for our store of straw. We still have no stove. Apparently some iron bunker stoves are on their way to us from Orel. Fritze Barth, a mason, is going to build us a first-class brick kiln tomorrow. To supplement our provisions we slaughtered a sheep, and everybody got a chunk: insatiable Erwin had a panful of roast potatoes. The bread, butter and tinned beef which arrived today are frozen solid. I toasted slices of bread on my bayonet before the fire, had a quick cigarette and then slept for three hours.

30 December 1941

We found bricks for the kiln and two long clay pipes for the chimney: the structure was completed and the fire burned perfectly. At last our bunker became warm and suitable for occupation. Only one thing was overlooked: the metre-high flames coming up through the chimney for Ivan to see. To hide it, towards the enemy side we set up boarding covered with snow. Our neighbours the MG group have their own oven. During the day we see its smoke coming up out of the earth and snow.

31 December 1941

New Year's Eve! Our reconnaissance parties established that Ivan is about 4km away in a village behind the wood. After our relief we made 'our' house cosy. We got Matka's oven going and what glorious warmth it provided! After dinner we sat at the table reading old newspapers or writing home: towards midnight every man received a bottle of liquor and shared half a bottle of champagne with someone else. At midnight we raised our glasses in silence. There was no happy spirit like at home. We all had a single wish: *Sieg um jeden Preis*! Victory at any price! And *Soldatenglück* for every man! Scarcely had we taken a sip than the house trembled and the windowpanes rattled. Outside we heard a dozen roars overhead. Our sentry came in to report that a whole salvo of Stalin-organ rockets had flown above our village and crashed into the frozen Oka river. 'It looked really wonderful, a whole row of fountains spraying sparks.' And the man said it with a certain joy in his voice! That salvo of rockets could have come straight into our village. It was the only salvo. 'We must let Ivan send us his New Year's greetings,' said someone drily. At the bunker relieving the other shift we shouted down through the chimney: '*Prost*! Happy New Year!' Then we shook hands wishing everybody, 'Good luck!' We brought a bottle which did the rounds quickly and was then flung in a high trajectory into the snow. The relieved shift hurried off into the village. On sentry duty I kept observation on the terrain between the bunker and the wood: the night remained quiet.

Grenadier Hans Rehfeldt in walking-out uniform, the *Grossdeutschland* Regiment cuff title on the lower right sleeve.

Unteroffizier Josef Kalinowski of *Grossdeutschland* Regiment, seen wearing the Iron Cross First Class. On 30 April 1943 he was awarded the German Cross in Gold.

Opel-Blitz 3-tonne lorries were the principal means of transport for the fully motorized Regiment.

Company Leader Dr Meier pointing out the important parts of the structure of Potsdam fort.

The Olympic Stadium in Berlin, venue for the 1936 Olympic Games.

The Rheinmetall 8cm (81.4mm) GrW 34 medium mortar was the principal weapon for which the author was trained. It was a well-proven high-angle infantry weapon, muzzle-loaded with a smoothbore barrel, in production before the war and used in large numbers on the various Fronts.

The mortar captain warns: 'Mortar ready!' Training on the heavy mortar at Döberitz.

'Fired!' The mortar crew learn to duck low to avoid the blast of the propellant detonating.

The author kneeling as No. 2 gunner. Near him is the ammunition case for three mortar bombs each of 3.5kg. Crouching to his left is the mortar captain, the troop leader is standing.

Rehfeldt as No. 2 gunner left, the mortar captain is at the sight bracket, No.3 gunner at right.

The author selecting a new firing position, the mortar bipod on his back.

Josef Dörfler, later a companion of Hans Rehfeldt, already wearing the Iron Cross Second Class.

A rest after the hard work.

Mortar crews wearing additional camouflage of tent canvas squares. With up to five propellant charges an 8cm mortar had a range of 4,500m.

The mortar captain with his No. 1 and No. 2 gunners. He also had up to four ammunition runners.

A short break in training, rifles stacked.

Souvenir photo of recruits at the Döberitz training depot, 1941.

Group photo in the shade of a tree at the sea barracks, Neuruppin, the author on the right.

Group photo of the honour guard at the funeral for a dead comrade, Neuruppin.

Group photo during training at the sea barracks.

The recruits during training at Neuruppin.

The author on guard.

The author before leaving for Russia.

The garages used by training unit Marschbataillon 3/16 at Neuruppin.

The author amongst field packs ready to move out.

A last group photo at Neuruppin train station, 26 October 1941.

The long train curving eastwards.

Late October 1941: a break in the journey to Orel.

First impressions of the destructiveness of war in the Russian city of Orel.

Ruins like these would soon become an everyday sight in Germany.

The collapsed bridge over the Dnieper at Ryetshitza.

The rail terminus at Tula. Digging trenches in the cheerless winter snows.

A pit for the protection of an MG team in the frozen ground.

November 1941. Hans Rehfeldt in his trench at Tula in temperatures of minus 30°C.

1942

Chapter 6

Ivan Attacks

---

1 January 1942

We had occupied the so-called Oka position on Christmas Eve. It had the character of a broad but shallow bridgehead. We had had to occupy the eastern bank of the frozen river because it was higher than the western bank. If Ivan had his position here, he would have been able to survey deep into our rear on the western side. Almost facing each other either side of the river were two villages. At Voronezh on the west bank was the battalion command post and our 8 Company *Nahtross* – advanced rearward services. Here was a battery of 15cm heavy infantry guns (known as 'the fist of the battalion commander') and some 2cm Flak. Well to the rear was the town of Bolchov. I never noted down the name of the village we occupied on the east bank. We used its houses for our quarters, the heavy MG and mortar positions were about 300m ahead of the village in open country and 10–15m right of the bunker. The foundations of our bunker were 1.5m deep in the permafrost. It was well covered over but gave better protection against the cold than enemy fire. At any given time, one mortar crew was on six-hour watch in the bunker and the other resting in the village. The houses there occupied only the eastern side of the road. Thirty-five metres left of our mortar bunker was the heavy MG bunker, to their left were infantry with light MGs in smaller bunkers and at the extreme left Company *Wackernagel*. The terrain to the right of our bunker was empty for about 300m, then came the heavy MG post of a non-*Grossdeutschland* unit adjacent to a wood. In this wood were pioneers and men of a security company, all lacking heavy weapons. The front line was therefore only thinly occupied: along 3–4km only two heavy MGs, two heavy mortars and then light MGs and rifles. Beyond the 600m of open ground in front of our position lay a flat gully about 80m wide on the diagonal: another 600m behind that stood a forest.

I had been standing sentry for about an hour when I saw dark points moving on the snow at the edge of the forest, confirmed with binoculars as Russians,

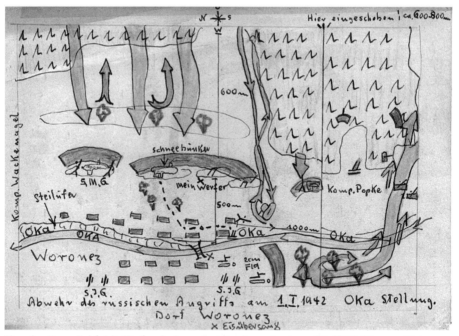

Map by Hans Rehfeldt, 'Defended against Russian attack on 1.1.1942 Oka position, opposite Voronezh village'. The River Oka with crossing point over the ice to Battalion command post at Voronezh is at the foot of the map. Steilufer = steep bank. Halfway up: SMG = heavy MG position, Schneebunker = snow bunker, mein Werfer = my mortar. Komp.Popke = Company Popke (security force). Ahead of these positions is the gully in which the Russian attackers sought cover and were later eliminated. The Russians broke through from the woods defended by Company Popke (right side), crossed the frozen river (bottom right) but were repulsed at the barrier by the 2cm Flak half-track.

some in dark uniforms but many in white camouflage, and towing sleds. Suddenly they began to pour out of the forest. I raised the alarm, and the heavy MG sentry did likewise. The groundsheets were cast off the mortar, ammunition laid ready, the barrels given another pull-through. Since we had worked out the range of our curtain fire, we would only shoot when the Russians got that close. The heavy MGs took a bead on the Russians advancing slowly through deep snow. Our bunkers and firing positions were level with the snow surface. The MG to our right opened fire first. The Ivans lay down in the snow and crawled forward. The first rifle rounds came singing and chirping towards us. A messenger ran for the village to raise the alarm. The intention of the Ivans was to reach the long gully before our position which would give them cover, and now they broke and ran for it in chaotic order. Our heavy MGs rattled: we saw the snow spray up, the first Russian casualties threw up their hands and let their rifles drop, falling dead or wounded into the snow. The rest all lay prostrate, shooting. Our mortar had not yet fired: we had zeroed in on the gully and wanted them all sheltering in it first. We remained in cover behind our bunker posing as 'snipers'. Even Unteroffizier Stedtler had joined in with a rifle! It was like being on the rifle range: take your time, aim and then – squeeze the trigger! Another of them fell. We noticed one gesticulating, shouting orders loudly. This would be a Commissar. Two of us took him in our sights. Two shots rang out – and he fell like a tree. Two Ivans tried to drag him into the gully but were deterred by our well-aimed fire. Another man fell and lay without moving. In order to shoot better we removed our gloves: very quickly the fingers grew white and stiff. It became impossible to open one's ammunition pouches. Rubbing them with snow helped. The mass of the attackers had now disappeared into the gully, preparing the next stage of their attack. Our moment had come! The first mortar bombs were in the two barrels. 'Fire at the aiming point!' This was the centre of the gully. We observed the fall of shot. It was accurate and we heard the first cries. The bombs would be dropped into the barrels: 'Flupp!' and twenty seconds later they exploded in the gully amongst the Ivans. The cries of agony increased. Next a Russian exposed a light MG, the type with the flat ammunition drum, and fired three or four rounds before it jammed. He withdrew it and then he could be heard hitting it with a hard object. After a short while he reappeared, 'tack-tack-tack' and it jammed again. We saw the funny side of this. 'Keep watch there! He'll be back!' But two of our 8cm bombs landed a metre in front of his MG and put an end to it. More Russian troops appeared from the woods, even set up a mortar, and though two rounds fell close, seriously wounding Ober-gefreiter Mochen, most were aimed far too long. As we carried him into the bunker we heard loud cries of "Urrah!", the Ivans arose, fixed their three-edged bayonets to their rifles, and were then met by a hail of our MG and rifle fire, forcing them to retreat back into the gully where we caused them more mayhem with our mortars. We needed more ammunition, which had to be fetched from the village. When I saw a man without an ammunition case I shouted to him, 'Hey! Go back, quick! Nobody comes here without bringing ammunition!' The man did not react at first, and so I shouted more brusquely. As he came closer, I recognized him as Oberleutnant Blumenthal, commanding a rifle company. When he realized the situation, he ran back to the village with the other mortar gunners and brought us two cases of three bombs each. The Ivans seemed to be uncertain, and we could hear loud scolding or commands. Finally they started the 'Urrah!' cries again and advanced. Over the last few weeks the sound of it had sent shivers down my spine. We mortars were ready to fire but the heavy MG to our left had problems. Then we saw something funny. The MG would not fire. Now whenever the Russians started up with their 'Urrahs!' the entire MG team would cry louder 'Floohrah!' and then the Russians would throw themselves down into the snow. This happened several times. The MG gunner ran back to the bunker with the iced-up lock of the MG to thaw it out. Oiling it was of no use in these temperatures. From experience many MG gunners carried it in their trouser pockets to keep the component warm and didn't put it back in the MG until they had to! We fired a few more mortar bombs into the gully and then saw a grey-white object rumbling towards us, pushing its way through the snow, throwing it high in the air! 'Tank ahead!' came a shout. The people in the bunker to our right came running towards us with their weapons and kept running – definitely not *Grossdeutschland* men! Now we became anti-tank-mortar gunners: a couple of bombs in the path of the tank and it turned away, its crew obviously thinking that we were Pak. If we had had more ammunition we might have done it serious damage, maybe dropping a bomb on the roof. Our comrades who had run for it received orders to return to their position. The T-34 rolled towards our village, fired a couple of rounds and then turned to its left, passing behind the woods. God, he could have wiped us all out in a flash. A 3.7cm Pak gun hit the tank twice with shells which bounced off. Why hadn't the gun fired before? While pinning down the Russians in the gully we heard sounds of fighting from the direction of the wood behind which the tank disappeared. Were they trying for the breakthrough at that point? Nothing much could happen to us here providing the Russians didn't bring up heavy weapons. Their mortars couldn't get the range and so far we had hardly any casualties. Individual Russians had begun to run back, drawing our fire. From the timber forest 600m in front of our position a sledge drawn by two horses headed for the gully at the gallop. Bringing ammunition? Therefore, fire at will! Our heavy MG fired a few bursts. The horses reared up, fell and remained on their sides but still moving. The sledge was abandoned, an Ivan getting back to the forest in wild leaps and bounds. To our right, there seemed to be more going on than we had thought. Our infantry alternated between pulling back and lying in the snow shooting: then we saw the reason – Russians in white camouflage dress on skis disappearing behind the wood to our right. The sound of firing was now coming at an angle to our rear. This was getting dangerous! We were short of ammunition but nobody was coming out to us from the village. Encouraged by what they saw as the success with the tank and skiers, the Russians in the gully were being required to advance. We heard some loud shouting, as when a Commissar was giving orders, but the 'Urrahs!' he drummed up were rather pathetic. As soon as they showed themselves our heavy MG opened fire and they put their noses in the snow. A messenger came stumbling from our village. Order: 'Dismantle one mortar and one MG immediately and return with the messenger.' It was explained as soon as we arrived that the Russians on our right flank had broken through and crossed the frozen Oka to threaten Voronezh directly. From our new firing position on the steep bank near the last houses of the village we could look down on the Oka and see the Russians crossing the ice, forming in large numbers only 300m from Voronezh village! In Voronezh itself all was quiet. The ice of the frozen Oka wouldn't bear the weight of a T-34 and so with a loud 'Urrah!' the main body of the infantry attacked. A 2cm Flak gun appeared at the village outskirts and fired its tracer into the oncoming mass. Large numbers of them twisted and tumbled to end up lying in the snow. Then the 15cm infantry gun fired into them, within seconds of each report black fountains of earth spraying up. Great black clouds of smoke formed over the scene. The Russians, undeterred, pushed forward in five to six waves, but the defensive fire was too much for them. This they had not expected. The counter-attack was led personally by our II Battalion Commander Major Greim. The half-track Flak guns with infantry seated on the superstructure headed for the Russians, spewing fire with all barrels. At this the Russians had had enough. First individuals, and then whole groups arose and ran for their lives, the 15cm gun and Flak firing into their backs. Our mortar was aligned on the ice of the Oka, the heavy MG set up in the middle of the village street. As the fugitives reached the ice of the river, the MG gunners used tracer to verify the accuracy of their bursts and our mortar bombs exploded amongst the retreating Ivans. The survivors who managed to cross the Oka climbed the high bank and disappeared into the wood. 'Halt! Cease fire!' We stood up, still deafened by the firing of the mortar and the rattle of the MG. The barrel was too hot to touch, around it lay the empty ammunition cases. Gradually it quietened down and the broken Front had to be restored. With the help of our battalion's infantry, Company Popke was able to reoccupy their former position by nightfall. Towards dusk at 1530hrs we returned to our bunker. We heard that the Russians had mounted another attack at Voronezh but found it a hopeless cause. After the danger there had passed, the spotter for the 15cm gun, Oberfeldwebel Schwappacher, arrived with his liaison people. He had no telephone equipment and at Voronezh had had to establish a human chain to shout his observations to the fire direction point. There was still a Russian force in the gully 600m ahead of our bunker to be flushed out before nightfall or they might have enough men there to eject us from our village during the night. The initial attack they made had been in battalion strength. About three companies had crossed the Oka. That was in all well short of a regiment. We could repel this strength with the pitiful remnants of II Battalion! 'From zero line – above me – 50 less! Range 700m. First group fire!' From the emplacement 10m lower at Voronezh four 15cm shells boomed out and passed so close overhead they almost grazed us. They exploded in the snow beyond the gully. Long. Fresh orders were issued and we had to take cover because the shell splinters could reach back this far. The next salvo howled over and landed in the centre of the gully. Now salvo after salvo of four shells pounded it. Black smoke rose up and we could taste the powder; in the gully terrible cries. One could feel sorry for the Ivans who were now being blown to shreds. A few managed to escape the gully, without rifles, some hobbling. Schwappacher added a few metres to the range, the 15cm gun pursuing the escapees to the edge of the forest. In the snow great black patches. By now, all those who were going to reach it had done so, but once inside the forest the shells would explode against trees spraying splinters far and wide. Schwappacher increased the range by 100m: dark clouds arose from the forest, trees splayed and branches split. The Russians had been driven off! At once a reconnaissance party set out. Dead and seriously wounded were scattered about the gully. The latter could no longer be helped. We heard the occasional 'coup de grâce'. It sounds cruel but in that situation was the lesser evil. The wounded would never have arrived at the dressing station alive. Near them were many rifles, automatics and the coveted Russian sub-machine guns, better than our own with a magazine for sixty to seventy rounds, always ready to fire even if left lying for days in snow or mud. The long diagonal gully was a picture of annihilation. The night was quiet except for a single Russian soldier calling for help from somewhere beyond the gully. At sunrise they found him, long dead in the snow. Shit war! Now we crossed to the gully to collect up the weapons. Our NCOs each had a captured sub-machine gun and three to four drum magazines on the belt. German sub-machine guns had a long magazine with scarcely thirty rounds, prone to jam for no good reason. The simple rifles had the accursed long three-sided bayonet fitted. There were also some light mortars lying around, and the MG that wouldn't fire more than three rounds, its gunner dead beside it. We took the gun in the hope that it could be repaired. In the upshot, despite all the oiling, it couldn't be made to fire. In the course of the next couple of days the pioneers set up a light barbed-wire fence and laid some mines. After that the Front remained quiet.

2 January 1942

The question now was, how much longer would this damned war go on? Naturally we felt better after our defensive success yesterday after all the retreats with our heavy losses. Our confidence had grown. We needed to improve the bunker, line the walls with straw and boards. A petrol lamp was hung from the ceiling. We had to maintain a constant supply of wood to feed our stove, in which a fire was kept going day and night. The rule was that the incoming watch had to bring dry wood, how each man 'organized' this being left up to him. My own source was the boards and beams of neighbouring houses but nobody must notice. These had to be chopped up when on watch, a difficult job when an eye had to be kept permanently on the distant forest and the open ground in front of us.

3 January 1942

In the early hours a fierce skirmish broke out in the woods to our right. Ivan's sub-machine guns chattered, our carbines replied unceasingly. In the wood the shooting sounded two or three times louder than normal. The MG bunker at our right told us that Ivan had attacked the 'security battalion' and tried to break through the Front there: apparently Ivan had learned his lesson from the debâcle in the gully on New Year's Day. At midday we were sent with one mortar and a light MG to the security unit as 'corset stays'. A depression led into the wood, small earth bunkers lined its paths and the edges of the wood. The infantry there ran cautiously from tree to tree, for Ivan fired between the trees continually with an anti-tank gun. He was using the wrong ammunition though, probably armour-piercing, because generally the shells failed to explode. They would crash into a tree and then keep going with a peculiar 'brrr!' noise before hitting some obstruction and landing harmless. A small wooden direction shield pointed to Company Popke's command post. We reported and were informed about the morning's attack, in which the Russians had been beaten off. Ivan had got to within 20m of the wood with a strong force of infantry, then had stormed forward, depth of snow permitting, shouting 'Urrah!' The defenders' MG had failed after the first round, resulting in a close combat skirmish in which the Russians lost thirty dead to rifle fire. In order to supplement our non-existent winter clothing, the fallen Russians were deprived of their gloves, fur boots, padded jackets and sub-machine guns. We set up our mortar and looked for a bunker in which to spend the night. These were equipped with a shooting aperture which was always open, and the bunker could not be heated. We crept inside the one of our choice and huddled close together, the cold of the naked earth walls freezing us to the marrow. If somebody had to leave – thirty-minutes' sentry duty – he would stumble out over his companions by the light of a match. It was a miserable, bitterly cold night. Sleep was almost impossible. I was roused for sentry duty. Outside, my carbine was missing from where I had left it against a tree. I gave up looking and took a rifle lying on the bunker roof. Rifles were longer than carbines. After half an hour I woke my relief, crouched in a free corner and rested my head on my knee, trembling with cold. I thought of home and of all that we were missing by being here. Somebody awoke and snarled, 'Always this shit cold. This damned shit war!'

4 January 1942

I awoke stiff and frozen through, crept out of the hole in the ground and ran about in an effort to warm up. Generally this was discouraged, for Ivan would notice and fire into the trees. Towards midday our No. 2 mortar crew relieved us. We explained the 'advantages' of the bunker and then with gladness made our way back to our village where our previous day's rations were waiting for us. It grew dark quickly and I was detailed to take a horse and sled over the frozen Oka to Voronezh to fetch hot food and cold fare. Our field kitchen had come up from Bolchov with goulash and noodles, and best of all, chocolate. There was field post too, and naturally ammunition etc. We loaded up the sled and were given a warm welcome on our return. There was no letter for me. Nine weeks without a word. I wrote a letter home assuring my parents that I was alive and well. The fire crackled in the stove, it was cosy and warm. We were just getting ready for sleep when we noticed a smell of burning. It didn't seem to be us and so we sent a man out to investigate. He ran back in shouting, 'Everybody out! The house is on fire!' In a flash we awoke those already asleep, tossed all our things into a groundsheet and got out fast. Bright flames had already engulfed the roof, sparks flew around, beams were collapsing inwards, the smoke and fumes made our eyes smart. It had started in a side room where the MG crew lodged. Now they waded out through the snow barefoot, one of them dressed only in his thermal underpants, each man clasping his belongings. Someone had forgotten his haversack and field flask in the living room, but by now the flames drove him back, the snow around the house had begun to thaw, the whole village was lit up with a garish light. Small explosions began inside the burning house, probably from ammunition, and one of the MG men shouted: 'Watch it! Get away from here, there are explosive charges and mines inside!' With our personal gear we wandered the street asking at every house whether there was room. Every house in this 'Front village' was occupied by infantry and nobody had space to take us. Finally we found a unoccupied house, filthy and in very poor condition, but at least we now had a roof over our heads. We had the MG crews join us for there was probably nothing else available for them in the village. The first task was to seal the windows, clean the stove and the living room. Everybody did his share and we soon had the stove going. The little house had been unoccupied for days and needed heating up. There were twenty of us in dreadfully overcrowded conditions, but soon every man had a hook to hang his things. We agreed the sleeping arrangements as follows: men found sleeping were to be carried to a corner thus creating more floor space. Once we had enough straw the remainder slept where they could, close alongside somebody, across somebody . . . infantry aren't fussy. When the shift came back from the bunker they looked at the situation in disbelief. A further reconnaissance of our new home resulted in the discovery of two sheep.

Chapter 7

A Soldier's Luck

---

5 January 1942

Returning the following evening to our new abode from the bunker, a colleague called out, 'Rehfeldt, you've got mail!' Despite my painful frostbitten feet I ran. My first letter from home, postmark 5 December 1941: it had taken a month to get here. My parents expressed the usual concerns, were worrying about the unusually cold winter and provided advice about taking care of myself at the Front. Finally they asked, 'When are you coming home on leave?' I had never dared think of such a thing. In any case, because of the critical situation on the Eastern Front all leave was cancelled. In closing they wished me *Soldatenglück*. I thought back over the last difficult weeks when my life had been governed by some lucky star. But if a bit of shrapnel or a bullet has got your number on it, it will kill you no matter what precautions you take. Kismet.

6 January 1942

Today something weird happened. Karl Viole was sitting with the others cleaning mortar bombs with an oily rag. To keep his fingers warm, he laid the bombs on the stove. Colleagues in the corner raised horrified objections at the danger of doing this, but Karl merely smiled and ignored them. Suddenly there was a tremendous crash, mud and bricks flew everywhere, we heard a short, loud hissing sound and Karl found himself on the floor near the wreckage of his stool. Everybody else had thrown themselves to the floor and lay flat! Upon investigation we discovered a hole the size of a man's head in the wall nearest the enemy, and in the opposite corner near the stove a smaller hole. Neither had been there seconds before. Mortar bombs are not armour-piercing, so Ivan must have accidentally fired an AP shell which went through our house wall. On its way through, it took off the leg of Karl's stool and came to rest in the corner near the stove. It must have been an AP, for an explosive shell would have left us with many dead and wounded. That was *Soldatenglück*!

7–14 January 1942

Along our sector of the Front it had fallen quiet at last. We stood the usual six hours on, six hours off, roster at the bunker. I was outside on sentry duty when the single Russian aircraft appeared which flew reconnaissance in clear weather. We took cover to avoid our positions being spotted. After a broad sweep he flew off. From behind the timber forest into which the Russians had withdrawn on New Year's Day, suddenly I saw a thick blue-grey strip of cloud approaching rapidly, soon obscuring the sun. The sky grew dark as the cloud arrived overhead. I was thinking that this might bring us another heap of snow when everything turned greyish-black, I heard a kind of 'singing' and 'whistling' unknown in my previous experience and then I saw a wall of snow falling behind Voronezh before the village was lost to sight. I raised up the collar of my greatcoat, muffled my face with the cap comforter and was then assailed by a whirlwind of huge snowflakes accompanied by a blast of wind howling and whistling with the most tremendous force. I got down into the mortar pit for cover: the snow on the wind got down inside my collar. It had grown so dark that a hand could hardly be seen before my face even when I forced my eyes open. Snow began to build up quickly in the mortar pit: the ammunition cases beneath a groundsheet were soon covered over. My attempts to shovel the pit clear were defeated by the storm. Soon the mortar was 50cm deep, I was up to my knees in snow, my carbine had acquired a thick covering of frozen snow which soon spread over my whole body. I gritted my teeth and stamped up and down, watching the level of snow rise to the muzzle of the mortar barrel. This first exposure to the might of a Russian snowstorm lasted an hour and ended as swiftly as it had begun. The dark clouds were driven for some time in the direction of Ivan and then the first rays of the sun broke through. Both mortars had disappeared under the snow and our bunker was so snowed under that only the projecting stovepipe betrayed its location. I had to shovel the bunker door free to allow the occupants to emerge. They looked at the scene in astonishment and then set to work to clear it. Of Ivan there was no sign. I warmed myself at the stove, my hands and feet hurting at so much sudden heat. By the time our relief came wading through the snow we had the mortars ready to fire and the bunker entrance totally free. In the village we found a tureen of wonderful hot pea soup awaiting us.

14 January–8 February 1942

I went to the doctor at Voronezh again, because the pain in my frostbitten legs was now intolerable, the affected patches being open wounds, suppurating and bleeding. This made them stick to my trouser legs and the itching from the lice drove me crazy. My leather boots were frozen solid and I cannot describe my suffering as they were removed. When the doctor saw my legs he said at once, 'Go back to the *Tross* [rearward services].' Then he cleaned the encrusted wounds with a pair of tweezers. I could have cried out with pain every time he touched them. I went back to Bolchov on the back of the field kitchen wagon clasping my few things and reported to the *Spiess* Stabsfeldwebel Maritzen, who directed me to the 'sickbay'. As I hobbled in I was greeted loudly by Gottfried Fritsch and other front-line comrades, all with more or less serious frostbite. It was a large room without beds and had a typical Russian stove at its centre: the patients lay on the straw-covered floor. Each man kept his 'personal belongings', mess tin and field flask at the head of his 'place'. Because the house floor was at ground level and not raised, every time the front door was opened a cloud of ice-cold air wafted in to embrace the patients. The doorway was hung with woollen blankets which made little difference. I had to report to the doctor every third day. It was a pitiful sight to see the wounded and frostbitten hobbling slowly and laboriously across the street to the doctor's little house, teeth clenched against the pain. These inflammations to cellular tissue, caused by frost and the subsequent effects of lice infestation, were treated with about ten different kinds of salves and baths, but those which had gone deep into the flesh would simply not heal. My legs were bandaged from toe to thigh, but unfortunately there was no delousing unit in the small town and so at night the lice raged. Sleep was hardly possible what with the pain and itching, every man groaning and not knowing the best position in which to lie. Often I would lie with my feet up on a stool to reduce the throbbing of the blood in the wounds. We had laced shoes, but even these I could only wear with the greatest discomfort. The doctors were initially powerless, trying all kinds of salve and ointment without success. In the first couple of days I slept as much as I could and warmed up through and through. Mail was delivered every third day, and we could receive parcels with a weight limit of 50g but the joy mail and parcels gave us was great. Lying around inactive led us to eat from pure despair – baked potatoes, toast, often three portions. Mostly we ate our rations in the evening. In that sickbay 'our Matka' lived with her three sons aged seven, five and one still in the cradle. She was a dutiful mother to us. When we called, there she would be in the kitchen doorway: she cleaned the sickbay, fetched wood for the stove, got the stove going, washed our mess tins. Because we were lying on the floor, the sickbay was never really warm, and so we wanted the fire going all day. In winter the Russians would live upstairs above the stove, and also store corn, sunflower seeds, other comestible items and their clothing there. Mostly we had a very good relationship with our Matka, and when she got annoyed we knew it would pass quickly. We learned that our Regiment, a regiment only in name, was being relieved at the Oka position as a result of the many casualties on the retreat and caused by the cold.

Chapter 8

Fighting in the Woods around Gorodok-Yagodnaya

20 January 1942

Task of II Battalion *Grossdeutschland*: Reconnaissance in the Yagodnaya-Tshuchlov area. Russian regiments and partisans coming from the north-east encountered in the woods around Gorodok-Yagodnaya.

21 January 1942

Strong Russian attacks on Yagodnaya in temperatures of minus 40°C: stubborn resistance.

23 January 1942

Evacuation of Yagodnaya. II Battalion transferred to Kudinov. Bolchov was protected by MG Battalion 5, Inf Regt 171, 17 Pz Div, 134 Inf Div, 80 Inf Div and 4/Pz Div 7. The enemy lay in the woods between Bolchov and Lowat. Strength of our companies: twenty to thirty men each.

25 January 1942

Oberleutnant Schwarzrock (2 Company/I Battalion) wounded: an Oberfeld-webel took command of the remnants of the Company.

29–30 January 1942

III Battalion dissolved. Its few survivors were transferred to the other battalions.

7 February 1942

After two days' rest our regiment arrived north-west of Bolchov at the so-called 'Karachev Woods' north of Orel with orders to wipe out three Russian regiments which had made great strides ahead of Ivan's offensive.

On my last visit to the doctor he had ordered 'bedrest', meaning I should lie still and not run around. In the afternoon came the order, 'Every man peel potatoes for the field kitchen!' Since that cannot be done effectively lying down, I sat on a case and set to work. During his evening rounds the senior surgeon saw me sitting up instead of lying down as ordered. 'Are you crazy?' The outcome was my discharge from sickbay back to the fighting front despite my still open wounds. Next morning the provisions lorry took me back to my Company, where I reported to my platoon leader, Oberfeldwebel Puls. He said I could be charged with disobeying an order. Then I reported to my group leader, Unteroffizier Stedtler. Having noticed that I was unable to walk properly, he put me in charge of a horse-drawn sled for carrying ammunition and other things. I relieved the previous driver who gave me a brief introduction to the secrets of controlling the horses and was satisfied I was up to the job. But who can know the moods of a Russian steppe horse? My sled was drawn by two of them. That evening after dark all of II Battalion set out for the battle preparation area. I cracked the whip and my horses obeyed. Two hundred metres from the village there was no more road to be seen, but every 50m was a stake with a wisp of straw. Was we supposed to know which side of the stake the road ran? The convoy halted. A horse had gone down and refused to get up. After ten minutes when the convoy resumed, my sled would not budge, its wooden skids having frozen in the snow. Then a Wehrmacht telephone line parted. Behind me was a long column which came to a halt again, cursing and 'mutinous'. It was not advisable to overtake: those who tried it ended up chest-high in snow. The telephone connection was restored, and with everyone pushing, my sled came free. Its load indicated its importance: ammunition, greatcoats, frying pans, potato graters, the carcase of half a cow, frozen hard as stone: axes, saws and spades: precisely things needed for everyday use. At the start there had been another sled ahead of me but this was long gone. In the darkness the stakes with the straw wisps could still be seen. Progress through the deep snow required much effort: my two horses refused to go any farther. All the pulling and encouragement with the whip served no purpose. One of the men ignited some nitrocellulose, tied it to a long staff and held it under the bellies of the two horses. The end justified the means and the sled resumed 'fully motorized'. We sweated and the pearls of sweat turned to ice on our forehead and cheeks. The curses I heard that night would have done justice to any trooper. Soon we caught up with the battalion, overtaking on the way several bogged-down sleds.

9 February 1942

Finally we reached the village of Ploskoiye. Here we formed up ready to advance next morning to the village of Werch. In the early hours the battalion was ready and left in three columns, the fighting troops leading the way, ourselves with the sleds close behind. Beyond the wood lay a broad plain. Here dead Russian soldiery lay strewn, their limbs at bizarre angles, hands holding a rifle or sub-machine gun. A heavy Maxim MG mounted a sled projected a little through the drifts. Our infantry advanced with intervals between each man. After 2km we saw Werch situated in a flat depression: the Russians subjected us to heavy fire immediately forcing us to take cover. Our infantry reached the first trees and a furious exchange of fire developed. A Russian mortar concealed in a gully ahead to our right caused our first wounded. Their rifle fire whistled by too close for comfort: we could see the path of enemy MG bursts in the snow, directly in line for us. Our own MGs were near the trees and firing at the Russian positions. When the enemy fire increased, we dug in deeper to avoid being seen. Our white camouflage dress was proving its worth on its first outing, having finally arrived at the Front in quantity. Our mortar bombs were fitted for the first time with five propellant charges, the authorized maximum being three, but the barrel proved up to the job and thus with these increments we increased our range. Our infantry deployed and headed for Werch a stretch at a time cooperating with our MGs in leap-frogging forward. We dismantled the mortar and went with the infantry, which now attacked the village with a loud 'Hurrah!', our men shooting from the hip as they trudged forwards. At the distant end of the village we saw Ivan turn and run for the woods with some horse-drawn sleds. The infantry searched the first Russian 'snow bunkers' and houses at the nearer edge of village: this drew Russian artillery fire on the houses and to the right of us. We got a move on to reach the village proper: here we found that Ivan had shot his horses and abandoned a number of sleds and carts. We found the houses empty, Werch was ours! We found a house in good condition and got a fire going. This winter a village would often be fought over simply for protection against the cold. Ivan let us have a few desultory rounds from his artillery. I was answering a call of nature near a haystack when a shell hit the neighbouring house and frightened the life out of me. I stood two periods of sentry duty that night, but it remained all quiet.

10 February 1942

In the early morning we headed for Kudinov. A reconnaissance party had established that the Russians had abandoned the village after softening up by a few salvoes from our 15cm infantry guns. We entered cautiously and stopped by a barn. We were fairly warm from the hard marching. A search of the houses came up with mines and explosive charges. The order came to cut all Russian telephone wires as a precaution against remote detonation. We were to advance further led by Major Greim. The bodies of men from our security company who had fallen during the retreat at the beginning of February and been left where they lay were now gathered up and loaded on a sled. Some had had the ring finger amputated by the Russians to steal the ring. Loud talk died away at the sight of the dead: how short a soldier's life could be, how quickly it could end. We set off for the woods beyond which lay Novolginsky. Ivan shelled us; we attacked; Ivan fled into the woods; our MGs mowed him down. We trudged through the deep snow to the village, searched it thoroughly and stayed the night.

11 February 1942

Once again we set off early, in single file through metre-deep snow, treading in the footsteps of the man in front, entering a wood very alert and reaching the village of Gorodok without encountering the enemy. Sentries were posted and we remained in the houses. We were some distance from the Bolchov–Melichov so-called 'Rollbahn' and our supply and ammunition sleds took a long time to come back.

12 February 1942

We plodded ever deeper into the forest taking the villages of Nogaya and Melichov without much of a fight. Our battalion commander Major Greim was wounded, however. Oberleutnant Senger took over as battalion leader.

13–14 February 1942

We pressed on to Nish and secured the flanks of (the remnants of!) Infantry Regiments 178 and 172 and MG Battalion 5.

15 February 1942

In the early hours our long, tiring and cautious advance through deep snow and forest brought us closer to Yagodnaya. Our 15cm guns bombarded the edges of the forest where Russian positions were suspected. Ivan had some very well-camouflaged snow bunkers there, but he was absent personally. We made a short pause for rest, maintaining an all-round watch. My back ached from towing the heavy ammunition cases. I sat down on one and delved into my haversack. The bread and butter were frozen hard as stone and the corned beef honeycombed with ice. I put the bread in my trousers pocket to thaw. In silence we resumed the march, clad in our long white camouflage shirts, and reached the small village of Fondeyevka. While our pioneers cleared landmines from the snow, our 15cm artillery fired at another village. We stood around freezing, then from curiosity investigated some stalls and found a number of cows which we milked. Even better, in a search of a house we discovered plum schnapps. I filled my field flask with it. 'Take up weapons and equipment, ready to engage!' We set off again for the small town of Yagodnaya. Two weeks earlier the Russians had tried to encircle us there. We went round a barricade of fallen trees across a path and glimpsed the first houses. Ivan must have forgotten to post sentries. With a loud 'Hurrah!' we attacked. Ivan, surprised, pulled out after blowing up two T-34 tanks. We searched every house, tossing hand grenades inside to make sure. From the centre of town we saw many Russians ascending the slope to the woods. The slope was thick with them attempting to flee with sleds and horses. In seconds our MGs and mortars were at readiness. 'Fire!' Everyone able to fire joined in, a fearsome display. The tracers of the heavy MGs flitted after them, our mortar bombs exploded amongst the fleeing enemy! I fired sixty rounds from my carbine from a standing position, my weapon resting on a plank fence. The MGs concentrated on the horses and carts and the groups of running Russians, we carbine-armed grenadiers aimed at isolated targets. My platoon leader grabbed my carbine as I reached into my cartridge pouch: 'Rehfeldt, give me the ammunition, I'd like to have a go.' I had the feeling this was revenge for the miserable days of the retreat. Ivan replied with rifle fire now and again, but not what one might call real resistance. Soon the last survivors got behind the crest of the ridge and disappeared into the woods, and we ceased fire. My God, the whole foreground was covered with dead Russians. None of them was a Siberian, for they wore neither the white padded jacket nor white trousers. Previously, the Russians had co-opted anybody capable of firing a weapon into the struggle against us, many of them 'Workers' Militia'. Lacking infantry training they paid dearly in blood. We posted sentries, and looked for a promising house for quarters. First we examined doors, ovens and cupboards for booby traps, Ivan could be very crafty with these things. During the night it was fairly lively in the woods with Russian stragglers surfacing here and there and firing like crazy. They had a Maxim MG somewhere: it was shooting red-yellow tracer upwards, but the point of it escaped me.

16 February 1942

The morning dawned sunny with good visibility. From Yagodnaya we could see several villages in open country ahead. No doubt the Russians could see us here too. We had received no rations the day before, but nevertheless we had to make ready to advance. Scarcely had we gone 500m than we received heavy fire from a village to our right and the edge of a wood. While still confused as to how to react, a motorcycle messenger came up from the rear: 'Halt! Stop the advance, new orders. Hot food, cold fare and post have arrived. Return to Yagodnaya immediately for rations! Advance will be resumed at 1000hrs.' We were happy to trot back leaving the war on hold for an hour. Ivan must have been very surprised to see us simply turn about. Meanwhile four SP assault guns had rolled up and guarded Yagodnaya while we ate hot pea soup. At 1000hrs we set off again led by the four assault guns, ourselves following in long files with wide spaces between. To the left was a large Rollbahn bridge from where our flank was protected. Moving up along the road we came under accurate mortar fire, salvoes of four down the middle of the road each time. Our assault guns kept going and we were obliged to follow. Near the entrance to the village we knelt behind a low wall of snow, listened for the mortar to fire, counted off the seconds and then jumped up and sprinted, still in single file with a space between each man, and arrived almost unscathed at the village. The assault guns had already driven Ivan out of the first houses by the expedient of firing a single round from the main gun into each. A number of houses were already burning. We infantrymen advanced between the houses but came under mortar fire again. Our heavy MG gunners suffered their first casualties. Battalion commander Papa Greim was wounded by a splinter. He was taken into a house and the wound was dressed. He insisted on staying, not wanting to be taken back, but the surgeon ordered it and he was carried off to one of the assault guns returning for ammunition. Sitting near the upper hatch, he delivered a stirring farewell speech to us. The sense of it was as follows: 'Comrade Soldiers! I am out of it, rotten luck! They've sent me back though I would have preferred to remain with you. Things must go forward without me, however. The assault guns are only going back to fetch ammunition, after which they will return to you. The reconnaissance troops have reported that the Russians are pulling back with long columns of sleds. They are retreating. After him! *Auf Wiedersehen, Kameraden!*' Then the assault guns roared away. We sat in a cottage to warm up or eat. Erwin Rieger told me I had two parcels from home, the first since October.

The Russians offered stiff but fruitless resistance to the assault guns at the entrance to the village. A Russian heavy MG stood before a bridge over the Wytebet. Passing by, I saw wreckage and two dead gunners burned to a crisp. A direct hit! At the far end of the village lay open country. Ivan would have no protection here. We set off in pursuit. The road ran ruler-straight to the second village: the assault guns led, we followed in file. Ivan's anti-tank guns fired at the Rollbahn itself where his shells failed to explode in the snow and bounced away. Since he persisted in firing 10m short of the assault guns there must have been some method in it but instead the ricochets came flying towards the rank and file behind, often a close call![1] From a wood to our right we saw Russians fleeing towards the next village, but the snow was deep, and even when they got there they would have to brave the shellfire at the village edges. After a hard struggle we arrived at the village and set up the mortars: there were plenty of Russians milling around and so no lack of targets. When fetching ammunition from our sled I heard: 'At 1648hrs, II Battalion reached village of Melichov. Continue advance to Rshevka. Out!' Ivan had mined the entrance and one of the assault guns had had a track blown off. The others detoured and were continuing to advance with caution. At the centre of the village we came to a barrier which Ivan had made by felling trees left and right, laying them across the road and filling the space between them with landmines. He had also mined the road. We advanced cautiously, weapons at the ready. The Russians were firing round after round of anti-tank fire between the houses, the idea being to spray us with debris and splinters. Our pioneers probed in the snow with a bayonet for mines. Now and again a wooden-box type mine would be found and carefully removed. We moved singly and cautiously in leaps and bounds from house to house to the far end of the village. Our heavy MGs were assembled, the gunners shooting from the prone position. We were ordered forward to fire our mortars at Russian MG positions and assemblies of infantry. Five propellant charges were used again to increase range (i.e. four additional charges plus one in the bomb). Many Russians were being hauled from hiding in the huts behind us and sent back as prisoners. Our mortars were being harassed by fire from a concealed MG somewhere to our left and were short on ammunition. We runners had to dash back, always risking fire on the village street. Our sleds were under cover somewhere in the first houses and had to be looked for. Finally we found them in a barn. The sleds were loaded and then back we went. Our No. 2 Group of heavy mortars had set up in the centre of the village, sending out bomb after bomb in rapid fire. We had just passed them when a shell hit a tree and exploded, breaking off branches, while fragments and splinters whirled in all directions. A black explosive cloud formed above the trees. Then we heard the shouts, 'Medic! Medic!' From the Group of Feldwebel Hinz, two men at the mortar were dead, and four or five seriously wounded. A motorcycle messenger lay with tendons in a leg cut through. After a brief period of confusion the wounded were stretchered away, the mortar dismantled and fire continued with a single mortar only. From our rear somewhere our Do-Gerät rocket launcher fired: the propellant was not smokeless and a single salvo left numerous broad trails overhead for some time.

Gasping for breath we reached our forward mortars and stacked the ammunition nearby. The accursed Russian MG was still firing into our flank from the left forcing our mortars to relocate behind a house. The artillery spotter for our 15cm gun had set up on the roof from where he scanned the territory through binoculars. I climbed up to him and informed him about the Russian MG. 'Well, shall we look for where the beast has his lair?' At that moment the MG 'blabbered' and its burst of fire clattered into a neighbouring house. I was studying a barn about 500m from the village when by chance I saw a Russian steel helmet and the muzzle fire. I pointed out my discovery to the artillery spotter. At once he gave new orders: 'Left hand, alone, from ground zero ten less. Range, 1,200. Percussion.' We heard the field gun fire and upon impact a fountain of earth rose up near the barn. The MG fell silent. The spotter issued a correction and the next round blew up the barn, boards and beams whirled in the air. Direct hit! Only two rounds had been needed to wipe out the MG. We watched in fascination. In the evening we set up something like a 'forward front line' as darkness covered the land. The night passed fairly quietly: from a constant distance north-west to west of the town of Shisdra, Russian

15.2cm artillery fired at us. The range gave us enough time to take cover after seeing the muzzle flash. So the Russian winter offensive had broken through as far as Shisdra, almost due west of us! The small local huts trembled under the impact, splinters reduced planking to fragments which clattered everywhere in the snow.

17 February 1942

Despite their artillery I slept deeply. After sentry duty I stretched out in the straw, greatcoat collar up and hands in pockets thinking, 'If I'm to go, best a direct hit,' and then I'm asleep. Early in the morning we looked to our front: apparently Ivan had evacuated the village of Rshevka. To our left the grenadiers of 6 and 7 Companies built snow bunkers: they protect only against wind and snow. Ivan began aiming at them with his 7.65cm general-purpose gun: our grenadiers crawled out on their stomachs. The white snow shirts are excellent camouflage. There – direct hit on a snow bunker. The grenadiers crawl back to retrieve a wounded man. When we had the stove going nicely in our house and everybody stood around it warming up, suddenly chalk and earth sprayed off the walls and MG rounds came through the windowpanes and into the wall opposite. Where was this MG located? Neither we nor the artillery spotter knew. When the remaining windows were shattered later by an anti-tank round, we decided to find another billet. Was it deliberate or coincidence? That same night, when some of Ivan's 'sewing machines' circled overhead, a direct hit destroyed the whole house. I had just gone on watch when I heard this ground attack aircraft. The Ilyushin 2 can really get on your nerves. (In my four years on the Eastern Front, I never saw one shot down.[2]) And now another one has turned up to lay his 'eggs'. I could see the flame of his exhaust clearly as he disappeared towards the village of Yagodnaya. Here the red-yellow fireballs of our 2cm and 3.7cm Flak flew at him like pearls on a string. Then came lightning flashes on the ground indicating that he had bombed something, after which he flew back above us towards the searchlight in the distance guiding him in. As my time on watch ends he comes over again at his usual slow speed. Holes cannot be dug in the ground for cover and so I stand behind the houses on the right-hand side watching. He circles there, and when he cuts his engine he glides down with a rustle, picking up speed and releases his bombs, sometimes as many as a stick of six. Once the last bomb has exploded, he starts the engine again, although often with many

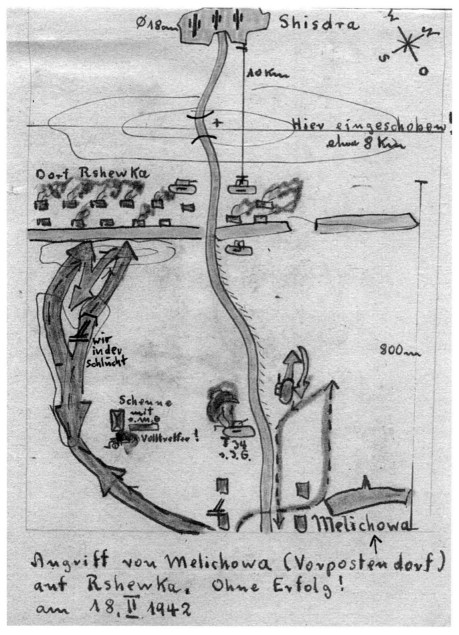

Map by Hans Rehfeldt, 'Attack from Melichova (advanced outpost) against Rshevka on 18.2.1942. Unsuccessful!' The author was in the gully on the left 'wir in der Schlucht': the 15cm infantry gun appears to have been located by a barn – 'Scheune'.

misfires! Then he heads back to his searchlight, from where one often hears the next one coming. We think that his bombing routine is as follows: after recognizing his assigned target, he cuts the engine, holds the control stick between his legs, grabs the bombs in his hands and throws them out when he thinks he's more or less in the right position. Usually he will have a gunner aboard who only shoots at the stars. On this last raid the pilot hit a couple of houses which we see burning. His bombs made deep and wide craters in the frozen earth. I believe there is nobody on this Front who has not had a bad experience with a 'sewing machine'.

18 February 1942

The morning began with bright sunshine and excellent visibility. Therefore we could not venture out on the village street. Ivan fired at anything that moved. From my perch in the roof of our house I could see the whole village and into the Russian positions. As several sleds approached from afar they were fired on by our MG. They turned about in wild disorder, some of the Ivans abandoned their sleds and ran for it, but the MG picked them off. The gunner was Obergefreiter Bolle, later awarded the German Cross in Gold. We stood on watch, our mortars ready. Apart from a few skirmishes during the day it remained quiet, the night too. We prepared for the assault on the next village, Rshevka.

19 February 1942

The attack on Rshevka began in the early hours supported by the assault guns. After softening up the occupiers with an avalanche of mortar bombs, the twenty men of 6 Company on our right led by Leutnant Horstmann reached the first houses. Ivan replied with his mortars. In a split second we were all under cover, I rolled into a burning house. Only the walls still stood but the warmth did me good. I lay for a while on some straw observing the attack. After fierce fighting our grenadiers took the village and secured it. The attack came to a standstill, but we needed to take the village of Tshuchlov as well. One of our Panzer IVs straddled the mined street, pouring shell after shell into the village attracting both wild and accurate MG and rifle fire from Ivan in response. Their mortars hammered. The heat of battle developed. From ahead came the shout, 'The lieutenant is dead!', and a little later, gasping and sweating, several grenadiers brought his body back in a groundsheet. Now

6 Company had only sixteen men, the lieutenant and two others dead, two wounded. The defensive fire was increasing: our heavy MG was forward in the thick of it: their group leader Unteroffizier Alois Rempke (he was my group leader for several days in the Oka position) was seriously wounded by a bullet which passed through his cheek and mouth. Suddenly the burning house, my refuge, collapsed inwards and the sparks burned holes in my white camouflage shirt. It was already sunset and fairly cold. When night fell the shooting died down. We could not hold Rschevka with only twelve men and so pulled out. We set sentries and got warm in the houses left standing. After the attack the fighting strength of the battalions was sixty men. 6 Company was attached as a platoon to Company *Wackernagel*. Regimental commander Oberst Hörnlein combined the infantry battalions into a single 'Schützenbataillon *Grossdeutschland*' led by Major 'Kiki' Gehrke.

20 February 1942

Very early in the morning a messenger came with fresh orders. Pioneers were to join our attack, so we mortar men had to lend them our white snow shirts. We were to set up in a long gully providing fire support for the pioneers' flamethrower attack. At 0500hrs our artillery at Yagodnaya opened the assault with a tremendous barrage cratering the edge of the village. A smoke screen was also laid which would enable the attack to proceed in leaps and bounds. While Ivan was temporarily blinded the pioneers would go in with their flamethrowers. We mortar carriers had been advancing as fast as possible to the cross-gully under cover of smoke but it lifted suddenly. Ivan could see us running and subjected us to MG and rifle fire. In our field-grey uniforms without camouflage shirts we were easily seen and had to run hell for leather. In the gully we were to stand by as reserves in the event of a Russian counter-attack. We zeroed our mortars in quickly and then the first wounded came back, hit by our own artillery at the edge of the village. This risk exists especially in winter if the guns zeroed-in the previous day are fired with the same settings the following morning. Therefore in this case the first salvoes fell on our own troops close to the village. The effect on morale can be imagined. The usual excuse was that the gun barrels needed 're-rifling'. The Russian defensive fire intensified: they had infested the village of Tshuchlov to the left of the road with snipers and many infantry armed with sub-machine guns and probably had some tanks hidden away there too; we heard their rumbling and the occasional round being fired.

The whole village was on fire, black clouds of smoke billowed into the overcast morning sky but the attack had come to a standstill. II Battalion consisted of just eight to sixteen men. In the gully we watched and waited. A messenger came back panting for breath: our people had advanced as far as the Russian snow bunkers where they received murderous defensive fire forcing them to retire to the nearest depression. And the flamethrowers had failed. The pioneers returned with the equipment on their backs, the hose and jet in their hands, fury in their faces. In our gully they took the things apart: the cause was the fuel, frozen solid. Our artillery was hitting the village and the guessed-at tank positions with continual harassing fire. Towards midday the sun broke through. It shone down almost vertically on the slope of our gully and we ran back and forth to keep our feet warm in the snow. Some of the men had stretched out on ammunition boxes enjoying the warmth. I climbed to the top edge of the gully where the occasional rifle round and ricochet whistled past nearby. A few metres ahead, three men were carrying ammunition and dressings to the forward infantrymen. From our gully the flat terrain sloped downwards to end in a depression: from the depression the terrain rose towards Rshevka. Our attacking infantry had taken refuge in this depression: they would draw enemy fire should they try to leave it and so were bogged down there. A surgeon and two radio operators had got to the depression on skis to attend the wounded. The latter had been lying motionless in the snow in a temperature of minus 45°C since early morning and could expect frostbite to be added to their wounds. A few metres away from me a small group of infantry was standing surveying the village with binoculars. A sniper bullet hit one of the party who threw up his arms and collapsed. They carried the casualty down into the gully, unbuttoned his greatcoat and field blouse and searched for the wound: there was no blood, he was only gasping for breath. Ah! The bullet had hit his Infantry Assault Badge and been deflected. The wound to the skin was relatively minor. It was now 1500hrs and we sent a messenger to Melichov to ask when we could expect rations. Two hours later he returned: 'Not until evening and only then if you have taken Rshevka!' The men were disgruntled but the mood improved with the issue of fifty cigarettes per man. The sun had set and a pale ice-grey light filled the sky. It had grown much colder and I was not tempted to remove my gloves to light up. Meanwhile the medic-sled with dressings had arrived. In darkness we would bring out the wounded. Now two T-34s appeared from the burning village at top speed and came down the Rollbahn, stopping short of Melichov. They did not know that the emplacement for our artillery was behind the first houses: in the absence of our Pak the 15cm gun fired at the leading T-34 from a range of 100m. The wreck burned long into the night. Its companion withdrew, probably much impressed by the direct hit. We looked at the burning wreck with satisfaction. Now that it was fully dark, we received orders to dismantle the mortars and withdraw into our 'forward outpost' of Melichov. The wounded were retrieved and treated in Melichov, later the poor comrades who had spent the day in a freezing depression also returned. Soon we had hot and cold food and post, we warmed up, sentries were posted and we turned in on our beds of straw. The Russian artillery fired all night but poorly, the shells landing in the open ground ahead of the village. His 'sewing machines' also paid us visits throughout the night and left two houses burning: a third house was set on fire accidentally by overheating the stove. The attack on Rshevka left Schützenbataillon *Grossdeutschland* with two dead: Leutnant Keiner (1 Company) and Oberleutnant von Garnier (Leader, 2 Company). Oberleutnant Senger (3 Company) was now its latest commanding officer.

21 February 1942

Three officers and thirty other ranks were all that remained of the once so proud 'Reinforced Infantry Regiment *Grossdeutschland*'. We were without heavy weapons and rearward services structure. And I was one of the lucky thirty!

To put this in perspective, here is the 'war footing' authorized strength of the battalions and companies:

I Battalion	Staff, Signals detachment
	1 to 3 Inf Companies
	Light infantry guns (7.5cm) Pak anti-tank (3.7cm)
II Battalion	Staff, Signals contingent
	5 to 7 Inf Companies
	8 Company: heavy MG and heavy mortars (8.14cm)
	Light infantry guns (7.5cm) Pak anti-tank (3.7cm)
III Battalion	Staff, Signals contingent
	9 to 11 Inf Companies
	Light infantry guns (7.5cm) Pak anti-tank (3.7cm)
IV Battalion	Staff, Signals contingent
	13 Company, light infantry guns

14 Company, tank destroyers

15 Company, heavy infantry guns (15cm)

16 Company, SP assault guns

V Battalion   Staff, Signals contingent

17 Company, motorcycle company

18 Company, pioneers

19 Company, signals

20 Company, Flak (2cm and 3.7cm)

Of nine standard infantry companies (authorized strength 150 men), 9 x 150 = 1,350 men, on 20 and 21 February 1942 there were only thirty fighting men left of which most were 8 MG Company with two heavy MGs and one Group (two heavy mortars).

The enemy artillery fired all night in front of the village, once or twice overshooting, these shells landing between the houses. At breakfast with all sitting at the table a shell exploded just outside, shattering all the windows, splinters clattering against the walls. One of the signallers in an adjoining room was wounded.

The air was clear and the visibility very good. Almost due west 10km or so away, we could see easily the houses of the town of Shisdra (on the river of the same name) through binoculars. The Russians who broke out from Moscow had headed there. Around it lies the great wooded area of Bryansk, home to many partisans. Today we were relieved by I Battalion, but came back in the afternoon and met at the village pond near the company command post, so few of us that 8 Company could all be billeted in a single house, being the crews of three heavy MGs and two mortars. All of 8 Company could be obliterated by a single direct hit on one house! I had to do my turn of sentry duty that night. I didn't dare walk about in the snow because of the pain and throbbing from the suppurating wounds on both legs. The bandages, soaked in blood, stuck my thermals to the wounds. With the permission of my group leader I was allowed to fetch a stool and perform my sentry duty seated. During the night several houses went up in flames from the artillery fire. The question of accommodation was gradually becoming problematic!

Notes

1. The idea was to ricochet the shell so as to damage the *Seitenvorgelege* (drive and drive sprocket for the tracks) and render the panzer immobile to await the *coup de grâce*. See: Richard Freiherr von Rosen, *Als Panzer Offizier im Ost und West*, Flechsig Verlag, 2013. (TN)

2. The Ilyushin 2 was a well-armoured two-seater ground-attack monoplane. In 1943, Reinhard René Rohr, a French national declared to be a *Volksdeutscher* in 1940, a conscript into the Wehrmacht, was sent to the Russian Front. On the afternoon of his arrival he was crossing open country to his unit when attacked by a 'sewing machine'. Rohr stood his ground and shot the pilot dead with his rifle. The aircraft then crashed. Rohr was immediately awarded the Iron Cross Second Class for this feat of arms. See Reinhard René Rohr, *Ma retraite de Russia avec la Wehrmacht*, Strasbourg, 1991. (TN)

The winter of 1941 at minus 35°C. Oberleutnant Greim, leader of II Battalion *Grossdeutschland* by his vehicle.

The Divisional Commander, General Hörnlein, at Tula on 8 December 1941.

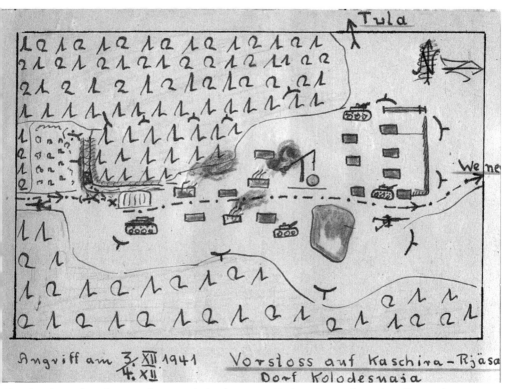

Angriff am 3. XII 1941
        4. XII

Vorstoss auf Kaschira-Rjasa
        Dorf Kolodesnaja

Map by the author showing the intended advance to Kashira-Ryasa from the village of Kolodesnaya.

A mortar team in white camouflage uniforms, winter 1941.

A Propaganda Company photo in an illustrated magazine showing a mortar team in action. The handwritten note reads: 'We never had a misfire, we never had anything freeze up.'

The mortar barrel elevated for long-range fire.

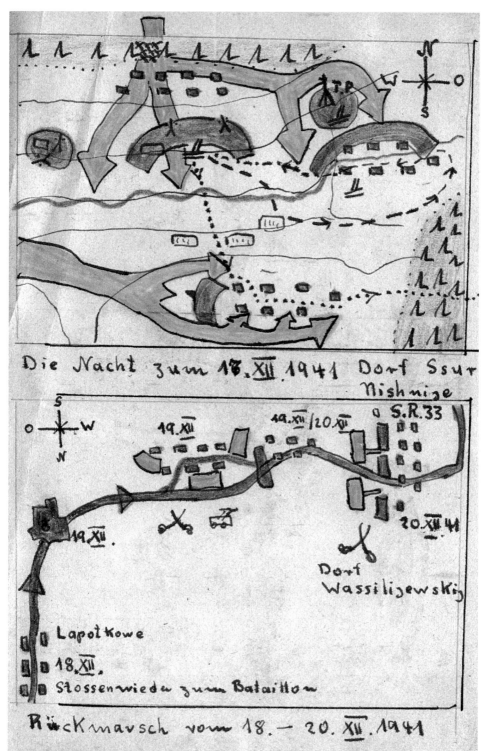

Maps drawn by Hans Rehfeldt.
(Top) 'The night of 18.12.1941, village Ssury Nishniye'.
(Bottom) Withdrawal of 18–20.12.1941 'to meet up again with Battalion'.

Abwehrkampf im Nebel

Infanterieregiment „Großdeutschland" steht unerschütterlich
Sibirier blutig zurückgeschlagen

Ein trüber Wintertag geht zu Ende. Im Halbdunkel bezieht unsere Batterie vom Infanterieregiment „Großdeutschland" ihre Stellung in der neuen Verteidigungslinie. Die Grenadiere haben tagsüber mit dem Bau ihrer Erdbunker begonnen. Mühsam muß Zentimeter um Zentimeter aus dem hartgefrorenen Boden herausgesprengt werden. Bald werden die Sowjets heran sein. Unser Nachrichtendienst hat längst im Anmarsch befindliche neue sibirische Divisionen festgestellt. Eigene Spähtrupps melden: „Die Dörfer am jenseitigen Ufer des Flusses noch feindfrei."

Im Ungewissen, über das, was der nächste Morgen bringen wird, strecken wir uns am Abend lang aufs Stroh. Eine wohltuende Müdigkeit überkommt uns. Die Sowjetkate ist gut gewärmt. Wir sind fast wunschlos zufrieden, nur die Läuse ärgern uns noch eine Weile, ehe wir fest eingeschlafen sind. Aber sehr lange dauert die Ruhe nicht. Der nächste Morgen bringt uns die erste Ueberraschung mit einem Artillerieüberfall auf unser Dorf. Mit den ersten Einschlägen, die uns jäh aus dem Schlafe reißen, kommt jedem von uns die blitzschnelle Gewißheit — jetzt sind die Sowjets da. Vorn tacken schon die ersten Maschinengewehre unserer Vorposten. — Alarm! Die Infanterie hat längst ihre Stellungen bezogen, und wir legen unsere Beobachtungsstelle in eine Scheune. Beim Morgengrauen wird der Gefechtslärm stärker. Infanteriegeschosse pfeifen durch die Luft, klatschen in die Holzwand unserer Scheune. Dazwischen tönt der „Ratsch" der sowjetischen Granatwerfereinschläge.

Leuchtzeichen unserer Grenadiere vom Infanterieregiment „Großdeutschland" — Feind greift an! Noch verdeckt ein dichter Nebel die Sicht. Der Gegner nützt diese Gelegenheit und arbeitet sich immer näher an unsere Stellungen heran. Die Waffen unserer Infanterie feuern aus allen Läufen. Links drüben kommt das Feuer langsam näher; jetzt „ratschen" die sowjetischen Werfer ihre Granaten dicht vor uns hin. Der verdammte Nebel verhindert immer noch die Sicht. Wir schießen Sperrfeuer, ohne beobachten zu können. Es ist zum Verzweifeln! Wir wissen nicht, ob wir im Augenblick damit Wirkung erzielen, andererseits können wir aber unsere Schüsse nicht näher heranziehen, um nicht die eigene Infanterie zu gefährden. Schon sind die Linien beim linken Nachbarn zurückgedrückt worden. An der Trennungslinie zu unserem dritten Bataillon drohen die Sowjets durchzubrechen. Wird die Infanterie dem ununterbrochenen Ansturm der Bolschewisten standhalten? Eine weitere Kompanie unseres Regiments „Großdeutschland" wird in aller Eile eingeschoben und wirft im erbitterten Kampf den Feind an der bedrohten Stelle zurück. Trotzdem hält die Gefahr weiter an. Beim G_ner macht sich zwar ein gewisser Mangel an

A newspaper article from December 1941 headlined: 'Defensive Battle in the Fog: Infantry Regiment *Grossdeutschland* stands firm as a rock: Siberians repulsed with bloody losses.'

The fine Russian Orthodox monastery at Bolchov, January 1942.

n the Stalin era most churches were used as warehouses.

Hans Rehfeldt was treated at Bolchov between 14 January and 8 February 1942 for frostbitten egs.

An 8.8cm Flak gun put out of action at Bolchov by enemy fire.

Grave of Obergefreiter Dumpe of 8 Inf Regt *Grossdeutschland* who fell on 25 December 1941.

Graveyard on the outskirts of Bolchov, February 1942.

Company strengths were greatly reduced by death, wounds and frostbite.

The Communist Party offices at Orel were used by the German occupying force as a cinema. The 'G' stands for Guderian.

The road to Bolchov at Orel 1941/42.

Seen from a German trench near Orel, a flare briefly illuminates the foreground.

Group photo with mortar at Melichov, February 1942.

Home-made jackets and coats gave little extra warmth and were used mainly for camouflage in the snow.

By comparison, the same troops without camouflage could be seen from a great distance.

A German 8cm mortar, to the right a captured Soviet mortar.

Gefreiter Fritsch at Melichov.

A German mortar at Kudinov, February 1942.

Group photo at Melichov.

Another side of the 'fully motorized regiment'.   Group photo, Alexandrovka, 6 April 1942.

Oberfeldwebel Puls (CSM), seated on the wall at left, in front of the orderly office.

Chapter 9

Relief from Neuruppin: Withdrawn from the Front

---

22 February 1942

I could not stand the pain any longer and reported sick. I could hardly walk: one leg in front of the other and then pause, and repeat. When he saw my legs the doctor said, 'Dear God, you're still able to walk on those legs? Get off to rearward services at once!' I scrambled with difficulty through the snow and over the ice of the Oka to my hut, packed my belongings together, took leave of my comrades, and after reporting my departure to our company leader Leutnant Hoffmann, I found my old platoon leader, Oberfeldwebel Otto Puls, and we parted with a hearty handshake. It was the last time I saw him, for he fell a few days later in Melichov village. Unteroffizier Berbrich, our quartermaster, took me on his horse-drawn sledge. I sat alongside regimental leader Oberfeldwebel Patzke who wanted to know what my wound was. When I showed him my legs, he said, 'Jesus!' We left the village at the gallop, reducing speed on the Rollbahn, pocked with huge black shell craters. Ivan had an extensive view over the Rollbahn here and liked us to keep our speed down so that he could pound our supply route. We were in luck, however, and reached Yagodnaya without incident. Our artillery was located here but we saw that Ivan's 'sewing machines' had been busy here too, large bomb craters and some ruined houses being the evidence of his nightly forays. Often enough on sentry duty at Yagodnaya I had watched his bombs explode and the Flak bursting around him. The next stage of my journey to the rear was a ride of 25km to Bolchov in a motor car, and we reached 8 Company *Ferntross* [distant rearward services] late that night. Here I reported to the *Spiess*, Stabsfeldwebel Maritzen, who knew me of old and after collecting my post I went to my 'old quarters in the sickbay'. There I met a few fellow-sufferers. I lit a candle, in agony removed my boots and lay in the straw fully dressed. Dear God, how good that felt. I was told that replacements would be arriving from Neuruppin. II Battalion was being rested for a few days before being withdrawn from the Front. Over the next days the replacements were sorted out and distributed to the companies. We met former recruits who had gone through basic training with us and had been held back. Scarcely had the newcomers got settled than they were tossed into the front line! When the Russians attacked on 7 March 1942, the whole battalion went forward. Thus they received their baptism of fire very quickly. On 29 February in defending against a Russian attack coming from Tshuchlov towards Melichov and Rshevka, the regiment's last assault gun was hit and destroyed.

March 1942

Spring is coming! A violent wind howled across the steppe and relatively speaking it was warmer. During the day there was a superficial thaw but at night the thermometer fell to minus 15°C. One night there was a very heavy snowfall and many places had a fresh metre-deep layer of snow on top of the frozen snowdrifts. Supplies from Orel could not get through and at midday some Ju 52s would appear and drop food and ammunition, also barrels of fuel and medical supplies suspended from small parachutes. Thus we were supplied by air for a week until the entire Rollbahn was finally shovelled free. By the look of it, the winter was not finished with us yet – already it had lasted from November to April, six months! A half year of winter, frost, bitter cold! And in addition the deprivation and demands of war. How wonderful it must be to be dressed only in light sports gear, stretched out in warm air. It was after 21 March: here it was spring but it remained bitterly cold with fierce winds. The Russian winter of 1941/42 had not complied with the calendar! But now that it was approaching its end I could say with pride, 'I coped really well with the worst winter in many years!'

3 April 1942

Yesterday the surgeon gave me a clean bill of health. And about time too. I left early with the provisions cart, sitting on top of the soup canisters. We went through Yagodnaya again and then bore left for my group in reserve at Alexandrovka. The groups relieve each other only every five days since the Front is quiet. The day after tomorrow we will go forward again. I reported to my company leader Leutnant Hoffmann and then found my group's small house at the end of the village. They were all busy dynamiting deep holes and digging. In some they buried dead Russians and in others dead horses. The graves of fallen soldiers are marked by a thick pole. Ivan often left his dead lying in the open for years. There was only a light covering of snow on the fields but still metres-deep in drifts. I joined in the work industriously.

4 April 1942

My group has been 'resting' at Alexandrovka since 2 April and will go forward to relieve on 7 April. On sentry duty at night the woods limit the view. Behind them, flares flicker up, one hears shooting and artillery fire. Then it falls quiet for a while, interspersed only by MGs chattering somewhere. When the rattle gets louder, perhaps scouting parties are at work. When the hated 'sewing machine' comes bumbling over we all have to take cover, for there is no knowing where his eggs will drop. If he bumbles beyond, the Flak and exploding bombs will show his target for tonight. Occasionally a few heavy bombers can be heard droning in the distance. Tomorrow is Easter. Maybe they will make an issue of cigarettes, or schnapps. Perhaps even champagne. A glance at the watch, my sentry duty is up. I wake the relief in the house. When he appears I report: 'All quiet, no special occurrence.' Then into the warm room. Our motto here is: 'Better suffocate in a warm fug than freeze to death in the cold ozone!' Boots off, stretch out, blanket over the ears. 'Many have frozen to death, but none has died of the stink!' Thus is the experience of a soldier.

5 April 1942

Suddenly all the talk in the room is of leave! Today we didn't work and so sat and wrote home or just talked. During the morning our whole crowd went to the 'delousing institution' they have set up at Afosonov. At midday we returned to our quarters deloused, bathed and refreshed. It was announced that we would be served sweet, thick milk rice pudding for lunch. A race to the field kitchen! Afterwards, 'round-bellied and fully fed', I smoked a big, fat Easter cigar. More letters were written, no more work for us. In the evening we slept in warmth on the straw until awoken for sentry duty.

6 April 1942

My watch was two hours from 0500hrs and I saw the most wonderful sunrise! By midday we could feel the warmth of the sun's rays doing us good. The weather is glorious. Finally winter is over. After so many months of icy cold, an indescribable elation for us!

7 April 1942

Today we should have been relieved. The word had gone round that we were to be withdrawn from the Front, perhaps out of Russia itself. But there had been lots of 'words' like this before. At last something official. Lemmelsen, Commanding General of the Panzer Troops, would be coming tomorrow. The most thorough spring cleaning was ordered! Sentries were posted at the village entrance and exit, Pak guns nearby. We mortar men had to excavate a firing pit. Instead we dug a deep hole in the snow in the corner of Matka's garden. Scarcely had we tossed out the first spits of earth than Matka herself appeared and brought to bear all her powers of persuasion to stop us digging there. We ignored her. Suddenly my spade encountered some trousers, a shirt and a bag full of clothing. Also axes, saws and other worktools, all buried deep in the snow. Now we knew the reason for Matka's objections. But there was no risk that we would confiscate any of this stuff. Triumphantly we paraded the treasure before her. Matka and the Malinki (two children) stood by, smiling. 'Just like the old Germanic people in the Thirty Years' War,' a historical-minded comrade said. We kept digging and more tools, cooking implements and even a wooden spoon came to light. Soon we had our position ready, assembled the mortar, laid the ammunition alongside and threw a groudsheet over the lot of it. In the afternoon we went over our quarters with a fine-tooth comb and cleaned out all the filth and grit down to the last millimetre. I believe that the village had never been so clean since the last visit of the tsars. The older Pans and Matkas admired our handiwork very much, praising us to the skies: '*Germanski monoga Kultura! Karosch!*' ('The Germans are very cultured. Excellent!')

8 April 1942

Today the general was supposed to visit but he went elsewhere. All our spring cleaning for nothing. Then came a radio message. Today we were to leave for Yagodnaya, we were relieved from the Front! At last! All day horse-drawn columns of advance troops arrived at the village and looked for quarters. Their officers went forward to the main battle line to be appraised of the situation. We got ready to leave and cleaned our quarters. All MGs, mortars and ammunition were piled on the lorry, the men retained their hand weapons and hand grenades.

9 April 1942

We relinquished our sleds to the relieving unit and set out at 1630hrs. It had been warm and sunny at midday and thawed, but only superficially. The meltwater could not drain away because of the still-frozen earth below it and soon the Rollbahn had a surface layer of liquid mud half a metre deep. The high snow walls at the sides prevented any of it flowing off. In places it was a lake, everywhere streamlets and rills flowed from the fields into the Rollbahn. The vehicles, engines howling, rolled and lurched through the morass up to the axles. After 5km we had to dismount with all our equipment. Now began the indescribable toil of walking through this mud. It would suck the boots off your feet. Our boots plus mud content weighed almost a hundredweight. We could hardly move our legs through the muddy slush, we had bootfuls of it and at every step the filthy meltwater sprayed up into our faces. Soon darkness fell and it was impossible to see where one trod. Many of the men caught their feet on obstructions and measured their length in it. Cursing was the only relief – *Schisskoyenno*! The march continued through several villages, but our aim was Yagodnaya. We came to a village in which the local brook had been swollen by the thaw. There was no bridge, only a couple of large stepping stones from one side to the other. For the men of the grenadier companies this was easy since they had only a light MG or rifle to carry. My turn came. With the mortar barrel (24kg) on my shoulder I found that the first stepping stone was already submerged: I misjudged and found myself standing up to my midriff in filthy icy water. I got to the other side but of course arrived without the mortar barrel. Mortar leader Günter Weidner said, 'Fetch the barrel out or I shall shoot you myself for dereliction of duty.' But even a Prussian wouldn't shoot you just for that. I got low in the icy water, it poured into my boots again, I grabbed the barrel on the river bed and climbed out. In a few minutes I had no feeling in my feet. The temperature was minus 15°C. Nobody laughed at my misfortune, for everybody had cold, wet feet. Soon we got to the large wooden bridge over the Wytebet and heaved a sigh of relief, for Yagodnaya was just ahead. We thought there would be quarters ready us. Bathed in sweat from the long march, our feet numb, we had to stand for a half hour at the first house. At this some 'mutinous talk' began. We steamed like horses in the cold air. Finally a messenger came to show us to our quarters. We had to chop wood for the stove and then sat at the table eating the remains of our rations. The problem taking off my boots was that my feet now fitted them perfectly and could not move inside them. My feet also burned painfully. Once all my colleagues were asleep I struggled for half an hour to remove my boots until I was successful. I hung the remains of my socks on the stove door: here they steamed and finally smoked, giving off an infernal stink. I consigned them to the flames and made rag socks for myself. Putting on the dried boots was also not without its problems because I could not angle my feet into the correct place for my toes.

10 April 1942

Well after 0900hrs the convoy of lorries with us aboard pulled out from Yagodnaya for Bolchov. The Rollbahn with its high snow wall either side was like a river, the lorries making a bow wave through the filthy flood, the wheels almost fully covered. The lorries' radiators ahead cleaved through the water. We floated rather than drove through the high mud. Motorcycle riders were being towed behind some of the lorries and had difficulty in keeping the machine upright and sat with their legs spread wide, their rear quarters almost touching the water. Upon our arrival at Bolchov nobody knew where our quarters might be and so we directed our lorry to the rearward services and the 'sickbay'. Matka was as pleased as the Snow Queen to see me and said, '*Ivan Ivanovich nasad? Kak djela?*' ('Ivan Ivanovich back? How are you?'). Then she served up a large tray of baked potatoes.

At midday we mounted up again and were driven to the city centre where quarters had been assigned to us in the old church. From a distance it looked very impressive with its two onion-domes and the tall round cupola, but the inside was bare. Like all Russian churches it had been used by Ivan as a warehouse and thoroughly plundered, but at least they had given it a fresh coat of white paint. We installed large iron stoves and much straw. It was only for a night. The best was the mail we received: I got almost fifty of the small 50g parcels and many letters – my birthday post. Sweets, cakes, chocolate and much more besides. Our rule is 'One for all and All for one' and in true comradeship it was shared out fairly. At midnight a messenger arrived with orders, 'Immediately five men to the rearward services, provisions for three days have been received!' This meant going down a slope, over a bridge which had to be located first, then up the slope the other side, all in the darkness, before returning the same way carrying on our backs groundsheets bursting with the supplies, a round trip which needed some planning even in broad daylight and with no bags to carry. I have no idea how we managed it. It was like a night exercise. In the morning we went to the cinema and saw our first film since October, *Pedro soll hängen*.

11 April 1942

At 0700hrs two lorries stood ready to take an advance party to Orel. The second lorry had had its motor taken out and would be under tow. This was the lorry in which I was to travel. The condition of the Rollbahn was the same as that between Yagodnaya and Bolchov, and we rolled and lurched alarmingly. The snow had mostly melted and now the problem was the swirling water and mud. The transition from deepest winter to spring was worse than the cold. The motorcycle riders were being towed, skidding and side-slipping and always up to the knees in water. They were happier making their own way ahead. The route was Tshern–Mzensk–Orel, the way we came. At Orel, the terminus of the rail line from the West where we arrived towards 1300hrs, we were given quarters in a large school and then had to go on the scrounge around the railway station for nails, wire and wooden beams to secure a rail cargo. 'Poor Germany!' We ate and warmed up at the station barracks, for the weather was far from warm. It seemed years since last we heard the hissing and whistling of locomotives, the clank and rattle of goods wagons. In the afternoon I weighed it all up. We knew that a rail journey was being planned, but to where? It was a great secret.

12 April 1942

The station at Orel was a scene of devastation, as was the town. Gutted railway wagons remained where they had burned out. Otherwise activity in the streets continued. Every corner and telegraph pole had its military direction shield, each unit being identified by its tactical sign (in our case the white steel helmet): the Army Vehicle Park, the Army Provisions Warehouse, the Front Theatre, the Soldiers' Cinema, the Bazaar, Eating House and Soldiers' Hostel – trees of shields. Huge numbers of cars, lorries and other vehicles filled the repair yards, noisy with hammering and welding, motors being lifted out or fitted. Close by was the panzer workshop, where damaged parts were replaced using large winches, new turrets installed, tracks fitted, minor shell damage repaired by specialists. At a crossroads lies a fallen telegraph pole, nailed up from top to bottom with every conceivable department needed for and by the troops in the forward lines. Long columns of lorries, fully loaded with ammunition and supplies, set off slowly for the Front, the leaders of the column no longer visible in the mist, while ever more pull out of the warehouses to form the tail. Lorries returning from the Front bring back the empties and ambulances the wounded. At the Orel railway terminus the material is stacked high. We looked at all this coming and going with interest. Here was only a small part of what one calls Organization! By the evening we had enough nails and beams [to use as large stabilizing wedges for vehicles on the railway wagons].

13 April 1942

Today II Battalion/Grenadier Regt arrived at Orel. We were posted at the crossroads as unofficial traffic gendarmes, directing the columns to the accommodation. Finding quarters in Orel was not easy. I had the task of drumming up a building for 6 Company: in the end I rang the town kommandant and asked if he knew where I could find one.

'For which unit?'

'*Grossdeutschland.*'

'Aha, that is Waffen-SS?'

Grossdeutschland, the Bodyguard Regiment of the German Volk, was directly subordinate to the Führer, I explained. I got my building quite quickly. Soon all our companies were housed. They asked us where we were all bound. The craziest rumours circulated. France. Holland. Another sector of the Front. We no longer cared. The main thing was, we were out of the 'shit'!

14 April 1942

After the morning parade we marched to the station to begin loading up. The individual lorries drove over a head ramp directly on to the transporter train. This was done very efficiently. 8 Company began at 1100hrs and was finished by 1300hrs despite rain, snowfall and wind, the roads under slush and mud such as we had never seen before in our lives. What a climate! After we ate, the *Tross* train pulled out at 1400hrs. We sat in goods wagons full of hope. We dared not speak of leave, only of plans for when we got leave. 14 April was my mother's birthday, and she had no idea I was on a goods train heading in a general westerly direction. Our field post takes four to six weeks to arrive. I pictured our reunion after appearing unannounced at the front door. The train roared ever onwards through the gigantic woods of Karachev.

16 April 1942

Ryetshitza is a small, undamaged little town south of the confluence of Beresina and the Dnieper. The river is therefore fairly broad here, 600–800m, and has a strong current. Midstream is a long, narrow island. There is a wide bend here.

Our pioneers have dynamited the ice, so that it drifts away in large floes. The sky is clear, the sun warm! We are in good spirits! Here our regiment, which had dreadful losses in the winter campaign, will arrive for rest and recuperation: reinforcements are coming and the regiment will be expanded into a division. Therefore a second regiment! In this period of so-called R&R, we will train with the newcomers, merge with them, try out new battle tactics, especially the cooperation of all arms of service and above all with our panzers and assault guns. In short, much is going to be expected of us. It is not really rest in the true sense, but deep in the rear, free of the enemy, we will prepare for the new tasks confronting us in 1942. Hard work lies ahead. That is how the Prussians like it! Militarily correct even in well-deserved periods of rest. But first a large contingent of the regiment is going on leave!

Ryetshitza is in the northern Ukraine. Everything here is much cleaner, the people are friendly and we notice the difference between the villages in the woods around Moscow and Tula, and those here in the Ukraine. First we looked to our quarters. It is difficult to believe how a simple empty classroom can be turned into a bright, liveable and cosy room with just a few materials and much effort and goodwill. Our room had a 'soldierly imprint'. I painted some images on the walls and added some fitting maxims. The light bulbs were given shades and potted plants appeared suddenly at the windows. The Reich war flag was painted below a large German eagle. Soon our room was ready for habitation.

17 April 1942

To put an end to sleeping on straw on the ground our carpenters made double beds out of boards brought from a large sawmill on the Dnieper, and after two days there were enough to go round. A 'reward' of schnapps, cigarettes and money was offered for the best room, and for three days we worked.

18 April 1942

From the window we can see the broad, mighty Dnieper with its ice floes wobbling sluggishly down to the Black Sea. Tomorrow is an 'on-duty' day. We 'veterans' are treated like recruits. We have to exercise and march exactly as if we have just come from the training depot. We are not pleased! But: 'Discipline is the soul of the Army! One must desire the impossible in order to achieve the possible.'

19 April 1942

We marched out stiffly to relieve the watch, who in turn marched stiffly back. The Ukrainians stood by and watched us in astonishment. At midday the sun is high and does us all good. Spring at last! How quickly we forget the horrors of those deadly, icy winter days now that we live beneath the glorious sun enjoying thoughts of leave and returning to one's family!

Chapter 10

Grossdeutschland Becomes an Infantry Division (mot.)

---

20 April 1942

We have discovered that the local population is keen to barter. They gather at our door with purses, baskets and sacks of commodities. We show packets of tobacco at our window which cause a stir amongst the grandfathers. They overbid and we are happy to receive twenty eggs in exchange for one packet of tobacco. The men prefer smokers' requisites, the Matkas and girls are more interested in sewing cotton, needles, brushes, cloths, etc. It is quite like an oriental bazaar in which the infantrymen are often the crooks. We are delighted to have butter, eggs, honey and bacon. It seems that the Ukraine is the land of milk and honey! What this land could become with good husbandry! Fruitful black earth! In the afternoon we had regimental roll call. The old 'Reinforced *Grossdeutschland* Infantry Regiment' is to be expanded into a division known as 'Infantry Division (motorized) *Grossdeutschland*'. There are to be changes within the regiments. A battalion will now consist of five companies. I Battalion, Companies 1 to 5, II Battalion, Companies 6 to 10 and so on. Ourselves, we are to become 9 Company/II Battalion/Regt 1 *Grossdeutschland*.

Divisional Commander:	Generalmajor Walter Hörnlein
Divisional Adjutant:	Hauptmann Theo Bethke
Inf Regt (mot.) 1 *Grossdeutschland*:	CO, Oberst Köhler
Inf Regt (mot.) 2 *Grossdeutschland*:	CO, Oberst Garski
II Battalion/Inf Regt 1 *Grossdeutschland*:	CO, Major Greim
Adjutant:	Leutnant von Mitzlaff
Senior Surgeon:	Dr Hahn
6 Company (grenadiers):	Oberleutnant Schulz

7 Company (grenadiers):	Hauptmann von Courbiere
	Leutnant Blumenthal
8 Company (grenadiers):	Leutnant Doege
9 Company (MGs/mortars):	Hauptmann Schmidt ('Afrika')
10 Company (heavy):	Hauptmann Peiler

Our Generalmajor Hörnlein published an appeal to his 'Old Hands': 'In the coming weeks we are going to work hard. The two regiments, the battalions and the individual companies must grow together so as to become a homogenous unit.'

21 April 1942

We are still busy renovating our room and actually enjoy the barracks discipline. Wilhelm, our provisions officer, summoned me to receive a bottle of schnapps for my nineteenth birthday. I had almost forgotten it after receiving birthday parcels at Bolchov and Orel. I celebrated with my close circle of friends.

22 April 1942

Ten days ago we froze through our greatcoats but today we no longer need a jacket. We do physical training in sports gear and are already talking of bathing in the Dnieper. From 1700hrs if off-duty we go into the small town, interesting because it is the first town we have occupied where no fighting had taken place previously. On Sundays the Ukrainians stroll the streets in their Sunday best. In the former Culture Park we sit on the balustrades with a cigarette watching the young men dancing the 'Krakoviak' with their Panienkas [girls]. For us it is fascinating to see here some of the customs of the Ukrainians. In our clumsy attempts to speak Russian we try to make contact with the local people, one of the reasons being that we need volunteers to work for us. In general the people are very friendly towards us. We can approach the Matka or her daughter to repair a torn shirt or darn our socks. Almost every evening we are invited to share roast potatoes, always with eggs and bacon. We have a good relationship with the Ukrainians although we cannot deny that some of our older comrades make unwelcome advances to the Panienkas. There is a surprisingly high number of very pretty girls, of impeccable character and not stupid! Many learned German at school. The girls have a better command of German than we do of Russian. I have some talent in languages and am the best of the Russian speakers: a Wehrmacht phrasebook helped me very much. The girls pronounce the Russian word for me and I imitate it. I also listen out for where the stress falls. We often kid the girls along, but there is never any ulterior motive behind it. Initially we were told to have no contact with the people because they were 'sub-humans' in the Nazi terminology of the time. This was a grave error of propaganda, for here our experience has been quite different. Later the official view changed. Late, but perhaps not too late?

23 April 1942

In the morning we had drill and sport. Before the midday meal the *Spiess* told us: 'This afternoon the company will proceed to the Varieté. A troupe of German artistes has arrived and we will enjoy some hours of relaxation!' After the meal we marched to the theatre singing. (A good company always sings while marching!) A comedian opened the presentation (we laughed till we cried!), then followed the girl dancers, acrobats, magicians and jugglers and the high point, a father-daughter duet using a violin bow and pruning saw. We regretted that it all had to end. When we returned to the barracks we found a list of leave-takers pinned to the notice board, but the Tula Reserve was not on it. We went to bed fairly depressed.

24 April 1942

I wrote home: 'Unfortunately no thought of leave yet.' Next a lorry took us to the Gomel delousing institution. After a glorious bath we were issued new underwear. It felt like Christmas but not quite so festive. We arrived back at Ryetshitza grey and covered in filthy dust. We were no strangers to this dust. The vehicles stir it up and it hangs in the air above the Rollbahn for hours if there is no wind. To my great surprise and joy, in the evening the notice board announced: 'Tula Reserve, make ready at once! Tomorrow last roll call for leave-takers!' By midnight we had our things packed and stowed.

25 April 1942

The whole company paraded with pack and baggage. Leutnant Hoffmann and the *Spiess*, Hauptfeldwebel Maritzen, looked us over from head to toe. 'Oh, I don't know whether I can let you go looking like this,' the officer laughed. 'Reminds me of how you looked at the Front. Smarten up! Fall out!' In the afternoon we wandered through the town and once more enjoyed the hospitality of the Ukrainians. Then: *Do svidanya*! *Auf Wiedersehen*!

26 April 1942

A Hauptmann Schmidt came to introduce himself as our new company leader. He wished us a happy leave and convalescence in the Reich so that we might return to our work well refreshed. Then we marched to the railway station in sweltering heat to join the entire 'Leave-takers' Regiment'. On the tracks stood a long train of goods wagons ready to take us to the Reich. We paraded before some high trees with a stork's nest. After loading our belongings we had to re-assemble on the platform to witness the award of the War Service Cross First Class to our *Spiess*, Stabsfeldwebel Maritzen, from the hands of our new battalion commander Major Köhler. Finally at 1700hrs the locomotive whistled and we set off for home in an unbelievably exuberant mood.

27 April 1942

The train rattled and shook me awake. The sun rose red behind us: we were still in Russia and towards midday reached Pinsk. It surprised us to see frozen snow still piled up everywhere. The air was colder too. The train clanked ever onward.

28 April 1942

During the night we passed Brest-Litovsk station and entered Poland. Here we could see a difference in the people and the whole land for there were no gigantic unfarmed areas as in the USSR. We passed through Siedice station (known to some from the Polish campaign) and then Warsaw came into sight. After a short halt for the distribution of hot food the train moved on. Soon night fell.

29 April 1942

In the early hours we crossed the frontier into the Reich. What a difference between the USSR and our Germany! Properly built, clean houses, smooth, straight roads, well-dressed people and – German girls! At midday we alighted at Posen for food. We had to queue for some time in front of the main post office where the female postal assistants showed themselves in picturesque fashion in the open windows. After an exchange of words a small white slip of paper came floating down with an address written on it. Finally our mess tins were filled with hot soup and we streamed back to the train. Some of our group absented themselves on the pretext of having their first beer back in Germany. The locomotive whistled once and began to pull out. The absentees returned with long leaps across the tracks, elegantly hurdling hedges and fences, then followed a long chase after the train. The girls waved and waved until we lost them to sight. We looked at each other. What kind of impression would we make on girls as we were? Unshaven, unwashed for five days and with the filthy dust of Russia on our boots and uniforms. *Nitshevo*! We were heading for Berlin!

30 April 1942

We arrived at 0300hrs at a Berlin goods yard. We jumped out and stretched, then unloaded our things on the platform to await the distribution of our leave passes. We stood joyfully discussing our plans for the hour while waiting for the passes to be brought from the Kommandantur. Once we had them (valid to and from Berlin) Leutnant Hoffmann gave each man his hand and then we plodded through the empty streets of Berlin, weighed down by our heavy packs and carbine, to the main stations from where the rail lines ran to all areas of Germany. I accompanied Obergefreiter Willi Klein to Münster: after Porta Westfalica it was only a short ride to the Hohensyburg Monument and finally Hagen station.

I passed through the barrier to report myself to the senior officer and receive my ration cards. Major Crede invited me into a back room. He wanted to know confidentially how it had really been for us at Moscow and Tula. When I told him that we were forbidden to speak of the subject, he assured me on his word of honour that whatever I told him would remain between the two of us. Thereupon I provided him 'more or less' with my experiences. On hearing them he thanked me with a grave expression, offered me his hand and wished me *Soldatenglück*. The newspapers and radio had reported it as the 'planned withdrawal to winter positions in the rear'. That made me think. From the market I took the omnibus to Emst, the same journey in reverse as ten months before. Everything looked very different. On the bus I met old friends. It was touching how helpful they all were. I was one of the first leave-takers from the Eastern Front after the winter of 1941. 'Emst – Mackensen Strasse!' I got off. On my way to the front door I met my aunt and grandmother. They were hysterical with joy. My mother was quite overcome by the surprise and sat weeping on the sofa. I was plied with questions, and had to tell so much. But I was happy at being able to change out of my uniform and get into the tub to wash off the last filth of Russia. 'How shall we surprise your father?' We placed my dirty, dusty jackboots on the front step. While happily splashing in the tub I heard my father return: thus I was able to greet him clean and scrubbed. He could only hold back the tears with difficulty.

1–21 May 1942: Home Leave

Wonderful carefree hours and days with my parents and grandmother in our 'garden city'. Cherry and other fruit trees were in blossom. My cousin Rolf (b. 1925) had not been called up yet, cousin Gerhard, now a Gefreiter, was home on leave from the Flak, as was another Flak soldier, neighbour Friedhelm Becker. From classmates I met in town I learned that many former pupils from my school had fallen. We drank our beer in silence and reminisced about our old schooldays. I visited the school and was invited into the home of Dr Reinert, our teacher. He had sent stereotyped letters to former pupils at the Front. The days passed too quickly. We had to be back in Berlin on 21 May. The evening before, I packed my things. My mother made me a small mountain of 'rations' for the journey. I looked like a baker's roundsman! In the evening we celebrated my departure and drank to my safe homecoming.

21 May 1942

My mother accompanied me to the railway station; my father also came. The Special Front-Leave train left at 0900hrs. I took my leave of my father with a handshake at Hagen. My mother rode with me as far as Bochum and waved until the train was hidden to view by smoke. It was a fast run to Berlin where we arrived at 1900hrs. The train was full of members of my regiment. We assembled in the large indoor riding school of the Watch Battalion *Grossdeutschland* at Moabit, reported ourselves and then went to a Berlin corner tavern for a last German beer before we headed east. Roll call was at midnight. All names were answered, ticked off on the register and then we were able to sleep in the riding school or look for private quarters.

22 May 1942

I slept wrapped in my groundsheet in the riding school. In the morning we were driven to the Lustgarten in a Berlin double-decker bus to the great exhibition 'The Soviet Paradise' to see what the USSR really looked like. Just to kill time. After that we saw some of the sights and memorials of Berlin then had a coffee and some bread rolls for which bread stamps were not required. We had to report back to the goods yard station Puttlitzer Strasse in Moabit punctually at 1400hrs. Boys in the street happily shouldered our backpacks and rifles. Many of our comrades had brought their wives or girlfriends. We were allotted to individual wagons and reserved our places with our belongings. Those of us without female friends sunned ourselves in the grass until the locomotive whistled and then the order came '*Fertig machen! Einsteigen!*' We climbed aboard the train which then set off eastwards. From the large sliding doors we waved to those left behind until they were lost in the smoke from the locomotive. Those men with the best places sat in the doorway dangling their legs outside and remained there until late in the night. Nobody knew if this was the last he would ever see of the homeland, but we were young, optimistic and fearless. Once it grew dark we settled down in our sleeping places. We heard loudspeakers announce 'Frankfurt an der Oder', but the train passed through without stopping.

23 May 1942

In the course of the morning we passed through Posen and not much later Kutno. A month ago it was cold and grey here, occasionally still snow-covered, today every tree and bush was adorned with fresh green leaves. In the agricultural fields wheat was sprouting. Villages and towns flashed by: for us there was no going back.

24 May 1942

We crossed into Poland and soon reached Warsaw for a brief stop. In the early hours it was cold there. I pulled my blanket over my face and did not stir until Siedlce. Then at every station we saw long trains carrying weapons and materials, and many fresh troops for the East! We also saw the new 7.5cm Pak, tank destroyers and, what struck us particularly, that our panzers and assault guns had all been fitted with a longer barrel. The Russian T-34 always had a long barrel. Today is Whitsun! The train thundered on beneath sunny skies until stopping along a free stretch to camouflage the wagons with leafy birch branches. There was a plague of May beetles, the air was full of them. As the journey resumed, grenadiers sat in the brake house, on the roofs and riding boards. After Baranowice towards dusk the train halted. We got out and stretched our legs. We remained there for three hours without explanation and had to post sentries.

25 May 1942

During the night the train was more often stationary than moving. We reached Minsk, the yards filled with one transport train after another. On a neighbouring track a long train had a load of new troop carriers – elegant all-wheel drive vehicles, said to be from Austria. How envious we were, comparing them with our veteran Opel-Blitz lorries. We climbed aboard the other train to look the new vehicles over. From the large bridge behind the station women shouted to us, 'Bread! Sugar!' and thus the barter started up again. Finally the journey resumed, and we passed through Gomel towards midnight. Early tomorrow we will arrive back at Ryetshitza!

26 May 1942

Exactly one month after our departure we are back. The train thundered over the great Dnieper bridge. The river flowed swiftly to the Black Sea with small waves. We saw the houses of the town and then the train ground to a halt. 'Everybody out! Pick up your baggage. Fall in!' We marched through the town to our school quarters. The first thing we did after unburdening ourselves of the baggage was have a sauna to rid ourselves of the dirt accumulated during the journey. Hot steam drove the sweat from all pores: then under the cold shower! We repeated it several times. Soon one could not tell hot from cold. A good rub down, get dressed and out! We go to the sauna as often as possible. On the notice board the duty roster for tomorrow has been posted.

27 May 1942

Our company has received reinforcements and we are fully up to strength. The steep banks of the Dnieper are outstanding for training: like the sand of Döberitz, nothing but sand! We trotted out with our heavy mortar components. Memories of our recruit time came flooding back. In the afternoon we had sports in glorious weather, mighty cumulus clouds drifting sluggishly beneath a blue sky with beaming sun! After duty hours a group of us strolled through town. White or blue lilacs are blooming in all gardens and the Culture Park. I have never seen so many before in a town! And the fragrance that hangs in the air! If we sit on one of the small benches to converse with the Ukrainians, and make them laugh with our jibberish, the young Panienkas soon arrive in their bright summer dresses and shyly hand us large lilacs, or fit them in our caps and buttonholes. I have the impression that the people are happy, and glad to be freed of the Bolshevist yoke. It is important to know the right approach to these people. I had a head start from the beginning. Instead of *Matka* – 'birth mother' – I would call a woman *Mamka – Mamuschka*, or if she were older, *Babushka*. A Russian lady told me it sounds nicer. The men – all *Opas* – I address as *Gospodin* – equivalent to 'Herr'. To call anybody 'Ivan' is always correct, in the same way that Russian soldiers and the civilian population call us us 'Fritz'. Children enquire as to one's forename: '*Kak twoyo imya?*' I am very well up on military terms. It is also a good thing to hear the pronunciation before entering an area, the stress is very important. I put a lot into it and have linguistic talent, I don't often have to say, '*Ja Vas absolutno neponimayu!*' Both Russians and Ukrainians have told me that I am easy to understand. If they ask the meaning of the words on our black-silver cuff title I tell them proudly '*Bolshaya Germania – Gardiya*' ('*Grossdeutschland* – Guards'). How wonderful are these glorious warm spring nights and the perfume of the lilacs in blossom! I cannot get out of my mind the song '*Warum hat jeder Frühling, ach, nur einen Mai . . .*' ('Why does every spring have only one May . . .'). It will be forever associated with my wonderful home leave. We returned to our quarters a little homesick.

28 May 1942

In the morning we trained eagerly in the terrain, practising new battle tactics – for example 'firing by platoons': all mortars aimed at a single target. It sounded like a Stalin organ. Also mortars working in combination with heavy MGs. All very interesting and new! Our old battalion commander Major Greim, now Oberstleutnant – came to observe us and take his leave of II Battalion. The winter has cost him his health. [Note: Oberstleutnant Greim died in the summer of 1943 as a consequence.] We heard for the first time the rattle of the new MG42 and its terrific rate of fire, theoretically 1,500 rounds per minute. The Russians call it the 'Hitler saw' and also 'electric machine gun'. Our workshops have not been idle meanwhile and all our lorries and cars have been repaired as much as possible. We had also received some new vehicles. We are ready for action.

29 May 1942

Today MGs and mortars worked jointly practising an attack. The new tactic involves 9 Heavy MG Company always being at the centre of an attack or covering a retreat. In the 'Offensive Year 1942' we are to work in partnership: that means no longer can we be detached to other grenadier companies. The Russians have their own mortar companies and we have the scars to prove it! German soldiers are urged to submit suggestions for improvements and accordingly I wrote in regarding the Russian superiority in mortars and for bringing up ammunition I suggested a 'Karrette', a low, lightweight, fast and manoeuvrable cross-country vehicle on caterpillar tracks which I saw in an Italian Army magazine.

The mortar is a dangerous weapon. During the fighting one hardly notices the sound of it firing. When the falling bomb is heard at the target there is little time left to find cover. Mortar bombs are HE, the splinter effect very great. In addition the splinters fly extremely low across the ground, hitting even troops lying flat. Classic indirect fire is possible from one hidden position against another. Thus six mortars can fire thirty bombs (five each) in a few minutes, all falling on a particular target or to act as a curtain of fire. Flight time to impact is twenty seconds (independent of the range). The hits then occur as if from a Stalin organ or one of our rocket launchers. The Russians with their 12cm mortars have inflicted heavy casualties in dead and wounded amongst our infantry. The 'Heavy Platoon' of a heavy MG/mortar group is our response. [Note: The most successful deployment of this tactic was observed on 23 July 1942 in the Don crossing at Melichovskaya.] At midday we were suddenly ordered to make ready to leave and we spent the whole afternoon dismantling and stowing. By evening we were ready: our group under Unteroffizier Stedtler is to remain behind as rearguard.

30 May 1942

This morning the whole regiment left early for the departure point. We waved them off then set up our tents at the railway station, remaining back with sentries from other units to watch over the food and ammunition compounds and barrels of fuel. The roster is two men on watch for two hours and then ten hours off duty. A masterly accordion player provided restful music. At midday we swam in the Dnieper: after bathing or sentry duty we basked for hours in the sun or shade. There is rarely any talk about our future movements, sufficient is the moment. We make the best of everything for surprises will surely come.

31 May 1942

Our regiment having left Ryetshitza, Slovak and Hungarian troops have arrived to replace them. Their wagons are drawn by small steppe horses, hanging their heads in the heat. Thus their motto: 'If we don't come today, we'll come tomorrow.' Their infantry wear yellowish-brown uniforms and high puttees. The Slovaks understand Russian and so we can talk to them in a roundabout way. It is more difficult with the Hungarians, with whom we have to resort to sign language. They occupy the quarters we have abandoned. They report that they came under fire close to Ryetshitza. Partisans?

1 June 1942

After sentry duty we had an hour's drill, marching up and down singing: after sports in the afternoon we swam in the Dnieper. With two colleagues I decided to swim the 600m across. The water is fairly dark and not clean. Our aiming point was a tall white pole on a sandbank. We set off dog-paddling. In midstream we encountered difficulties. The white pole seemed to move quickly to our left upstream. Had we misjudged the current? Finally we got to the sandbank exhausted and from the protection of the rushes saw some naked Ukrainian girls bathing. When they spotted us they screamed and fled laughing in a small canoe. From the sandbank to the far shore was only 100m. We rested for a half hour in the warm sand working out the best point from where to be drifted downstream by the current to our starting point. When we arrived we all got a dressing-down and were sent off to the sauna to clean up.

2 June 1942

Amongst the supplies we guard are some flasks containing schnapps. We wondered if some of it might be evaporating in the hot sun and made a short check of the contents. Some of it then evaporated and we put the remainder in two litre-flasks and re-sealed them. When the watch was relieved we staggered down the high street. A Slovakian corporal hailed us, we partook of a 100g *Stakan* with him, he fetched out his mandolin and we stayed until evening listening to Slovak folk tunes.

3 June 1942

Our duty schedule is about the same every day: sentry duty, sports, drill. This afternoon we called on our Slovakian friends. Since they have occupied the vodka distillery in Ryetshitza, the alcohol is inexhaustible. Soon there was some shooting tomfoolery in which much damage was done and then all of us went to the Soldiers' Cinema to see *Unser Fräulein Doktor*. On the way back we made eyes at all the girls. While we watched *The Last Days of Pompeii* here, the regiment was rolling from Gomel – Merkuluvichi – Sherikovo – Bryansk – Karachev to Orel in the area near Kursk!

4 June 1942

In the Culture Park pavilion a Russian dance orchestra played for the Pans and Panienkas. We watched for a while then went to the cinema with the Hungarians. Whenever I leave the cinema having seen culture, beautiful women, German cities and lovers it is like waking from a dream to find myself back here amongst the Pans and Matkas in their primitive small houses. If I close my eyes and breathe in the wonderful perfume of the lilacs I can imagine I am at home.

5 June 1942

Today we were ordered to strike the tents and load up. A transport train had already pulled into the station. Sweating and cursing we dragged our heavy boxes on the wagons. By midday all ammunition and fuel was aboard. We were not due to leave until 2000hrs. Until then the mosquitoes plagued us, though as soon as the train was under way, the wind of its motion saw them off. We went through Gomel and the great woods near Bryansk. We had to wait at a small station nearby for two hours. Partisans had blown up a train loaded with barrels of fuel.

6 June 1942

We saw the damage: tracks ripped up, overturned wagons, the locomotive blown off the rails and lying on its side. Burned, misshapen barrels of spirit scattered around, auxiliary railway vehicles beginning the clear-up. We passed the site slowly. This could happen to us.

7 June 1942

After a really long journey we reached Orel. We had disembarked here for Tula in the winter. Orel was an end terminus. We were shunted in and then shunted out backwards. The whole station yard was full of fuel-, transporter-

and materials-trains, panzers and guns of all calibres stood on flat cars. We were going south! And then we rolled out again.

8 June 1942

At midday we reached the small terminal station of Svobodka about 30km from Kursk. Here we de-trained and unloaded. Our MGs were set up on the Flak mounts to watch the sky. We erected and camouflaged our tents. Once ammunition, fuel and provisions were off the train we stood watches. Scarcely had our transporter train left than another pulled in, this time bringing panzers and assault guns. Not far from the station is a large Luftwaffe airfield. We talked to the Luftwaffe men who think this is the starting point of our summer offensive. The unloading continued until late in the night. When I was on watch some Russian night bombers flew over on their way to Kursk. From there we heard bombing and the fire of many Flak guns. I could see the muzzle flashes and the Flak rounds exploding while searchlights swept the skies. Ivan is very active there at night.

9 June 1942

In the early morning our regiment's lorries arrived. Everything unloaded from the train had to be loaded aboard them. Finally, after endless drudgery we ourselves climbed into the last lorry. After passing through some villages we got on the Rollbahn to Kursk and drove into the town followed by a gigantic plume of dust. We crossed a bridge protected by a quadruple Flak, and then drove up a small hill into the town proper, swarming with troops. Long columns of a horse-drawn unit drove down the streets, outside a Flak division wormed its way through. It all looked chaotic but was actually perfectly controlled by the field gendarmes. Already the tactical shields of the various units had been nailed up, including our white steel helmet emblem. Some of the infantry referred to us as the 'Steel Helmet Division', which made us laugh. On the other side of town we came to a real concrete Autobahn from Kursk to Fatesh, but after a few kilometres bore off it for smaller roads, field paths and then cross-country, the route marked all along by shields with our emblem. Finally we came to where many parts of our regiment had lain in the woods for three days, well camouflaged. They had built huts and other accommodation and disguised the tents under birch branches. Our only source of water was from a small hole in the ground, although there was a kind of swamp nearby with countless croaking frogs, and so we erected our tents and slept unwashed, four men to a tent. Despite the hard ground it was quite comfortable apart from the ants. Here we were well hidden away from prying eyes in the skies. Russian bombers droned over nightly to attack Kursk.

10 June 1942

I awoke to the rays of the sun, a May beetle climbing the tent wall, mosquitoes buzzing, birds twittering, a cuckoo calling. How wonderful is Nature! We washed in a basin – twenty men sharing the water – and then toiled transferring loads from one lorry to another, the ammunition was looked over, weapons cleaned and then we turned to the industrious life of the field kitchen. A 'Platoon Evening' was to be staged. So great was the enjoyment that it grew to be a traditional event. An arena would be set up and each man had to do something solo – tell jokes, sing – whatever he did best. An unlimited supply of alcohol was essential. In the afternoon some promotions were announced – another reason to celebrate. Gefreiter Martin Scharfenberg was promoted to Unteroffizier (Corporal) for bravery in the face of the enemy and thus had the distinction of being a *Tapferkeits*-Unteroffizier.

11–12 June 1942

Camped in woods in the assembly area north-west of Kursk. At roll call, General Hörnlein awarded the Knight's Cross to Oberstleutnant Greim (our battalion commander in the winter of 1941). From 1800hrs until 0300hrs we were driven to another resting area in another huge wood and put up our tents for one night. At 1900hrs we set off again for the whole night. Via Ukalov-Kartashoka, and then around 0300hrs continuing to the east via Svoboda. Aircraft warning. The road is impassable, and so we had to wait six hours in open country. Dig in!

13–14 June 1942

Ivan's 'sewing machines' are looking for targets. The new 2 Regiment *Grossdeutschland* drove past us. We continued back to Svoboda and twenty-four hours later reached Savrashevka and occupied the edge of a wood near the Rollbahn, the lorries well camouflaged. Then we went deeper into the wood and made camp. The paths and bridges are often very poor. We set off again for Kuliga via Tshigri. During the night Russian bombers were active, possibly

Ivan has noticed all these troop movements and assemblies? We made camp with bivouacs near a brook. Three Russian aircraft were driven off by our Flak. During weapons cleaning a twin-boom reconnaissance aircraft flew over and dropped a message. 'Better camouflage necessary!' Our lorries became bushes on wheels!

15 June 1942

We went back to woods via Tshigri, camouflaged our vehicles, erected tents, posted sentries. The weather cleared. We had instruction in aircraft recognition including Luftwaffe types. In the evening we had another drinking bout. This mostly happens on the eve of an attack.

16 June 1942

We remembered our old '8 Company', our dead, and comrades in military hospitals. After the reorganization we are 9 Company/II Battalion, 1 Regiment *Grossdeutschland*.

17 June 1942

A straightforward heavy MG company with one platoon of heavy mortars exercised, exercised, exercised on the mortar. Weapons inspection.

18 June 1942

Paraded in battledress with all the trimmings!

19 June 1942

Instruction: 'Mine clearance'. We left everything unnecessary on the lorries and checked through our things. I kept some blue egg hand grenades in my haversack. If I had not had at least four of these during our retreat from Tula, we would not have got out of the house alive. We were given notice to pull out at 1400hrs, but this was put back twenty-four hours on account of sudden rainfall. We are gradually growing restless.

20 June 1942

Instruction: 'How to destroy weapons with explosives'. We were put on notice to pull out at 1500hrs, but this was postponed. The roads are too soft and unsuitable for vehicles. Bivouac again!

21 June 1942

Finally towards 1500hrs we went to Tshigri, 4km behind the winter positions now held by occupation troops. During our arrival we watched aerial battles above the town, in which two Russian bombers were shot down. Our advance being spotted by the enemy, we turned about to pass behind the town. Our convoy was bombed, three bombs exploding close to our lorry, two ahead and one behind. Earth flew around our ears! The blast threw us into a heap in the back. Now we are sitting up on the lorries without any cover. We stopped for rest in a small wood.

22–23 June 1942

The weather has improved. We lay down near our lorries to sleep. Ivan's bombers were very active again during the night. They have noticed that something is going on here. In the bivouac weapons training, rangefinder exercises. Washing underwear in a pool. We practised shooting with the new '38' pistol. Handling is a bit safer than the good old '08'. We checked weapons and ammunition.

24 June 1942

First we checked gas masks. A strange feeling crept over us. Will they do something like that? Then a sudden handball tournament was arranged. This made us 'veterans' wary. It nearly always preceded a sudden operational order. And as they suspected: up came the motorcycle rider: 'Make ready at once, you pull out in one hour!' So, back quickly to the bivouac – 'Load up! Executive order! Ready to pull out!' A long convoy of vehicles in broad daylight! Over the suburbs of Kursk nine Russian bombers came straight for us. We halted. 'Take cover against aircraft!' Our 8.8cm Flak shot down two of them, then our Me 109s appeared from the nearby field aerodrome and we saw three more ex-US Boston bombers shot down almost overhead. Bits of wreckage shining silver spun down to earth, the pilots in their parachutes following. Motorcyclists carried soldiers on the pillion to take them prisoner. The first fright had been warded off. The roar of the motors in the falling wreckage sounded awful.

We reboarded and moved out quickly, stopping later at the big phosphates factory at Shtshigrygostshick. 'Unload with equipment!' Then we had to march 5km through vast fields of rye to our 'departure positions'. We found communications trenches and set up our firing positions in the middle of a field near infantry trenches dug in the winter. We excavated a deep mortar pit then camouflaged the earth with wheatsheaves. My trench is near Group Leader Stedtler. From here the Great Summer Offensive will have its beginning!

25 June 1942

Our holes in the ground lie in the Polywoiye area. Sunrise 0300hrs! Still dripping with sweat from the march, we crouched in the holes and were glad of the sun, for the nights are cold. During the day it gets very hot. Both sides exchanged light artillery fire. Focke-Wulf reconnaissance aircraft are frequently seen. During the night a 'sewing machine' circled us. In front of our position the pioneers cleared mines. All kinds of preparation for an attack are in hand. Scouting patrols are sent out after dark – the flares rise up and sometimes a skirmish occurs. To our rear they are busy improving the roads and paths.

26 June 1942

What a night! Ivan came flying many throaty ex-US bombers and unloaded on our positions. It was like an earthquake. We got down very flat and low in our hole. Fortunately most of the bombs fell short in the field ahead, but a scouting party suffered three wounded. A 'sewing machine' unloaded many small bombs 'with the coal shovel'. These also fell close. During the night a landmine exploded. I stood sentry from 2100hrs to 2300hrs in the foremost trench. All quiet. During the day the artillery zeroed-in. Our rocket launchers (Do-Nebelwerfer) fired too, the projectiles make a howling noise and leave a long tail from the powder smoke. This makes it easy for Ivan to locate the firing position. One can hear the Stalin organs being fired, but their rockets use a smokeless powder and they fly quieter. Another surprise was a sudden storm and torrential rain. We took shelter in our holes beneath groundsheets held in place with bayonets and spades, but the water got in wherever it found a gap. I bailed as fast as I could with mess tin, cup and empty butter tin but I still have a wet behind!

27 June 1942

In the early hours the pioneers came forward and marked 'mine-free alleyways' with tapes. Ivan bombed very violently to our rear, and also the town of Kursk. Then he gave us a taste of his artillery. Russian reconnaissance aircraft flew at very high altitude overhead. Our company leader, Hauptmann Schmidt (Afrika), had us zero-in the mortars. The following night many Russian bombers came over. We can see the ground behind us very well for we are on an elevation. Ivan raised hell there. A hundred metres to our rear he hit a house which began to burn furiously. A woman was running around shrieking in distress crying: '*Dom kaputt! Malinki w dome!*' ('House done for! Child in house!') Some of our men went into the burning house and fetched the child from its cot. The mother collapsed saying, '*Oh bosche moi! Spassibo, spassibo!*' ('Oh dear God, thank you, thank you').

2300hrs: Readiness for the Great Offensive both sides of the Polywoiye – Dubrovka. The rations carriers went back again – we heard there was an issue of beer! Everybody feverish with excitement! Assault pack on the back, steel helmet buckled up, all weapons ready. The rations carriers appeared with the beer at 0030hrs. Carried for a half hour in mess tins: 'It tastes like piss!' One couldn't enjoy drinking that. Then somebody had a good idea, and we washed our cooking implements with it. It was a good start to our summer offensive!

Wie ist die Stukowirkung? Ritterkreuzträger Generalmajor Hoernlein, Kommandeur der Infanterie-Division „Großdeutschland", beobachtet von seinem Befehlswagen aus die Wirkung deutscher Bombeneinschläge.

Divisional Commander General 'Papa' Hörnlein.

A photo from a newspaper article showing the divisional commander during the 1942 summer offensive.

General Hörnlein at one of his division's radio posts.

O.U. denIiO

O.U. den IO.April I942.

Inf. Rgt. Grossdeutschland.

Regimentsbefehl!

Kameraden!
Der Führer hat mich vor kurzer Zeit zu einer neuen Verwendung
befohlen. SchwerenH Herzens muss ich heute die Führung des
stolzens Inf. Rgts. G.D.abgeben.
In den 8 Monaten in denen ich das Regiment führte, habt Ihr
in allen Gefechten, in denen Ihr kämpftet, in beispiellosem
Einsatz von Blut und Leben stets den Sieg errungen.
Ich danke Euch dafür und bin stolz darauf!
In erfurchtsvoller Trauer gedenke ich der toten Kameraden.
In dem neuen Verband den der Führer für uns befohlen hat,
werdet Ihr das Stammregiment sein ,das unter Entbehrung
und Opfern die Geschichte des Regiments und damit der Division
GROSSDEUTSCHLAND geschaffen hat.
Meine Wünsche begleiten Euch alle bei Euren zukünftigen Kämpfen
Der Führer wird viel von uns verlangen!
Wir weden halten was er von uns erwartet!

Alles für GROSSDEUTSCHLAND !

gez. Hörnlein
Oberst und Regimentskommandeur.

Oberst Hörnlein's letter of departure to his regiment upon being appointed to the Division 'Grossdeutschland-Einheit (unit)' with the rank of General. He wrote: 'Comrades! A short while ago the Führer ordered me to a new post. It is with heavy heart that today I have to give up my leadership of the proud Inf Regt GD. In the eight months in which I led the regiment, you were victorious in all engagements, unparalleled in blood and sacrifice, in which you took part. I thank you for that and am proud of it! I remember our fallen comrades with deep sorrow. In the new formation which the Führer has ordered for us, you will be the assault regiment whose privation and sacrifice has created the tradition of the regiment and with it that of the Division *GROSSDEUTSCHLAND*.

My wishes accompany you all in your future battles. The Führer will require much from you! We shall provide what he expects of us! Everything for *GROSSDEUTSCHLAND*!'

A page from Hans Rehfeldt's diary.

An important infantry motto: 'Even watchful with a glass eye.'

Retshitza on the Dnieper, May 1942.

At the latrines in the warm sunshine.

Flirting with the girls.

Russian women at Retshitza on the Dnieper.

A smartly dressed Russian girl poses for the camera.

A gas-mask canister still-life with through-and-through!

The 'sidewalk' at Retshitza on the Dnieper. It had an important function during the muddy period.

Ferdinand Spiegel on the 'thunderbox': both comrades fell later.

The smart lines of a crew tent erected from triangular camouflage sheets.

On 16 April deserving men received decorations at Retshitza.

An officer in the background calls out the name of a man to step forward.

Regimental commander Oberst Köhler in conversation with his officers after the distribution of decorations.

Retshitza railway station, from here the few survivors left on special leave.

Men of IV Platoon, 8 Company, II Battalion *Grossdeutschland*.

The lucky leave-takers before their departure for Germany.

With Unteroffizier Mehl in June 1942.

Jupp Dörfler (right) in the shelter of the woods.

Camp life before the great summer offensive.

At Kursk-Shtshigry.

Austrian comrade Adolpolla under cover of a pile of hay.

Field exercises with the mortar. The author is sitting in the centre right.

Rehfeldt, marked by an 'x' (middle row, second from right), with his comrades.

Passing along a muddy road after a downpour.

June 1942 in the readiness position. On the slope is the high-backed carrying pad for the mortar bipod.

Arriving at the readiness position, 9 June 1942.

Motorized column at Kursk.

The Kursk–Fatesh Rollbahn in June 1942.

The vehicles were camouflaged with bushes. Feldwebel Rhedanz is to the left of the divisional emblem.

Men of Rehfeldt's company watching the Stuka attack of 28 June 1942 marking the beginning of the summer offensive. Rehfeldt is at the far right of the picture.

In pursuit with horse-drawn carts while aerial battles rage overhead.

Chapter 11

The Front Rolls Forward across the Olym and Tim

28 June 1942

The German Front rolled at 0215hrs, before first light; *Grossdeutschland* advanced. Our artillery and Do-Nebelwerfer fired from all barrels. Fountains of earth, dust and smoke from the impact of all calibres rose up on Ivan's side: the earth shook. In the midst of this deafening racket panzers, assault guns and tank destroyers came up from our rear and headed for the Russian positions. High above us appeared formations of the Luftwaffe: He 111s to bomb the rear areas, Ju 87 Stukas to circle the Russian advanced trenches and then, sure of the target, fall almost vertically to attack with 'Jericho sirens' howling. After bombing, the Stukas climbed steeply and made a similar attack, this time firing their cannons. Ivan had gone to ground and even at the outset there had been no more than desultory fire from his artillery. 'Mortars! Forward! Maintain intervals and keep a watch overhead!' The grenadier companies had already advanced and now we were between the panzers and assault guns with our heavy components. We reached the forward Russian line unopposed. Everything bombed to rubble. Resistance came in the form of a few rifle rounds at which we ducked our heads involuntarily. We had broken through. Now we saw their many dead, destroyed MG posts, mortar pits – all ruined. They had been very well built, but not well enough. We pursued the fleeing enemy to the river Tim. Here we came across a 7.62cm battery which had not even fired. This gun was dangerous against panzers, bunkers and with HE shells for us infantry! With us we had the best anti-tank gun, the 8.8cm Flak so feared by the enemy. Me 110 ground attack aircraft hounded the retreating Russians and struck at every attempt to build resistance, diving like hawks repeatedly on recognized targets. We had captured a horse-drawn wagon and loaded our ammunition aboard it.

As far as the eye could see our German forces were advancing. Panzers, assault guns, light armoured personnel carriers (MTWs), half-tracked armoured personnel carriers (SPWs), twin-barrelled Flak, quadruple Flak and the 3.7cm Flak, all pushing forward: in the next line grenadiers with carbines and MGs, ambulances, ammunition vehicles, amphibious vehicles of the unit commanders and ourselves with our horse-drawn wagon. We had never expected a success on this scale and now we all believed that we would be victorious in the East within a short time.

As the terrain became more difficult we had to abandon our wagon and proceed with the heavy ammunition cases and mortar parts on foot. The sun was beating down and the sweat from our renewed efforts stung our eyes: after a short while the dust caked our faces like a mask. Suddenly some tank or anti-tank rounds from ahead passed between us and exploded: they had been aimed at our panzers and missed. Ahead we saw our panzers reply: suddenly two T-34s were blazing after direct hits, thick black smoke rising from their burning crude oil. Soon we saw many wrecked Russian tanks. A Panzer IV was hit and its crew abandoned the vehicle: a Kübelwagen came up quickly to pick them up. We reached some demoralized Russian prisoners and they expressed willingness to help carry our load even though we had fallen so far behind that now we had to run. Finally we hitched a lift on a towing vehicle for a 5cm Pak: overhead, at very high altitude, Russian airmen looked down more than they attacked. 'Mortars! Climb down with gear!' We had to continue on foot, but we had made good much lost ground.

We formed a hedgehog: at its centre the panzers and assault guns, barrels pointing in all directions, all other weapons around them in a broad circle, and beyond that circle the infantry, heavy MGs and mortars. The radio wagon was very busy but we failed to understand much of it. I stood watch from 0100hrs to 0200hrs, when Ivan found a new ally – rain. It turned all the paths to mud, and even towing tractors and tracked vehicles found the going difficult. The lorries side-slipped as though on soft soap. Our advance continued, however, if rather slower. On the first day we penetrated beyond their front line to a depth of 22km and reached the river Tim. Here we received supplies and food but had to press on. After another 8km we took up positions to control the Rollbahn. It was still raining and had also grown colder. Russian aircraft tried to knock out a railway bridge just ahead but found our Flak too strong. The Russian resistance seemed to be increasing, however, and we had to dig in and secure.

29 June 1942

At 0500 we set off again despite heavy going but a halt was called to it and we erected our tents near the Rollbahn. I found out that the advance had gone as deep as 60km – that's the value of wheelpower! It would have been much more but for the rain. All the same we reached Alexandrovka and crossed the river Olym in the evening. We secured some meadowlands, excavated firing positions, and individual slit trenches were dug. The depth of these depends on the military situation: here about half a metre. Russian bombers came over during the night but searched for us in vain.

30 June 1942

In the early morning we continued. Most of the regiment was now across the Olym. The mortar components and ammunition were a heavy burden for our shoulders. We found that tying a leather strap between the grasps of the ammunition cases enabled us to carry them on the right or left shoulder alternately. This left our hands free for the pistol or carbine. Today we had to watch our rear because other panzer divisions following up behind us were attracting the Russians. The leading units of our division had crossed the Stary–Oskol–Kastornoiye–Yeletz railway line and built up a bridgehead across the Olym with a reinforced company – ourselves! We were the spearhead projecting deep into enemy territory. To our left, therefore north of us, 9 Panzer Division was in action while 24 Panzer Division was hanging back somewhat on the southern flank at Gorshetnoiye intending to wipe out the enemy there. Our battalion advanced once more: we, the reinforced 9 Company (heavy MG and reinforced mortar platoon), reached Nasarovka and Michailovskaiya after skirmishing, secured and occupied these villages. A signpost in the countryside read 'Voronezh 100km'. So on we went. Our convoy was attacked by Russian aircraft at low level on the Voronezh Rollbahn. They came for us from ahead. This was a new tactic, previously they had only attacked at right angles across a convoy, which exposed them for less time. They feared our Flak but these pilots were bolder! We jumped down from the vehicles and engaged them with MGs and carbines. One was hit and crashed trailing smoke a few hundred metres behind us. Everybody claimed the kill. We advanced to the village of Kuyashnoiye along the railway line. Our panzers fired on a long Russian armoured train coming from Voronezh, and Stukas bombed the tracks behind it. We continued past Gorshetnoiye, encircled by 24 Panzer Division, to the eastward and while proceeding to the left of a railway line suddenly we saw between twenty-five and thirty Russian T-34s rolling towards us. Our convoy took cover behind the embankment: we lay along it ready to shoot. During the course of the day thirty-two of their tanks had already been destroyed and now these here! Our '8.8cm Battery' took up a position protected by the embankment. The duel began. The 88s were accurate. Every time a tank burned, the Flak gunners rejoiced. It was not long before twelve of these tanks, whose aim had been to attack us on the flank, lay burning beneath a tall column of smoke. Then the Stukas arrived. We were well protected and watched the destruction of the tanks: now and then a stray tank round would come to rest on the embankment without exploding. T-34s were even knocked out if a Stuka bomb exploded only nearby. One of them had the turret blow off. We celebrated each victory. The battle lasted two hours before the surviving Russians gave up. The approaches to the embankment were strewn with burning enemy tanks. Our vehicles used the distraction to slip away unnoticed. Two kilometres to the south, fighting flared up in the area around the village of Gorshetnoiye where Ivan had attempted to break out of the encirclement using thirty to fifty tanks, but 24 Panzer Division kept them bottled up. The exchange between tanks and our Paks lasted for hours. The short night fell quickly, the sound of fighting never dying down until daybreak.

2 July 1942

In the early morning we advanced motorized to Yassenki, which had been taken by other battalions of our regiment. 24 Panzer Division had not yet captured Gorshetnoiye and our Regiment *Grossdeutschland* 2 (the later Fusiliers) was called up to do the job. As we heard in the evening, they managed it against fierce resistance. Ivan had many tanks there. The general's Fieseler Storch flew in with General Hörnlein and General der Flieger Richthofen aboard. The divisional command post was to be set up here at Yassenki. Stukas engaged tanks and our artillery softened up outlying villages for our assault. Almost on the horizon we watched our bombers attacking fleeing columns of Russians.

3 July 1942

After listening to hours of raging tank and Pak fire, close enough to see the respective muzzle flashes, we slept exhausted beside our lorries. As soon as it was light we advanced to a village where air reconnaissance had reported eighty enemy tanks ready to strike at our flank. Before midday we attacked the strongly defended high ground at Krasnaya Polyana, overwhelming many bunkers. It fell to us at noon. Bathed in sweat we stretched out on the ground totally spent. From this high point we could see for miles: it really ought not have been possible to capture it. Our force consisted of panzers, assault guns, Flak, 8.8cm Flak, tank destroyers, and light and heavy infantry guns: two more of their tanks were destroyed by the 8.8cm Flak. In the late afternoon an attack developed up a slope to a village and the spot height 166.2 – Yandovitshe and the village Stary Semlya. Our force took the height towards 2300hrs. We rested near a signpost.

4 July 1942

Today was another exciting, successful day! We set off at 0300hrs perched on assault guns and pushed deep into enemy territory without contacting Ivan for 30km. Stukas were our vanguard and dived like hawks on anything identified as hostile. Fires burned in many places. The inhabitants of the villages through which we rolled were speechless with surprise. Trains still chugged along the railway line. We wiped out Russian support services and other columns. Ivan was taken completely unawares. But then the situation became ticklish. We had advanced too far and within an hour Russian tanks had encircled us. Their low-level aircraft attacked but achieved nothing worth mentioning. We broke out: our joyful battle cry now was 'The Don! The Don! And Voronezh!'

We could see the city ahead in the haze. First we had to take heavily fortified positions on a high ridge. Many Russians were hidden in the cornfields. We shot five of them dead for refusing our order in Russian to drop their weapons and raise their hands. Another fired at one of our men, hitting him in the stomach. This Russian was beaten to death with rifle butts. Several civilians we chanced to come across driving artillery tractors for their fighting troops were given a short trial in the field and executed by firing squad. 'Shit war!' Because this whole area might be infiltrated by hidden Russian soldiers, that night we formed a hedgehog for all-round defence since there was no cohesive front in existence. Russian stragglers could suddenly appear from anywhere. Many villages were on fire that night on the approaches to Voronezh, which lay well to the east of the river. We worked forward to the Don. A large railway bridge over the river, unfortunately not in usable condition, was bitterly defended and denied to us. An armoured train heading for the bridge had been hit by our guns and set afire, and the fire had spread to the bridge, making it impassable for panzers and other traffic. Another bridge was found several kilometres north of the rail bridge and taken later by a few men of 7 Company led by Oberleutnant Blumenthal. This was a road bridge thanks to which our units were able to establish a small bridgehead on the far side of the river. From the high bank we could see far over the land south-east towards the large city of Voronezh. Our bombers circled overhead and dropped on identified targets. Our aim was to establish a bridgehead over the Don. The pioneers had brought up inflatable boats.

5 July 1942

We were to attempt the crossing of the Don with the pioneers this morning. The Don flows south. The village of Potklodnoiye on the eastern bank of the Don is to the north-west of the city of Voronezh and is our objective!

We could see many fortified bunkers nearby with concrete caps and rifle apertures. The 8.8cm Flak on the high bank with us engaged them. We could see the trajectory of the shells as they have a tracer attachment behind. Round after round hit the small bunkers in the light of dawn: with every hit the tracer attachment flew off in a high arc. We saw clearly many good direct hits! We crouched behind the guns to avoid the enormous report when they fired. General Hörnlein and our regimental commander reconnoitred the terrain from where we would advance in a few hours once having crossed the Don. At 1900hrs the pioneers paddled the large inflatable rubber boats over the river and at 2000hrs, when the mass of the companies were on the eastern side and had establish a small bridgehead there, the order came to advance. We had crossed the Don without casualties but Ivan was not keen to let us through his defensive line: he had good positions from where he could read our intentions. The night passed restlessly: Ivan even tried a few minor counter-attacks.

6 July 1942

Around 0900hrs we set out to attack Potklodnoiye, defended by Ivan with everything he had. Approaching the village, we found swampy ground covered with many shrubs and bushes and emerging from there the defensive fire was heaviest, forcing us to return to the bushes. With our mortars we fired on identified targets to assist the infantry attack but were soon out of ammunition. We runners now had to return to the Don crossing point

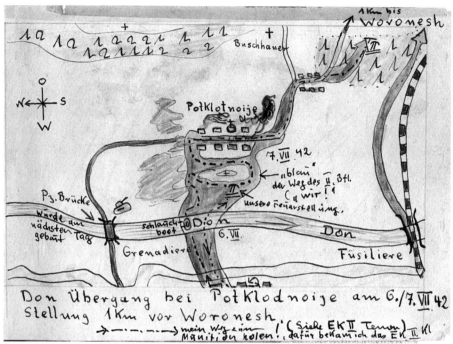

Map by Hans Rehfeldt showing the crossing of the Don at Potklodnoiye, 1km from Voronezh on 6/7 July 1942. Key: + Buschhauer fell, 'Unsere Feuerstellung' = our mortar position, 'Pz.Brücke wurde den nächsten Tag gebaut' = Panzer bridge was built next day, 'Schlauchboot' = pioneer inflatable, 'Grenadiers' = Regiment 1, 'Fusiliere' = Regiment 2, bottom line, 'Mein Weg zum Munitionholen, dafür bekam ich das EK Kl. II (siehe EK Tenor)' = My route to fetch ammunition, for which I got the Iron Cross Second Class (see Iron Cross citation).

to find some more. I went with several other men through the very heavy barrage being dropped by the Russians on the crossing point, and chanced it to the western bank paddling a pioneer's inflatable dinghy while under fire. Our II Battalion supply vehicles were so well camouflaged and hidden that I could not find them, and after a search I found a I Battalion motor car full of mortar ammunition. I knew the driver, Hans Leuwer, who hailed from my hometown Hagen, and convinced him to let us have the bombs. While we were adjusting the cases with leather straps for portability I noticed that the pioneers were building a bridge for panzers 100m upstream under artillery fire. We now had to return the way we came, paddling the rubber dinghy, great fountains of water rising up from the near misses, then scrambled out on the eastern shore and ran hell for leather for the bushes beyond which our mortar position was installed. We were soaking wet, not only with sweat but from having had to throw ourselves down so many times in the swamp for cover. There was little time for rest, for we had to repeat this dangerous supply run three more times. Runner Akteris was wounded in the hand. The danger to which we were subjected on each of these journeys cannot be overstated. Finally, after fifteen minutes' 'rest', we had the pleasure of joining the infantry for the attack on Potklodnoiye which was being bitterly defended and where we had sustained losses to their snipers. The village had been bombed by Stukas and shelled by the artillery of both sides and was basically a ruin, but we eventually found shelter in the remains of a convent. Now the pioneers' panzer bridge had been completed, our panzers and assault guns crossed by it, together with another unit which had recently arrived, and this was too much for the enemy resistance. Black smoke hung over Voronezh. We followed close on the enemy's heels. Beyond the village was more swamp and morass through which the vehicles could not venture and had to detour. In the evening we parked in a sinister wood not yet totally vacated by Ivan and so had to dig a mortar pit and then each man prepared his own slit trench.

7 July 1942

Voronezh is in our hands! We removed to another wood about a kilometre before the town. Suddenly in the night: 'Alarm!' I awoke to the sound of rifle rounds pinging, excited voices shouting: 'There they are!' Some Ivans were trying to escape from the woods. There were two of them still trapped above us in the trees. They could have massacred us from there! That was an eerie night!

8 July 1942

This morning was peaceful. We were relieved by other troops following us up. Our task here is finished. 24 Panzer Division had got to Voronezh before us and took over the fallen city. We walked to our battle wagons and secured on spot height 166.2. The terrain here has very deep gorges but from above we have a very good panoramic view. At night Ivan bombed the rear areas with heavy bombers which flew over with a tremendous roar. From our ridge we could see the distant bomb explosions. We fired 2cm and 3.7cm Flak, MGs and carbines at bombers. On the Rollbahn coming here we shot one down. Perhaps we shall be lucky again.

9 July 1942

New orders! Now we are to go from the north, after our direct frontal breakthrough from Kursk to Voronezh, to the south, to the Lower Don (Caucasus), far behind the virgin Russian Front to the south-west, cut through it like a knife and sever the Russian supply lines, roads and railways. The sun beats down, often up to 41°C (In the winter we had days when the thermometer sank to minus 52°C!) The columns whip up clouds of dust, often hiding the following vehicle from sight. We wear green rubber goggles against the dust, with sun protection. The dust and sweat sticks, and one gets grit even between the teeth. Our entire division is roaring lock, stock and barrel southwards, long yellowish-white clouds of dust ahead pointing the way. Under clear skies we reached Reyevka – Peduna and later Sitishtche. We overtook Hungarian troops. The thermometer reading was plus 50°C. We drove through abandoned Russian field positions, past earth bunkers and crossed anti-tank ditches. The word is 'The Caucasus – but where afterwards?' Countless prisoners in earth-brown uniforms came towards us – mostly Ukrainians – hapless, moving towards the rear almost without guards. I asked some at a stop: 'Where have you come from and where are you going next?' They begged for water and a cigarette. We gave them what they wanted then pressed on for Sitishtche under the relentless sun. Apparently we are going over the Caucasus to meet up with Rommel once he moves out from Egypt. There was even talk of an advance to India. Here it seems as though Ivan has been defeated. In a field post letter to my parents I wrote: 'The Russians here have had enough, the war will be over soon.' The extent of our penetration is fairly narrow however. The special danger is that our flank to the east has little cover. 24 Panzer Division which accompanied us for the attack on Voronezh is now headed for Stalingrad via Rossosh.

We passed countless prisoners trotting to the rear: whole Russian units behind us were flowing back. Our support services and the 'Staffeln' (repair units for motorized vehicles) often get mixed up with retreating Russian columns in the dust or darkness. Both sides usually recognize their error only on stopping in a village. Once a Commissar, standing on the running board of a lorry, threated a German driver with a pistol because he would not move aside to let the Russian convoy through. He didn't have the chance to rue his mistake! There were many similar unpleasant meetings – our Unteroffizier Walter Pfeil from Hagen was wounded in one of them. We had a prisoner on board whom I interrogated with my much-improved knowledge of the Russian language. He told me that the retreating Russians were going to assemble around Rostov-on-Don in order to establish a new Front there.

10 July 1942

Ever onwards to the south. After Krasnoye Waluiki we ground to a halt in open fields, out of fuel, and had an enforced rest waiting for Ju 52s to bring us more in barrels. We used the time to get a haircut, clean weapons and answer roll call. Sentries were posted, heavy MGs and mortars set up. Then we 'organized' eggs, honey, milk and even cream. Many of the gardens had trees with ripe cherries. Many Russian soldiers in earth-brown uniforms and burdened with sacks and packs passed heading northwards. When I asked where they were going, they replied, 'Home, to Mama and wife. The war is over.' We are also thinking the same!

1 July 1942

The three-engined Ju 52s landed in the open fields and unloaded barrels of fuel. It was very troublesome to refuel our vehicles because it first had to be decanted into 20-litre canisters. The panzers pump it directly into their tanks from the 200-litre barrels. Now we can get on with the war!

12 July 1942

It was a very short night and at 0245hrs we set off again to the south. Along the way shields had been put up with the letter 'K' for Panzergruppe Kleist. Our vehicles still bore the initial 'G' for Guderian who had led 2 Panzerarmee around Tula in the winter of 1941. Hitler had relieved him of command for not wanting to sacrifice his troops without good reason. He had made it possible for us to set up a winter position on the Oka. Today we travelled 170km to Olchovka, halting for the night in open fields. It really looks here as though Ivan has had enough.

13–14 July 1942

It is hot, almost 50°C in the sun. All vehicles, including those on tracks, have been refuelled. We moved out at 0300hrs. Ivan offered some weak resistance today and then faded away. We were approximately north-east of Rostov-on-Don and pursued the fleeing enemy as far as Kashary. At night we settled down outside the location.

15 July 1942

Today we took Kashary against token resistance. This enabled us to reach and block a railway line running west–east. At night before digging in we had to report to the regimental command post. We were told that we were to set up as Battle Group *Köhler* (our regimental commander). Our task is to sever the rail lines running west–east.

16 July 1942

We ran across more retreating Russian columns. Near Tazinskaya we halted in a gigantic field of sunflowers. Out of fuel again. The advance came to a standstill. The Ju 52s arrived again with fuel. Our Luftwaffe is far ahead of us. On the horizon we can see great clouds of black smoke darkening the skies. The Me 110s are very active. Excellent air support! While the panzers and assault guns were refuelling we secured the right flank. With the naked eye about 1.5km to our right we spotted Russian soldiers with horse-drawn carts in an area of bushes no doubt waiting to trick their way past us. Remnants of units such as these can always be a danger to our support services in the rear and to our so-important supplies. When some of the NCOs discovered through binoculars more and more Russians in hiding, my troop leader Unteroffizier Martin Scharfenberg decided to go over there with me and another man, take the soldiers prisoner and search the civilians. We set off with two carbines and Scharfenberg's sub-machine gun between us and a few mortar bombs were fired over beforehand to make an impression. About halfway there a sub-machine gun opened up on us from a haystack. Covering fire from our heavy MG and a few rounds from ourselves silenced the enemy sub-machine gun. Upon approaching the Russians, about fifty of them, we saw that all were armed with rifles or sub-machine guns. This did not look good, but we kept going, weapons at the hip, and stopped 50m short to plant ourselves before them with grim faces. The Ivans looked indecisive. Between the various groups was a fully loaded horse-drawn cart with some civilians. I called out: 'Weapons down, bayonets in the ground and hands up!' This order '*Shtiki na semlyu*' (bayonets in the ground) appeared on our leaflets giving Russians instructions how to surrender. There was now a period of palaver amongst them, some of them detached from the group and approached us with a leaflet containing a 'pass' for defecting soldiers. Some had already thrown aside their weapons, others remained indecisive. We pointed our weapons at them and insisted that they disarm. This did the trick and now we were able to search their pockets and rucksacks. We discovered large quantities of ammunition. I told them they were all now prisoners of war and eventually they all formed up in three columns as ordered. We had probably been lucky: the Russians had been able to see all our other regimental vehicles including the panzers on the road. A saloon car drove up with five or six reinforcements to relieve us of the prisoners. We had not lost interest in the horse-drawn cart with refugees' belongings, and they had even brought along a portrait of Stalin. The man in charge was the head of the collective farm, and he wanted to return there with his family. We found no weapons but confiscated a can of honey, several buckets of eggs and a milk churn full of schnapps. We let them keep the rest. We set off once more, to some extent rested, refuelled and resupplied with ammunition. When we came to melon fields the giant greenish-yellow melons were good for quenching thirst. There were also smaller ones, yellower, called 'Dinya', more like bananas and sweeter. Our Opel-Blitz was stacked with melons, tomatoes and onions. The tomatoes were also grown in the ground in huge fields. We headed through blinding yellowish banners of dust towards Taszinskaya where II Battalion took the town after a brief battle.

17 July 1942

We advanced motorized to the Lower Don and crossed a railway line towards Novo Konstantinovskaya/Alexandrovskaya. North-east of the towns we encountered fierce resistance. Ivan defended from positions in field and town and got help 'from above' when it began to rain heavily. In a short while the earth was slippery as soap (the well-known black earth of the Ukraine) and our wheeled vehicles were hardly able to proceed at all. Even tracked vehicles encountered difficulty. Then came a violent storm. Nevertheless II Battalion advanced to a crossroads 3 or 4km north-east of Novo-Konstantinovskaya where we secured. Now and again a round was fired at us from the town. On the road were some abandoned carts.

It was Sunday and we lay with our group, which from the fighting on the Don had acquired the designation *Sturmgruppe*, before the town of Novo Alexandrovskaya. Our assignment was to use our two mortars and one light MG to prevent the Russians encircled in the town from making an attempt to break out, but we were not to engage a superior enemy force. From our position the Rollbahn ran dead-straight into the town and we placed one mortar either side of the road. Our visibility and field of fire were good. Beyond the Rollbahn, the ground was covered with steppe grass parched by the sun. Our other security positions lay in a wide arc around the town.

The situation here had come about as follows: our troops, panzers and assault guns pushing forwards had circumvented the town to avoid losing time in the pursuit of the fleeing enemy. Panzers were waiting to put an end to them. We had to ensure that none escaped. We had dug our mortar emplacements and slit trenches, zeroed-in the mortars and got the MG ready for firing. Now we lay in the sun waiting. Our Unteroffizier did not like our firing position. We had enough fire power for ahead, but had only four ammunition runners protecting our left-hand side. No other weapons were available. While observing the entrance to the town through binoculars I saw a fully loaded wagon in the middle of the road. On top of it were two Russian Maxim MGs and ammunition cases. We could make good use of the two Maxims. The Rollbahn could be overseen clearly from the town and the Russians had a clear field of fire for their MGs. The wagon was about 400m ahead and the same distance from the town entrance. It looked too risky to do during the day, at night probably more so. When I mentioned it to my Unteroffizier he was enthusiastic but thought I should wait for nightfall. During the morning, however, a 2cm quadruple Flak came up and took position in a depression near the Rollbahn. We now had very good protection all on the right flank! I decided to appropriate one of the Maxims in daylight. I requested my NCO's sub-machine gun, unbuckled my belt and set off, two egg grenades in my pockets. First I ran, ducked low in the Rollbahn ditch to the Flak gun which had already zeroed-in. They had also been watching the entrance to the town. I explained my plan to the gun commander and asked for covering fire if necessary. The gun crew closed up and I ran ahead, ducking low, through some fairly thick bushes. When I ran out of bushes I had to crawl. Raising my nose I saw that I was quite close to my objective. Suddenly a lorry came out of the town driven very fast, a bright yellowish cloud of dust following it. As it neared I saw it to be a tanker. At that moment the quadruple Flak opened fire: I saw the tracer flying towards the tanker which was hit and began to burn immediately. Soon the blaze flared up fiercely and a thick black cloud of smoke rose lazily from the burning fuel. I was 20m from the wreck. I sprinted to the cab: it was empty: the driver was on fire in the roadside ditch calling for help which I could not give. The dry steppe grass all around had also begun burning. Under cover of the smoke I reached the wagon with its two Maxim MGs. They had wheels, bulletproof shields and were water-cooled: this made them heavy. I climbed up and looked them over. One had a broken wheel and damage to the shield: the other seemed undamaged apart from a few small holes in the cooling jacket. I found two cases of ammunition, bound them together with a leather strap and dropped them down to the roadway. But the chosen Maxim was much heavier than I thought, a job and a half to get it down. The smoke and fumes from the burning lorry made my eyes smart and affected my lungs. Carrying in my hand a third ammunition case which I had discovered, I dragged the Maxim behind me, the two other cases of ammunition around my neck. The iron wheels rumbled nicely although it was more heavy to drag than I thought. Scarcely had I got 10m from the wagon when I heard a 7.62cm anti-tank shell hit it. It had been my intention to blow up the other weapons and ammunition on the wagon with my hand grenades but in all the excitement I had forgotten to do this, and it was in any case no longer necessary, for Ivan had done it himself.

In the rays of the midday sun I sweated like a pig as I ran low to my position with my trophies. Ivan fired at me all the way with the same anti-tank gun. The quadruple Flak gave me no covering fire and when I passed it the crew grinned at me from their slit trench. In safety I inspected the Maxim and saw how simple it was. Raise the fixed sight, move the gun on the target, fit the belt. Now it was ready to fire. Rate of fire was a notional 500 to 700 rounds per minute, half that of our MG42. I lay on my stomach and aimed at a group of wild horses running around wildly. The belt was of a cloth material, not metal, and had tracer rounds. My NCO shouted, 'Fire a burst, Rehfeldt!' After a burst of four rounds the MG jammed. I removed the jammed round with my pocket knife. The breech was filthy with earth and oil. The third ammunition case had cleaning materials including a canister of gun oil but no MG belt. After cleaning the gun I tried it again and this time it worked perfectly. When the material belt with the bullets was wet, the gun did not fire so well. Next I fired the gun to check for accuracy using the fixed sight. This was good. I fitted a new belt and touched the water cooler jacket with my hand. Ow! It was hot: the water must have escaped through the small holes in the jacket. At least now we could protect our exposed left flank against an attack. I laid a groundsheet over the captured gun and placed the two ammunition cases beside it. That night we had a thunderstorm with lightning and all the works, sky black as pitch and heavy rainfall to go with it. Our foxholes were soon full, like bathtubs. On watch I sheltered from the torrential rain between the concrete bases of a giant pylon but only until lightning hit the electric cables 100m away. Blue-ish flames flickered up like St Elmo's fire. The thunder was extremely loud, but the storm soon passed. During the night I saw some figures in the field which I suspected might be the Russians coming for their Maxim and I fired a few bursts: but in the light of day the figures were seen to be wild horses. During the morning we had to make ready for the advance: I could not take the Maxim with me and so destroyed it with a hand grenade. I had gone to all the trouble to capture it for nothing.

19 July 1942

Today we attacked! Artillery in position, our panzers went off. The Russians' anti-tank fire had no success, the panzers entered Novo Alexandrovskaya, we followed, took many prisoners and captured the town with no losses (to our mortar crews). We assembled and were relieved by another unit. Now the direction of advance was changed to Michailovskaya on the Donetz where our advanced troops had discovered a Russian bridging-ferry. Ivan had tried to destroy it but our pioneers restored it. After we had made several ferry crossings, Russian bombers arrived to destroy it again, but all of us got across the river unscathed.

20 July 1942

We assembled on the far side and battled through to Kertshik against Russian tanks. At a brief stop in the evening, after dusk about 2km ahead we saw motorized and horse-drawn units crossing in front of us from right to left. We could make out the dimmed headlights of the lorries with the naked eye. The column was closed up, moved at a good pace and took all night to pass us. We were too weak on the ground to think about an attack. Our officers informed the Luftwaffe. If possible we wished our presence to remain unnoticed. In the first rays of the sun we could still see the column. It was a Red Army column consisting of lorries, horse-drawn and motorized artillery, between them T-34s, infantry in large groups, cavalry – all heading for Rostov-on-Don. Finally they spotted us. Some horsemen approached through the cover of bushes. We stood ready to fire. Our tank destroyers watched the Russian tanks, our heavy MGs lay in ambush and the mortars were prepared for any eventuality, ammunition close to hand. Our Pak guns and artillery took up interception positions beside the road along which the column had begun to roll back. Their tanks stopped, their guns turning towards us. Before the Russians could act, we heard the sound of our Stukas arriving. We released orange-yellow markers to indicate our position, the smoke rising up sluggishly from various places, the Stukas flew a circle and then the first tilted downwards with siren howling followed by the other five. The first bombs exploded amongst the Russian columns. Confusion on the ground turned to panic. The horsemen in the bushes turned and galloped off. We emerged from cover to watch the bombardment. The Stukas dominated the battlefield, first bombing and then on the second and third attacks strafing the fleeing Russians with MG and cannon fire. We were shocked by the blast pressure. The Russians fled *sauve qui peut*. Burning lorries, wrecked tanks and artillery lay strewn everywhere: the horsemen were no longer to be seen, infantry ran around bemused. To conclude the event the Stukas made a feint attack on us to which we replied waving our swastika flags. Our knees felt weak at hearing their 'sirens of Jericho' and the mere sight of the machines diving down at us almost vertically.

21 July 1942

Today the Motorcycle Battalion attacked Kertshik while we took up positions on an elevation. We saw long Russian columns (motorized and horse-drawn) passing about 2km away, much of their artillery drawn by heavy tractors. We also saw tanks and a large number of infantry.

22 July 1942

The sun shone all day from a clear blue sky, the thermometer read 52°C and as usual during the drive the vehicles whipped up the dust so that our faces (except for the rosy rings where we wore our goggles), and just about everything else, are encrusted with it. Now that the sun is sinking in the west, we grenadiers sit or lie by our trusty old Opel-Blitzes and are glad for a rest. Today we fought our way 60km and now we wait, panzers, assault guns, armoured personnel carriers, our heavy MGs, we mortar gunners, 2cm and 3.7cm light Flak and our lorries while the platoon leaders and group leaders attend the chief's conference.

The platoon and group leaders returned. 'The company will remain here until early morning. Dig in.' We set to work digging our individual foxholes and then the pit for the mortar. Sometime later Unteroffizier Stedtler came back: 'Fall in around me, 3 Group!' We formed up in a semi-circle. 'Listen up, men! An advance section will be leaving Battalion this evening for the town of Shachty to maintain contact with the fleeing Russians. It is assumed that they are going to gather at Rostov-on-Don and help defend that town. We are leaving with two armoured cars, one group of heavy MGs, us, 3 Group with the mortars, and also a tank destroyer with 7.62cm gun.[1] Our task is to prevent if possible the retreating Russian forces occupying the town of Shachty. So, make ready, board the vehicle and as soon as you're standing by to leave, report to me at once!' What a shit way to organize things. We had dug our foxholes, excavated our mortar pit, were looking forward to a few winks of sleep and now we're off again. '3 Group, heavy mortars, standing by for departure!' Two lorries roared away: one with the MG crews, the other with the mortar gunners; the men remaining behind, soon to sleep in their foxholes, gave us a wave. On the Rollbahn we met up with the other vehicles and drove slowly to the battalion command post in a drainage ditch at the side of the road. The drivers received their orders. The tank destroyer was to lead; the two armoured personnel carriers were to be staggered laterally left and right in the wheatfields up to 200m away. We two, and two other lorries, would remain on the Rollbahn. We headed west towards where the sun had left a red sky on the horizon. The Rollbahn, neither asphalt nor concrete, was no more than a good field track. As we came to a bend and rose up a slight hill Ivan greeted us with one round. 'Dismount! Set up gear!' Our lorry continued on for a short stretch. In the gathering darkness we saw quite clearly muzzle fire coming from two or three T-34s about 800m ahead of a village. They landed close and exploded. Because of the dust whirling around, the Russians could not estimate our strength. Our lorry stopped. 'Dismount with equipment!' The moment we were all standing near the tailboard to dismount a tank shell hissed between us. It looked like a short horizontal flash of lightning. We all felt the air pressure as it passed! While sprinting to the other side of the road for cover in a shallow trench, I saw one of the MG gunners collapse 5m away in the middle of the road as if struck by lightning. Several fist-sized fragments of shrapnel clattered against my steel helmet. A moment later I lay breathing heavily in the shallow trench. A soldier asked me, 'Who was the man whose head was blown off by that tank shell?' I told him, 'I don't know.' Later I discovered that it was Gefreiter Wäschenfeld. This name was then confused with Rehfeldt and someone going on leave was to tell my parents. Fortunately this error was prevented. Our tank destroyer returned fire and after a short, inconclusive duel Ivan's panzers retired into the village.

We were ordered, 'Dig in!' Being interested in survival we had already started: in a few minutes we had shovelled out a 1m-deep hole in the soft brown earth and the mortar pit was also ready. The degree of haste in digging a foxhole, and its depth, depend on the situation and the motto, 'Who digs deepest has more chance of life!' The tank destroyer was concealed in a spot with a good view and the two armoured cars took up position to the left and right. After eating we got to sleep early: I was roused at 2300hrs for sentry duty. The night was dark, no moon, but the sky was bright and clear. Although summer, the nights here are cold. A lot of noise could be heard in the village ahead. Engines starting up, the neighing of horses, artillery tractors, tanks roaring. I could not believe my eyes: full headlamps blazed as vehicle after vehicle pulled out of the village. There was a road high up to the right where the long column was heading. I reported it at once but the Hauptmann commanding the tank destroyer told me, 'Let them run, they won't get far to the right, 24 Panzer Division is coming from there.' I spent the rest of my sentry duty watching the spectacle of Ivan's column slowly climbing the height towards disaster.

Once relieved I hit the sack and fell asleep at once. At 0400hrs I was awoken. 'Hans, there's lots of vehicles coming down the road, lights blazing from the ridge on the right. Are they ours?' By now it was light and I took the field glasses. 'No, that's Ivan. Probably the same ones who fled up the hill a few hours ago.' Now I could see very clearly Russian lorries, heavy Stalin tractors towing artillery and crowds of infantry, also tanks with infantry seated on the hulls. Countless guns, tanks and other vehicles all rolling back to their starting point. Most of the men were up now, watching the great Red Army column only a kilometre away. We stood for a while watching this gigantic enemy force right in front of our noses apparently unaware that this here was just a Germanski forward outpost. The commander of the tank destroyer appeared. Everybody tried to convince him to start shooting! 'The trouble is,' he explained, 'if the Russians see how weak we are, they will just steamroller over us.' The order came, '6 Mortar, range 1500m, five propellant charges! One round, fire!' I laid the mortar on the tank with the infantry on the hull, dropped the bomb into the barrel and the first round was fired. The men all waited keyed up for the effect, thought five seconds was too long, began to complain about the slow 'pancake', about this gypsy artillery, and then after twenty seconds there arose a black cloud of smoke in the centre of the Rollbahn close behind the tank aimed at. How the infantry jumped off and sprinted in all directions! 'Forward a bit! Two rounds, fire at will!' Two more mortar bombs left the barrel, both perfectly placed. Ivan was running in crazy circles for he could not detect from where the fire was coming, the Russians were making too much noise to hear the mortar being fired. Suddenly came a deafening noise as our tank destroyer fired. We could hear the shell in flight, and then the impact! 'Good, good'. Now round after round followed, falling amongst the great convoy. Large vehicles blocked the road, soldiers ran blindly hither and thither. 'Save yourself who can!' Ivan in terrible confusion! I thought to myself, 'All they need to do is bring up two field guns and they can make mincemeat of us!' But they didn't. Instead they sent a whole troop of cavalry. Through our binoculars we could see some of them, probably the commanders, looking back at us through field glasses. Finally they came to a decision and galloped in our direction, maybe 100 or more mounted men, and pulled up 800m short of us in the bushes and opened rifle fire. The range was a little long for accuracy seated on a horse. Our heavy MG replied with a few bursts which made the riders indecisive. Our No. 2 mortar fired no more than a couple of bombs in order to spare ammunition. We heard by radio that Stukas had been called up. Now we searched the skies waiting for them to appear. Meanwhile our armoured cars had rounded up about twenty-five Ivans from the fields of wheat and sunflowers. The cavalry troop was on the point of making an attack when the Stukas arrived, twelve of them. At this the cavalry, some mounted, others on foot, turned tail and ran for cover. The Russian fear of the Stuka appeared to be enormous. Our prisoners standing near us threw themselves down and looked up fearfully at the aircraft. We have noted this behaviour amongst the Russians so often that we consider that the Stuka dominates the battlefield. First they circle the target like vultures, then one machine after another tilts over one wing in steep downward flight at fantastic speed. The bombs are released almost directly into the target. The howl of the 'Jericho sirens' is an additional psychological factor. The walls break and the howl gets on your nerves. It all makes Ivan deadly quiet, but for us brings – relief! The circles become tighter, the target has been identified and the nose tilts – towards us! Crippling horror! They are diving on us! Flares! Smoke signals, quick, quick!' The flares hiss upwards and orange-yellow smoke is borne on the wind. Our position is marked and the tank destroyer shows the swastika flag. At the last moment, already in their dive, the Stukas realize their mistake and, with a blood-curdling howl of sirens close overhead, veer and climb in a steep curve upwards. 'Well, that went well!' They circled again and this time bombed the Russians: total chaos ensued, the bombs exploding in the midst of wildly zig-zagging tractors, tanks and fleeing soldiers. An ammunition truck exploded – some tanks zig-zagged off the road, bombs dropping between them: Ivan made no reply. In conclusion the Stukas strafed any vehicle in the open, and soldiers fleeing in panic. We watched the scene wordless and spellbound. Whenever a Stuka bomb exploded, we felt the blast wave a kilometre away. Thick clouds from the explosions hovered over the battlefield. Finally the Stukas made a pass over us at low level waggling their wings, a sign of greeting and victory, and then they roared off without climbing.

Wreckage was strewn everywhere, in the fields and at the roadside countless tractors with artillery pieces still in tow, exploding ammunition, thick black smoke above burning vehicles and many dead in between it all. After we checked the village and loaded the few Russian wounded into the lorries, we set off in pursuit of the enemy division, the tank destroyer in the lead, the other vehicles a short distance behind. Our weapons were at the ready and a light MG was mounted on the roof of the cab. Whenever we came across damaged T-34s, we dropped a hand grenade through the hatch. Our panzer, the armoured scout cars and armoured infantry-carriers led the chase in line abreast. Whenever the lorry crested one of the many low hills we would see ahead the fleeing Russians – artillery, cavalry, infantry and support services – trailing a bright cloud of dust. The tank destroyer would occasionally fire a round into it. We assumed that they were heading for Rostov in a desperate attempt to reorganize, and we had to prevent them entering the city. Our few vehicles and weapons had put a division-size unit to flight. Our morale had seldom been so good as on this advance. On the way we saw many Russian soldiers, some wearing greatcoats in the sizzling heat, emerge from fields of wheat and sunflowers holding a rifle and a sack containing their belongings. Mostly upon searching them we would find in the sacks bread and sunflower seeds, ammunition and stolen goods. As we reached the top of another hill we came under MG fire. A few hundred metres ahead lay a village, and behind it a brook with a narrow bridge. The Russians needed to halt our approach here to enable their vehicles to get across. Our tank destroyer fired, round after round. At the edge of the village we saw the muzzle flashes from four T-34s, the shells arriving and exploding before the sound of the discharge, and then they pulled back with some deliberation. On a road to our right with an uphill slope we saw a bright grey cloud of dust trailed by Ivan as he retired hastily to the large town of Shachty. This town had been bitterly defended against us last winter, the prisoners confirmed it. Would we be able to take them by surprise, chase the Russians through the town and eject them at the other end? Two T-34s had been posted as a rearguard as we advanced. We entered the village cautiously and saw beyond it a broken-down T-34 blocking the middle of the bridge. It would take some time to shift it. Therefore we dismounted, assembled and primed the mortars, then released gunners not required at the weapon to make house-to-house searches with fixed bayonets and pistols at the ready. Every slit trench and cowshed had to be searched for enemy soldiers in hiding, but all we found were great-grandfathers, Matkas and Malinkas of all ages. Naturally very anxious, they offered us basins and baskets with fruit, eggs and melons but we 'organized' milk, cream, eggs and home-baked white bread for ourselves. Their fear of us dispelled very quickly, they brought us water and some Matkas even brushed down our dusty uniforms. When an aircraft flew over they wanted to take shelter in slit trenches and told us, 'War no good, rifle no good, peng-peng, man, woman dead.' As one of Ivan's tanks began firing at us from the high ground a strange-looking motor car came bumping through the fields to our left. The vehicle stopped short 100m away, turned about and made to return the way it had come, pursued by rifle fire. A light infantry gun fired, forcing the driver to steer in wild zig-zags into a wheatfield where two men jumped clear of the car and disappeared into the tall crops. Our No. 5 mortar fired off two rounds before they found the cover of a depression. At that the shooting stopped. In the meantime the bridge had been cleared of the broken-down tank by pushing it into the brook. We remounted and set off again for Shachty. As we got to the high ground, a tank appeared either side of the road. The column halted, somebody fired a heavy Panzerbüchse[2] and the victor proudly wrote in chalk on the turret: 'Three rounds heavy Panzerbüchse – IR Grossdeutschland 1' and sketched our divisional emblem. Our unit kept going along the miserable Rollbahn towards Shachty. The rearguard called out 'Tanks to the rear!', three of them. Our panzer fought them for a while but they must have been pretty green, for two were destroyed by shellfire, the other bogged down in swampy ground.[3] During the tank battle our lorries drove off the Rollbahn into the fields where five sleeping Russians were found, disarmed and made prisoner. One of them was identified by the others as a 'Bolshevik Politruk': when our NCO approached him he drew a pistol and fired at him but missed. The NCO shot him dead with a sub-machine gun. We took the lesson that in future we needed to be more careful taking prisoners. From our prisoners' ID/paybooks we saw that they were Ukrainians. We sat with the four prisoners on the superstructure of the tank destroyer and farther along the Rollbahn came to a Stalin organ which had had engine trouble and been blown up. Our tank destroyer stopped and we crossed to another Rollbahn which bore the track marks of many panzers. I asked some Russian civilians who confirmed that yesterday a thousand tanks drove through here. These can only have been German panzers coming from the town of Grachevsnoye. But a thousand? The Russians like to exaggerate and so a thousand was probably 'a lot'. At least we now knew we were not completely alone in the district. About 2km ahead to our right was what looked like an overland electrical sub-station and for the sake of caution our tank destroyer fired a round into it but all remained quiet. From the next elevated section of road we saw in the distance the town of Shachty. We thought it must be a mining town by the pyramidal slag heaps between the houses. We approached the town at a fast speed, saw road blocks and tank obstacles but encountered no resistance. The tank destroyer fired a single warning shot into the town and then we entered the deserted streets. Soon the first inhabitants appeared from their cellars and slit trenches, shocked by the round the tank destroyer had fired. Then the girls and children waved to us. We thought back to Rostov in 1941 when the same happened and our men were caught in an explosive trap which cost lives. The people here did not seem to have any malicious ideas in mind. In general I have the impression that the population in the south is friendlier than in the wooded areas south and south-east of Moscow and Tula. At every street corner the people called out to us 'Hitler olé!' The girls had bare legs, wore colourful headscarves and seemed well disposed to us. Damn war, they didn't look at all bad! They were better dressed than the people we saw last winter. The houses were neater too – not only of wood, but sturdy houses of stone.

It was an industrial town with pit-head frames, thus the slag heaps: on the streets trams had been coupled up to form barriers and barricades were built on all sides of crossroads. Many houses had been reinforced into bunkers with sandbags. 'Man, imagine it if Ivan had taken this town, it would have been a hard nut to crack!' We learned that the fleeing Russians had passed by the town in order to get to Rostov-on-Don, 'the Fortress', as soon as possible. We marked out a route through all the obstructions and reached the main road leading to a large open square, the Krassnaya Ploshyad (Red Square) with Lenin, bleached white by the sun, on his pedestal in oratorical pose. Our tank destroyer rolled past the monument and secured all streets running into the square. Later a quadruple Flak arrived. We made our position left of the brickworks, the heavy MGs being set up in a circle around it. We were ready to defend ourselves: hand grenades on our belts and fixed bayonets (always makes a good impression, very martial), and so there we stood, fifty German soldiers in the middle of a large industrial town as the advanced detachment well ahead of our regiment and only in contact with it by radio. The following message was sent: 'Advanced detachment *Grossdeutschland* – Battle Group *Köhler*, 1430hrs took town Shachty without a fight. Secured Lenin Platz, town centre, enemy fleeing south-south-west.'

With our bayonets we had difficulty holding off the huge crowds of towns-people who came to welcome us, but they meant us no harm. They brought us water, apples and pears. A girl handed me a basin of sugared mulberries: they were unknown to me but looked like blackberries. I invited her to try one first for which she laughed at me. They tasted wonderful. A couple of our 'organizers' raided a shop window and brought us a large round Swiss cheese but aha! made of papier-mâchée. We assembled all the men of the town to check that none were military in civilian dress: all were released later. A couple of hours afterwards other German soldiers arrived at the town preceding an armoured scout car flying a general's pennant: a tall slender figure climbed out, walking stick in hand. Hurrah for Papa Hörnlein! The commander of the tank destroyer reported and the general walked down the line, looked each man in the eye and said, 'I am proud of you grenadiers!' Then he returned to his command vehicle. A long rope was attached around the neck of the Lenin monument and pulled down by ten of the townsfolk to loud applause. Thus the outward sign of the Leninist spirit tumbled into the dust at least here. Soon we were relieved by III Battalion and attached to 7 Company as 'Heavy Weapons'. Afterwards we returned to our 9 Company/I Battalion. Later Panzergruppe Kleist took over the town.

Notes

1. This would be a 7.62cm Pak 36 (r = Russian) mounted on a PzKpf II version D1/ D2 chassis Sd Kfz.132 Marder II. The calibre indicates a captured, unmodified Russian anti-tank gun in a fixed mount with limited traverse. Top speed, road, 55km/hr. The Sd Kfz.132 entered service in April 1942: 185 were built and were highly thought of. Alexander Lüdeke, *Panzer der Wehrmacht Band 1, 1933–1945*, Motorbuch, 2014, pp. 76–7. (TN) (Ed: The photograph at the foot of p. 201 is a tank hunter of this type.

2. The 2.8cm heavy Panzerbüchse 41 was a light Pak gun (229kg) with chassis (spreading legs and wheels), recoil system and shield, and capable of firing up to thirty rounds/min over an effective range of 800m. The 2.8cm barrel tapered to 2cm at the muzzle for firing tungsten-core shells at a muzzle velocity of 1,440m/ sec thus enabling penetration of 66mm of armour at 500m. Alexander Lüdeke, *Deutsche Artillerie Geschütze 1933–1945*, Motorbuch, 2016, pp. 44–5. (TN)

3. The author does not state the types of Soviet tanks engaged, but the Sd Kfz.132 was at a great disadvantage in having its gun in fixed mount with no traverse. (TN)

Resting by the wayside in the summer heat.

Grenadiers of the *Grossdeutschland* Division waiting to mount the hull of a self-propelled assault gun, two of which are seen on the road. Hans Rehfeldt is indicated by the arrow.

Unteroffizier Stedtler in his slit trench, behind him is Rehfeldt.

Unteroffizier Stedtler in his slit trench, mess tin, cutlery and haversack close at hand.

In the woods at Karachev: Becker, Hinz, Rhedanz and Lorenz at a table.

A group photo of the platoon corporals, summer 1942.

Motorized advance through the Ukraine, summer 1942.

NCOs in front of their tent in a wood near Kursk.

Motorized advance in the back of an Opel lorry. Hans Rehfeldt at the centre.

A Panzer IV with 7.5cm gun during an advance.

A Marder II tank destroyer. Seen at Svoboda, the conversion is a Panzer II chassis fitted with a captured Russian 7.62cm 'all-purpose' gun.

A dozen Panzer IIIs climbing a hill towards Voronezh.

NCOs in the Ukraine, 1942. Many fell in the course of the war.

Unteroffiziers Stedtler and Starost at Ryetshitza.

The market at Ryetshitza on the Dnieper shortly before the offensive.

Final bartering before pulling out.

Cars lashed down on rail low-loaders.

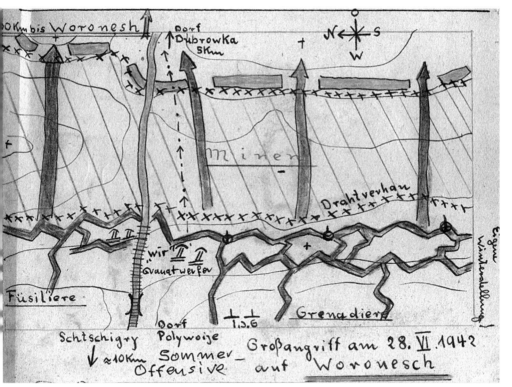

Map by Hans Rehfeldt showing the offensive towards Voronezh on 28 June 1942.

A light field howitzer ready to fire, ammunition handlers to the right.

An 8cm mortar firing in the open.

The No. 1 gunner drops the bomb into the mortar, which fires immediately.

'Better a rough ride than a gentle walk' was the motto of experienced infantry.

A Panzer IV halted for observation purposes.

Heavy 15cm howitzer of the *Grossdeutschland* Division on the road.

An eight-wheeled armoured car on the steppe at Voronezh.

The typical Russian Maxim MG with wheeled mount and two crew. This MG had a slower rate of fire than German heavy MGs but was very reliable.

Die Kriegsfreiwilligen-Division „Großdeutschland" grüßt die Heimat!

Sturmgeschütze und Grenadiere

8. (9.) Komp. II Btl. Pz Gr Rgt.

Grossdeutschland Division self-propelled assault gun with grenadiers aboard.

Die Kriegsfreiwilligen-Division „Großdeutschland" grüßt die Heimat!

Panzer rollen vor

Finally Panzer IVs with the longer 7.5cm gun arrived at the Front to tackle the superior Russian T-34.

Die Kriegsfreiwilligen-Division „Großdeutschland"
grüßt die Heimat!

SMG in Feuerstellung

A heavy MG34 in firing position. Mounted on a tripod the gun had a range of 2km.

Die Kriegsfreiwilligen-Division „Großdeutschland"
grüßt die Heimat!

Leichtes Inf.-Geschütz im Einsatz

The 7.5cm light infantry gun ready to fire.

A column of the *Grossdeutschland* Division on the move.

A five-man *Grossdeutschland* Division mortar team advancing.

Italiani, mandati in Russia!

Noi, otto soldati italiani della divisione „Celere"—art. Trabbcchi Ezio regg. art. a cavallo 3 gruppo 6 batt., ed i bersaglieri del 3 regg. bers. 18 btg. della divisione „Celere"—Santangello Paolo, Tartaglino Verginio, Gervasini Carlo, Marchetti Umberto, Montis Eliggio, Folli Giuseppe, Gorla Ernesto—sono volontariamente passati dalla parte dell'Esercito Rosso.

L'abbiamo fatto perchè abbiamo carito che ci hanno mandati a morire per gli interessi tedeschi in Russia. Ci ingannavano da molto tempo, promettendoci da ritornare in patria, ma infatti ci tratterranno qui finchè saremo morti tutti.

Ci ingannavano, dicendoci le solite fesserie che l'Esercito Rosso è stato distrutto, in realtà l'Esercito Rosso da giorno in giorno diventa più forte.

Ora i tedeschi sono abbattuti su tutto il fronte Orientale. Hanno già perduto la guerra, e bene che loro periscono, i cani maledetti! Perchè noi dobbiamo aspettare il nostro turno da morire! Non è meglio a vivere!

Noi tutti otto vostri fratelli abbiamo deciso e siamo coraggiosamente passati dalla parte dei russi.

Ebbène! Credete che si sono giustificate le barzellette stupide che ci raccontavano i nostri ufficiali sul trattamento dei prigionieri in Russia!

No, ci hanno accolto fraternamente, ci hanno riscaldati e dato da mangiare. Noi stiamo bene, non ci manca niente, e dopo la guerra noi ritorneremo presso ai nostri padri, madri, moglia e figli. Così noi siamo salvi della nostra vita.

Fratelli italiani! Fate come noi l'abbiamo fatto, passate dalla parte dei russi. L'Esercito Rosso vi tratterà bene, come noi. Alcuni giorni fà ci hanno letto l'ordine di STALIN, nel quale si dice che l'Esercito Rosso non ha nessun odio verso a qualsiasi popolo o razza. L'Esercito Rosso stermina i soldati ed ufficiali che con le armi in mano hanno aggredito il territorio russo e continuano la lotta, rifiutandosi da darsi prigionieri. Ma l'Esercito Rosso assicura la vita e un buon trattamento a tutti coloro che depongono le armi e si arrendono.

Fratelli italiani! Vi nasconderanno quest'ordine di STALIN, come vi nascondono ogni verità. Lo sappiate dunque e senza paura datevi prigionieri! Salvate la vostra vita! Finite questa sanguinosa guerra che è insensata per voi!

From 1942, Hitler's ally Mussolini sent an Italian army into Russia. The Russians knew that the Italians lacked commitment and worked on them with leaflets in the effort to get them to defect.

Back of the leaflet.

Chapter 12

Bridgehead over the Don

---

23 July 1942

At 0415hrs the attack on the Don began. We were to capture the village of Melichovskaya on the northern bank. Ivan tried to frighten us with an attack by a tank (not a T-34) first, but it was destroyed. Then came perfect collaboration between the heavy MGs and mortars. At the raised northern bank of the Don at Melichovskaya we saw large quantities of military equipment at the river's edge which Ivan had had to abandon – many lorries, heavy guns, large tracked towing vehicles and even tanks, some of the latter putting up a fight having been knocked out by our tank destroyers. We advanced swiftly and took many prisoners. A cadre of commissars put up very stiff resistance in a house but were wiped out.

Now came the time for plunder. From clothing stocks we took linen underpants and khaki-coloured officers' shirts. Among the many vehicles we found a strongbox containing a great bundle of banknotes. These would be handy for bribery: later when preparing for home leave we exchanged them for Reichsmarks through the company paymaster. Ivan had also left behind butter (liquid at 45°C), and we found mulberry trees at the water's edge. The pioneers rowed or paddled us across the Don in inflatable rafts. The river was 300m wide at this point and fast-flowing. We came under fire from heavy mortars, causing metre-high water fountains to rise up around us but all missed, otherwise with our own heavy mortar aboard we would have been sunk. On the southern shore was a loam-sandy slope about 3 to 5m high. A few metres inshore came the order to dig in. The ground was soft and the foxholes were soon ready, mortars and heavy MGs in position. The sun beat down, our thirst was severe, our field flasks empty. Some of the men went to drink the dark waters of the Don but were deterred when the first bodies of dead Russians drifted past. The inflatable boats brought all of II Battalion across to establish a bridgehead here. It was not very large, about 300m deep and 2km long, but our heavy guns could protect us from the far bank if necessary. Ivan was not very active; finally evening came and the temperature fell. After our meal, which included stewed mulberries, sentries were posted and we deepened our foxholes. Our bedfellows were sand flies, small frogs, and even small snakes and so we relocated instead to the infantry trenches, which were no better. Had we not been so exhausted from our efforts during the day we would not have slept.

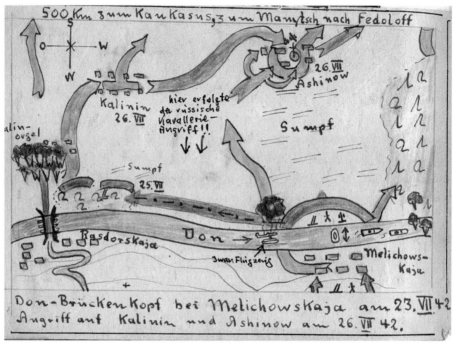

Map by Hans Rehfeldt, '500kms to the Caucasus, to Manytsch after Fedeloff'. (NB: this map has south at the top, see top left indicator). Bottom legend: Don minor bridgehead at Melichovskaya (bottom right of map) on 23 July 1942, attack on Kalinin and Ashinov on 26 July 1942. Key: Sumpf = swamp, hier erfolgte etc = this was where the Russian cavalry attacked!! Ivan Flugzeug = Russian floatplane. Left margin, 'Stalinorgel'.

24 July 1942

During the night three Russian gunboats passed noiselessly downstream towards the Sea of Azov. Unfortunately they got through. In the early morning, after a weak Russian attack had been broken up, a floatplane painted with the red star landed elegantly in midstream. The two crewmen climbed out on a float to discover with horror Germans on both banks! They got back on board swiftly, the engines howling but the alert men of Leutnant Konopka's regimental pioneer platoon took them prisoner. The floatplane was brought to the bank and loaded up with 2cm Flak rounds. To the south of our bridgehead was a swampy area which was difficult to cross, especially for vehicles. Farther upstream after heavy fighting our forces had established a second bridgehead at Rasdorskaya. The ground there was sandy and firmer, providing better prospects for our advance. After carrying out a survey, the pioneers had erected a pontoon bridge there over the Don. Noting the development, Russian resistance had stiffened at Rasdorskaya, and we received the order to move upstream with all weapons and equipment. We had gone 10 to 12km towards the objective under a baking sun when we heard infantry fire from the III Battalion bridgehead and now for the first time in the war we experienced a genuine cavalry attack, a dreadful sight, the first and last I ever saw.

The earth rumbled from the horses' hooves, which threw up a huge cloud of dust, and through which we saw the flash of long sabres, held high pointed towards us. Some of the Kalmucke riders fired at us from the saddle. We lay in full cover watching this spectacle galloping fast in our direction. To our right a 2cm quadruple Flak gun was brought up as our heavy MG42 began to rattle. Soon the Flak fired too. Ivan replied with a Stalin organ located in a village due south of the Rasdorskaya bridgehead and also raked us with his 7.62cm anti-tank guns. The explosive Flak shells fired into the mounted formation caused panic and the groups of riders began to separate and gallop back to the village of Ashinov from where they had originated the attack. Many were killed in this retreat. The whinnying of the horses in their death throes was awful to hear. Hardly had we emerged from our foxholes believing it to be over than with the same verve and élan the attack of the Kalmucke cavalry came again. At that came the order, 'In the bridgehead – heads down!' The quadruple Flak on the other high bank of the Don now took the riders under fire, terrible to witness! Horses collapsed only a few metres from us, the rider dead, wounded or thrown clear, though most survivors had serious injuries. The few mounted survivors returned to Ashinov village. Our Flak guns ceased fire: Ivan sent us some Stalin-organ rockets and anti-tank fire before it fell quiet to the south. Such incredible madness! Cavalry against MGs and Flak guns! Our infantry went forth cautiously, pistols drawn, to deliver the *coup de grâce* to seriously injured horses. A few Russian cavalrymen were found alive and taken prisoner. All the sabres were collected up as trophies. Our drivers had two sabres each to

fit crossed on the radiator of the lorry. Oberleutnant Konopka attended FHQ
to present the Führer with an officer's sabre.

Now we lay in scorching heat parched with thirst in a fairly open wood on
the Don. Against the strictest orders and all reason I went down to a pool
and laid a handkerchief over my field flask to filter the lukewarm, dirty water.
In the flask I had a soup of brown water inhabited by water beetles, filth and
small spiders. I used it as mouthwash and then took a swig. It had a vile taste.
Later in the same pool we discovered a dead horse and some dead Russians.
We were no longer so thirsty. At Rasdorskaya pioneers, naked but wearing
steel helmets, were making a large pontoon bridge able to take the weight of
panzers. We watched the first vehicles testing it. Soon an unbroken convoy of
vehicles of all kinds, panzers, assault guns, rocket launchers, infantry in lorries
and armoured personnel carriers was heading towards the Manytsh reservoir
and beyond it to the Caucasus. We changed our position to some kilometres
upstream and rested. While standing stark naked at the river's edge, some of
the men already swimming, suddenly we heard the sound of a Stalin organ.
Everybody lay flat, and twenty-four rockets exploded in the river and on the
shore. In the evening we stretched out in the grass near our position. During
the night I had two hours' sentry duty. It was damned cold. The summer nights
here in the south are very short. At sunrise I had barely stretched out when we
heard the things in flight and forty-eight Stalin-organ rockets exploded around
us. I turned immediately onto my stomach and pressed myself flat against the
ground, my head behind the two ammunition cases. I glanced up once and saw
how the splinters nipped off the tips of grass haulms at 30 to 50cms height. I
got my head down quick again! Ivan played his organ a second time, mortally
wounding a motorcycle rider and lightly wounding two others, but our group
got off scot-free.

26 July 1942

Today we started by taking the first village of Kalinin without resistance, but
came under anti-tank fire on the way to Ashinov. The worst of it is that the
shell explodes before you hear the report of the gun being fired. Sound travels at
333m/sec, but a shell is much faster. Nevertheless we drove out the Russians and
took many prisoners, troops from Kazakhstan and Siberia. Ivan's last reserves?
There were about 100 horses loose in the village, a tall breed, saddled, some with
portmanteaus buckled, the long cavalry sabre still in the scabbard on the saddle.

The animals were crazed with thirst. Where was the well? When a couple of us drew water and filled some wooden buckets, the horses saw this and we were almost trampled in the crush. Those seriously wounded we shot. In front of the village and in the street lay many dead horses, bloated in the heat, some with bellies burst open. The wind swept the sickening-sweet smell of their cadavers far and wide. The Russians were long gone and we dug in forward of the village.

27 July 1942

Our sentries brought in some prisoners. Amongst them a youngster from the 110th Cavalry Division, scarcely 17 years old and three months a soldier! He told us that boys were now being called up at age 15 and received little training. He was sick of it and wanted to join with us as a Hiwi [*Hilfswilliger* = voluntary assistant]. We can use Hiwis for all types of jobs, and nearly all of them can be trusted! This morning we drove 8km to the village of Fedoloff and occupied it without a fight. It lies in the direction of the great Manytsh reservoir – general direction Caucasus. Here we secured and 'organized' eggs, honey and fruit, set up our tents on a flat elevation and set up our mortars, Flak and Pak. The heavy MGs took up position at the village entrances. Here we have been detailed to wait until all our division has crossed the Don over the pontoon bridge at Rasdorskaya. Eggs, tomatoes, cherries and other fruit are in abundance. The Russian ovens stand outside the houses because it would be too hot to have them inside: sunflower stems are used as fuel. The Matkas were surprised at how well we made omelettes. Late in the night we watched Ivan up to his scorched earth tricks on the horizon. We slept in our tents and posted sentries. The night was not quiet with all the goings-on in the distance. Our artillery fired on some of the villages at a range of 5000m.

28 July 1942

During the night there was a tremendous explosion, rather like an ammunition dump being blown up. It was a good way away and did not disturb us much. When it was getting light at around 0200hrs, a sentry came running to rouse us with much ado. We surveyed the situation. Everywhere before us in the low ground, what looked like a greyish-white mist was pushing towards us. When the sun rose, it shone down on great expanses of water, behind and around us, that hadn't been there the night before. Without a round being fired, the so-feared Panzer Grenadier Division *Grossdeutschland* had been put out of action by a great flood. We could no longer advance. Some of our units had got as far as the great wheat silo at Elista, others tried to cross the Manytsh and its tributaries. It had been our fortune to set up tents at Fedoloff on an elevation. And the cause? East of us lay the great Manytsh reservoir, 300km long and between 20 and 30km wide. Ivan had blown up the dam and flooded the land for many kilometres. In some places the water was up to 3m deep, at others as shallow as 50cm. A number of villages higher up had become islands and remained dry. We could not advance, but Ivan could not attack us with cavalry or motorized troops. The Russians had few aircraft here with which to make our lives unpleasant: we had a fairly good opportunity for rest. Countless dead cattle floated around: huge formations of ducks and geese arrived on the water or islands. On a small 'neighbouring island' were fields of tomatoes and so, clad only in belt and haversack, we swam or waded forth for the harvest. '*Achtung!* Nobody else go in the water – we're going to shoot some duck and geese!' I had never eaten so many of them in my life. From Manytsh a canal led to Starottsherkassk on the Don, a waterway which connected the Don with the Caspian Sea. We learned later our advance had been halted by the Russians blowing up a bridge over a tributary of the Manytsh, otherwise we would have gone on some way to Salsk. This area is a great plain, and surprised by water there we would have been marooned.

29–31 July 1942

Our regimental band came and played both military marches and hits! It raised our spirits. They ended the performance with the beautiful melody, '*Freut Euch des Lebens*' ('Enjoy Your Life'). Next day we saw our first camels, harnessed to carts. That night we experienced a tropical storm with torrential rain. Swarms of mosquitoes made our life hell and we could not sleep at night for them. We have no mosquito nets. On the 31st we speculated: could we be going to cross the Kalmucke Steppe to Astrakhan?

1 August 1942

It is like Army service in peacetime here. We awake at 0500hrs, receive instruction, one hour's drill, sport and swimming. During the day we swim, collect tomatoes from distant islands and shoot some geese. In the evening, we had a platoon get-together, the high point of the day being my promotion to Gefreiter [Private First Class]: a reason to celebrate but watch out! 'The enemy shoots first at the man of higher rank!' Then a football tournament was arranged for the morrow. We knew what this meant. Previously a handball or football tournament preceded pulling out.

2 August 1942

Sunday, the traditional travelling day for *Grossdeutschland*. We were free of duty, rested and watched the football. At midday the field kitchen served us an excellent meal, roast goose (again!). The supply here is inexhaustible. At last, towards 1700hrs came the order to move out. There began a hurried packing and stowing, our MGs and mortars were thoroughly cleaned and greased for a long journey and then loaded aboard. The men retained their hand weapons. Farewell, restful days! At 1700hrs on the dot the columns of II Battalion rolled out, and no more than hours before the flood had receded, we had the dust back! We headed north-east, sitting up in our good old 3.5-tonne Opel-Blitz lorry, our home. Directly behind the cab we put our field packs and laundry bags, in the centre was a rack for stowing the mortar and below it the ammunition cases. The lorry walls either side were lined by benches with space below for more ammunition. Food for any eventuality was stored in the back of the lorry. Buckets, empty or filled with tomatoes, melons and even chicken or geese: salt, masses of sunflower seeds, and on every lorry a box with 'iron rations' for the occupants. These would be at least ten to twelve tins of pork and the same number of bags of dry biscuits. Iron rations could only be eaten on the orders of an NCO in special emergency situations, such as when the troops had had no rations over an extended period. All the iron rations we received at Neuruppin were consumed at Tula in the first winter without waiting for orders. The pork tins were then filled with mud, the empty biscuit tins with small sticks of wood, and they passed muster in all subsequent inspections. To the rear under the benches were containers of water and fuel. Many lorries bore the marks of damage from splinters and shells.

During our journey the whirling dust had settled in a thick layer on our sweaty faces. To protect our eyes against the sun and dust we wore the already-mentioned rubber-framed goggles like the motorcycle riders had. We looked as though flour had been thrown at us. We reached the great pontoon bridge and here joined a long queue, for columns of vehicles proceeding to the Front had priority. We saw our own panzers, drawn up in long lines. Finally we crossed at Rasdorskaya to the northern side and drove along the Don to Melichovskaya.

Here we had made our first crossing of the Don in rubber boats. Quarters were assigned and occupied. After the evening meal we made ourselves cosy and let our minds wander. Would we be sent to France for rest and recuperation? Some of the men pictured themselves already in Paris!

3–10 August 1942: Melichovskaya/Don

Just like the peacetime Army again. Marching, weapons practice, barrack-square drill. All to maintain discipline. We bathe in the fast-flowing Don when the opportunity arises. We remained at Melichovskaya until 10 August. We attended the mobile delousing wagon at a neighbouring village some kilometres away. Our clothing was almost grilled there ('By order: No kind of ammunition or hand grenades to be left in your clothing!') and we were allowed an hour to bathe in the Don, run around on the shore stark naked or lie in the sun. Some of the men wanted to try fishing with hand grenades. Suddenly an old man in baggy red bathing trunks griped, 'That is forbidden, it kills the spawn.' We said, 'What does this old Opa want of us?' and then somebody shouted in shock, 'That is the general!' In bathing trunks he was unrecognizable. Clothes maketh the man! When our uniforms and underwear were returned they seemed almost cooked but apparently it was the only way to get rid of the lice. At midday the field kitchen served a wonderful dessert of pudding and stewed pears. We always had good cooks at 8/9 Companies of II Battalion. One of them had been trained at the famous Vierjahreszeiten (Four Seasons) Hotel in Hamburg. In the afternoon we had choir practice. A troop which does not sing is not worth much! The soldier must always be 'moved' and not have much time for brooding.

10 August 1942

Today we had 'smart' weapons training and in the afternoon instruction by the company leader regarding 'Behaviour on extended train journeys; Behaviour in France'. Aha! we thought, Where would this long train journey be heading? III Platoon went 'organizing' in the vicinity and also searched for abandoned Russian weapons.

11 August 1942

We were awoken at midnight to prepare to move out at 0200hrs. The columns rolled through the coalmining district of Shachty and after a long journey arrived at an industrial area of large towns with many slag heaps and pit-head towers. Crossing a railway line we saw that Ivan had destroyed the tracks with a 'rail-ripper'. This consisted of two powerful locomotives towing a very heavy steel frame which in a single operation tore up the sleepers down the middle and thus contorted the rails. Naturally this would make it very difficult for us to repair the line for we would have to ship in new sleepers and rails. After 134km we came to a halt to eat but afterwards had to sit while the mine precaution teams did their work and the Rollbahn on both sides was secured for several kilometres with a safe corridor. To the thin iron stakes supporting the cordon were fixed small metal shields or pennants of cloth bearing a white death's-head insignia. We slept in tents or on the lorries: the drivers preferred to sleep beneath the lorries. The nights here in the south are very short and cold.

12 August 1942

In broad daylight at 0400hrs we continued our long journey via Kuibyshev to Sneshnoiye–Chisskonoiye–Charzisk–Makeyevka to Stalino (today Donetz). Here we set up our quarters between houses at the edge of the town. Make and mend, tidy, clean weapons. In the evening we went to the theatre to see *Der Graf von Luxemburg* with Russian actors! At the end of each act the ballet dancers jumped down amongst the public and we infantrymen were overjoyed to be able to see girls again at close quarters. They even let us touch them! It was a very pleasant experience. Stalino is a big industrial and mining town. Wandering through its streets we saw that the large official buildings have a pleasant façade at the front but the sides and rear are pitiful, naked stone without plaster. The small houses are unattractive, the workers' cottages are better and have small gardens between them.

13 August 1942

While we are away from the Front here the railway is bringing up many divisions. Many Italians! We also saw units of the SS-Regiment *Germania*. Entirely freshly equipped with weapons and vehicles. We can only gaze upon them with envy from our 'battle-proven Opel-Blitzes'.

14 August 1942

During the night a storm raged. We had put up a tent in a garden near the lorries, but the torrential rain all but swept us away. We sought refuge in the house of the district administrator. The family is Caucasian, the administrator works in a bakery in town, his wife's name is Rosa and they have two children. The furniture is nicely arranged but very old-fashioned for our taste. Rosa speaks really good German which she learned at school. We bought a kilo of bread from her husband. On a low cupboard, a row of elephants made of soapstone served as book-ends, to the left and right each fifth elephant was larger, making a stepped formation. These small figurines were really attractive and I thought to myself that I would organize the finest as souvenirs. In the end I took the smallest. If I had taken one from each end, perhaps it would not have been noticed but Rosa saw that one was missing and what a fuss and lamentation! I felt a real heel, especially when our platoon leader asked if one of us had swiped it. (It stands today, as it always has, alongside a photo of myself on operations beside the bipod of our mortar.)

15 August 1942
Weapons inspection, drill etc. We were notified that we would soon be leaving: the advance party was already on the way to the railway station.

16 August 1942
At 0600hrs we rolled down to the goods yard at Grishinev, about 70km from Stalino. The advance party had done good work and by midday II Battalion finished loading. We remained with our vehicles on the open transporter wagons, all MGs were assembled for use as Flak or to fight off possible attacks by partisans. Two wagons with sand ballast were coupled up ahead of the locomotive to set off pressure mines on the track. We got settled in comfortably, for we were sure we were going to France. We had to wait until 2000hrs until the section of line was free for Rasdovi–Freymark–Usel, after which we crossed the Samara. Soon we were all stretched out and talking about France. The monotonous rattle over the tracks was like music to our ears. It grew cooler, sentries were posted and soon we slept.

17 August 1942
The sun rose at 0445hrs. The train rolled ever onward, often stopping but making good progress despite that. After Usel the long train thundered over a bridge crossing the Samara, and in the afternoon we reached Dnyepropetrovsk on the Dnieper, the train reducing speed through gigantic

industrial installations. We saw huge ruined steel constructions, gutted factories, jumbled steel girders, large thick steam pipes, electrical cables tightly stretched this way and that to tall wooden masts for no apparent reason. The overall impression was of a massive wire entanglement at the Front. A huge two-tiered bridge spanned the 500m-wide Dnieper, one tier for the railway below, one for road traffic above. Much had been destroyed by military action although the Russians had blown some of it up themselves. One of the colossal dams had a large hole blown through it by demolition charges. Evening came. Throughout the day I had sat in the cab of the lorry for its good view. At the last stop for signals several of our comrades had left the train to answer the call of nature. The rule while squatting was to watch the signals ahead or for the white smoke of the locomotive whistle: then one had to hurry! The moon was bright, the train moved off, and our comrades failed to make it back. During the night the train reached Krementchug. The river Dnieper here is almost a kilometre wide.

18 August 1942

We reached Dnyepropetrovsk–Krementchug on the Dnieper, straddled by a gigantic bridge. One hundred metres farther on is a large bridge put up by the pioneers, the Rundstedt Bridge. We passed Chorol and Romney through green, fruitful land. The fields looked already harvested. After many more hours the train arrived at Gomel. On 5 June two months previously coming from Ryetshitza we had left here for the great summer offensive at Kursk. We had come full circle!

19 August 1942

If we were being taken to France, the train would bear left at Gomel for the west, but instead it kept going to Rogatshev. A certain air of disquiet and tension began to creep in. Doubts were voiced, but even our officers seemed to know nothing. According to the map, Orsha was the last possible point for the tracks to convey us westwards. The train continued to head north and at midnight squealed to a halt at the station called Orsha. I fell asleep and awoke to the sun shining in my eyes. From where does the sun shine in the morning? From the east! Therefore our dream of France was an illusion. On the radio one of the men had heard that the Russians had been pounding Rzhev for weeks without pause and broken through the Front, and were also making heavy attacks on

Voronezh. There was talk of Ivan using 2,000 tanks in the attacks of which 1,068 had been destroyed according to Wehrmacht bulletins. But Ivan was not deterred. These attacks on Rzhev and Voronezh had been maintained merely to tie us down! Our troops heading towards the Caucasus could not be so easily supplied with men and materials. The pressure on these two points made it even more difficult. I wrote in my diary: 'Since the Russians attacked Rzhev with 2,000 tanks and broke through the Front, will our division, whose advanced units have come as far as Lemberg, be re-routed to Smolensk as a reserve in case of emergency. Will that turn out well?'

20 August 1942

We unloaded at Smolensk. It was not far to a rest area. Because the division had to re-assemble here from many trains, naturally a lot of time would pass until the last one unloaded. Weapons cleaning, spit and polish, physical training, drill. We were trained on the rangefinder. We saw the musical film *Die leichte Muse*.

21–26 August 1942

Our NCOs set up a shooting competition for pistol and sub-machine gun. Our platoon leader, Feldwebel Rhedanz, was drafted to Cottbus to a reserve brigade. He received a very militarily correct send-off. The local population is very friendly. They are tremendously hard workers. This year they doubled the wheat harvest! A Russian administrator explained: 'In 1933/34 there was a great famine here. Many people died.' We heard the same in the Ukraine. The old folk told us about it with tears in their eyes, always pointing to the cemetery with its many crosses. He also said that if the Bolshevists had broken through here in 1941/42, the population would have retreated with the German forces.

27 August 1942

1 and 5 Panzer Divisions are also here at Smolensk. We loaded up and went along perfect concrete roads to Wyasma. The villages, with our infantry spread everywhere, have a very cared-for and clean look.

28 August 1942

The farther we travel, the worse the roads get! And soon much worse! The vehicles suffer from the jolting. From Sychevka a log road many kilometres in length leads towards Rzhev. Great woodlands everywhere offer us protection against aerial reconnaissance. We, the Grenadier Regiment *Grossdeutschland* 1, are rolling towards Rzhev. From the Front we can hear heavy artillery fire and also Stalin organs, tank guns and Pak. Our Fusilier Regiment *Grossdeutschland* 2 is attacking supported by large formations of Stukas and bombers. We have camouflaged-up in the woods and set about making much-needed improvements to the roads. Our troops are everywhere in these woods. We feel that here at Rzhev, Ivan is intent upon achieving a major victory – with everything he has!

29 August 1942

All units lying here in these woodlands are busy with the road improvements needed soon for the fast inbound movement of troops and supplies. The ground here trembles under the explosions from the Front. The loud crack of panzer and tank guns firing are such as we have never heard before. Ivan has brought up huge numbers of tanks for his impending attack.

30 August 1942

Today we drove up, we believe unnoticed by the enemy, to about 4km from Rzhev. The woods end here in log roads, bushes and swamps. For our four-man tents, camouflaged with bushes and branches, we can dig down no deeper than 1m. It is not pleasant to be a tent-dweller here! We are in range of Russian artillery, and all hell often breaks loose no more than a couple of kilometres away. The ground trembles with the shelling and bombing by both sides. Quite often we find ourselves in the line of fire, often before hearing the report of the gun, and we take cover upon hearing the flight of a shell, for one never knows where it might hit. But it does not seem as though Ivan knows exactly where we are. We are very close to him here: if he aimed at us personally our chances would be slim.

31 August 1942

Heavy artillery fire continued throughout the night. Ivan dispersed his fire across the terrain – he knows we have troops everywhere here. I would have felt happier in a one-man foxhole. German and Russian flares light up the horizon and then soon fade out, ours white, the Russians a greenish-white. Continual panzer, tank and anti-tank fire. All day much aerial activity. Our Stukas concentrated on the Russian trenches or tank assemblies, first bombing and then strafing before flying off at low level above us. Ivan sent over some aircraft, but our Me 109s shot down an Ilyushin 2 'sewing machine' and a Rata fighter. We are at maximum alarm readiness!

1 September 1942

During the night Russian tanks fired random rounds into our area of bush and scrub. They still don't know where we are exactly. During the day the Stukas and Ju 88s attacked their positions with fighter protection. We checked our weapons and equipment for the umpteenth time. When will we finally do something? Are we here only as a reserve for the counter-attack, or will we make an attack ourselves in the future? The waiting is the worst. We had another 'platoon evening'. The weather is wet and cold and a nip of schnapps did me good. After quite a few nips of schnapps one can sleep better and then we forget this shit war. Perhaps that is why they issue it. At 0200hrs the Russians attacked over there in the darkness. Our flares and their flares rose up. Artillery, panzers, infantry created a terrible racket on both sides. For us it's just like watching it at the cinema. 'Alarm!' After an hour it's called off. Our fighters shot down a Russian bomber. It made a dreadful noise as it fell, its engines still at maximum revs.

2 September 1942

Worn out with lack of sleep we greet the new morn. People sit writing home: 'An accursed useless feeling to lie here inactive before the Russian guns awaiting the order – "Make ready! We're attacking!" – the order that never comes.' We heard that the total number of enemy tanks destroyed here has risen to 1,580! Today we did some road building and other work.

3 September 1942

The Russians began a heavy artillery bombardment with Stalin organs from 0400hrs. Our Nebelwerfers replied, our artillery laid a defensive barrage; involved on the ground were our panzers, their tanks and both sides' anti-tank guns and MGs, many aircraft milling around in the sky. Their offensive lasted until 0700hrs when it began to peter out: our Front held. We all sat or stood in our foxholes ready to fight, smoking one cigarette after another. Later we heard that this battle had cost the Russians another 108 tanks. We have to admire the soldiers in their bombed and shelled positions in the forward lines. When our turn comes to reply, we shall force Ivan back to the Volga! We have the self-confidence! Throughout the day heavy bombing by both sides, Ivan was well represented. If he knows where we are and bombs the bushes and undergrowth he will be bound to hit somebody, we are so thick on the ground here. We had weapons practice, i.e. dismantling and assembling mortars, moving from position to position, etc.

4–5 September 1942

One notices Ivan's determination to break through here. It is also an attack to tie us down because our troops have advanced into the Caucasus. An order has been circulated that we must not mention the name of our division. Ivan must know nothing of *Grossdeutschland*. We are now *Walküre* – 'Valkyrie'.

6 September 1942

'Wash underwear!' A rest day for us but for the first time Ivan's tanks are aiming at us!

7–8 September 1942

Today a tree-felling party worked from 0500hrs to 0700hrs. Trees are required to make a log road. We are in woods where heavy fighting took place in the winter of 1941. We found old bunkers, skeletons, weapons and equipment and much ammunition, all Ivan's.

9 September 1942

Heavy defensive fighting in the form of an attack to the south and on the outskirts of Rzhev attached to XXVII Armee Korps. We are lying here with other divisions and regiments as the Army Reserve of Army High Command 9. This morning the enemy artillery fire became persistent. Panzer Grenadier Division *Grossdeutschland* lay in the woods and bushy undergrowth south of Rzhev at maximum alarm readiness, 6 to 8km behind the front line and within range of the Russian guns. Tents were taken down, our vehicles stood ready, on our belts hung everything necessary for action this day: haversack with hand grenades, entrenching tool, ammunition pouches, bayonet and sidearm; the mortar and its ammunition lay to hand and the groundsheet was rolled up. We sat on our benches in the lorries smoking 'cigarettes to soothe the nerves'. When the platoon and group leaders returned from the commander's conference their faces looked grim. Feldwebel Hinz had been drafted to Cottbus: Unteroffizier Stedtler as the new leader of the mortar platoon now addressed us briefly on the situation:

> The Russians, who have a bridgehead here at Rzhev on this side of the Volga, have made a renewed heavy attack with tanks and artillery support. Our front-line troops, who have been fighting here since the winter of 1941 and weakened by the slow retreat begun at Kalinin in December 1941, have held the Front only with difficulty and by the heroic dedication of each individual soldier. It is our task to repulse the enemy back over the Volga by means of a powerful counter-attack and so shorten the line, and there we will build our positions for the coming winter.

Our destination was the Front a little south-east of the town of Rzhev. Rations were issued in the evening and at nightfall our column set off under a bright moon cautiously and with headlights dowsed, ourselves silent in the lorries, wrapped in blankets. Above us, as every night, the Russian bombers dropped bombs and parachute flares. Ghostly in the light of the latter the columns of vehicles headed towards the action at the Front, company after company, the entire II Battalion and the two regiments. At 0300hrs we halted. 'Dismount with equipment!' With a few moves of the hand each man scooped up his things, shouldered the barrel of the mortar or buckled the baseplate or bipod of the mortar over his back, bound two ammunition cases together and fitted them with a leather strap over his free shoulder. The lorry drivers called out, 'Come back safe, boys! Good luck and success!' We trudged towards the Front over poor tracks and log roads laid by the pioneers, passed through villages battered by artillery where our troops from other units, lying in bunkers and other shelter between the ruins, recognized us by the black-silver cuff title. *Grossdeutschland* is attacking! We gave them a wave of encouragement as we kept going. Entrenching tool, equipment and mess tin clattering: this was the familiar sound of marching infantry as we had often heard it in this war. At first light we occupied the old positions and held ourselves ready for the order to advance. We had time to smoke one cigarette and then the order came: 'Advance! Ten paces distance between each man, no racing! Hand weapons ready to fire. Go!' Ahead lay a flat plain, 500m beyond which began a rocky terrain with bushes. The Russians occupied it. Our artillery barrage pinned them down, we ran forward, the grenadier company ahead of us infiltrated the Russian trenches with a great Hurrah!, we followed. We had broken through. On account of the noise made by our own artillery we heard little Russian defensive fire.

10 September 1942

Now and again the odd rifle round would whistle by. Ivan was on the run, and we were just congratulating ourselves on our success when suddenly the Russian artillery responded with shells of all calibres. Luckily the entire bombardment fell too short. Some of it must have fallen amongst their own people. We had sought and discovered the abandoned Russian positions and trenches in the scrub, and took cover. Then came a second surprise, fifteen to twenty Martin bombers flying right to left in a strict formation. Our Flak and MGs opened fire at once, the rounds exploding beneath the bombers, the heavier calibre shells above, then six Me 109s appeared through cloud. At that moment they were immediately overhead. Kneeling in a foxhole I watched one bomber after another release its load while its cannon fired furiously. The flames from the muzzle made it seem as though the aircraft was on fire. I waited for the impact of the bombs, which seemed to have been aimed directly at us, curled up as small as possible in my foxhole, cowering against the cold, wet soil of the wall and saw for the first time that the floor consisted of a layer of mud 15cm thick. The bombs exploded. The noise was tremendous, the earth trembled and shook me, I had the feeling of being lifted up bodily. Sods of earth flew about me, I seemed to go partially deaf. I saw that I was in the company of a frog with large eyes. A second bomb exploded: I clutched at the mud, hearing the Flak putting up a curtain of fire as the bombers flew on, still in strict formation. This suited our fighters, sitting on their tails and waiting for the right moment to shoot. I heard the rattle of an aircraft cannon. 'One's on fire! Now he's crashing!' The machine lost altitude trailing a long, dark banner of smoke and crashed into a depression hidden behind bushes. A mushroom-shaped dark cloud of smoke rose up and then came the explosions. He had crashed with his bombs aboard. Everywhere our men surfaced from cover to continue the advance into the artillery barrage. This was reluctantly done so as not to be called a coward. Shells exploded very close, splinters whirred past, making us duck instinctively. Everything went well until we reached a shallow gully. We thought we were protected against direct fire, then shells began falling on the opposite slope and exploding in the undergrowth. I found a ditch and laid out flat in it. The enemy fire increased, most of it falling on our side. 'Quick! To the other side!' With mortar component and ammunition each man sprinted across the gully. My mortar team was running in a line and close together. I was just about to shout, 'Split up!' when something flashed with a bestial din 5m ahead of me on my right-hand side, the air pressure seized me and swirled me around my own axis. Splinters whizzing past, I collapsed and fell. Acrid powder-smoke burned my eyes and lungs. I had felt a sudden blow to my upper arm, and my right knee had a burning sensation. There was a hole in my field blouse and trouser leg at the knee. The shell had exploded in our midst! My comrades all lay on the ground, either under cover or wounded. The mortar No. 1, a Berliner, shouted: 'I am wounded, cannot walk, get me out of here!' The mortar captain was shouting out and the youngest ammunition runner, a robust Viennese, lay with wounds to his back and face. I heard him say, 'All four cheeks injured!' That is what I call humour. We were a team of six: three lay on the ground wounded; though injured I could walk and helped the other two drag the wounded into nearby slit trenches or shell craters. When I opened the uniform trousers of Fritze Barth I saw that he had a splinter wound to his thigh. He seemed to be in a lot of pain. Two grenadiers about to return for ammunition took him with them. A brief handshake: 'Good luck, be glad you're leaving this shit – and don't forget to write from hospital!' Then they carried him away. The other two wounded went back as well. I was seated in a shell crater and could not kneel because of the great pain. My upper arm hurt too and there was blood on my uniform jacket but 'Thank God, it's only a scratch.' We were now under such heavy fire that our NCO decided to move us into the scrub ahead. A Russian assault gun on the edge of the scrub turned towards us and opened fire. Some of the men began to shovel out a spit of earth to protect their heads. Rounds fell all around but we escaped harm, although the noise almost deafened me and I breathed in a lot of dust. Some 7.5cm light infantry guns had moved into the gully, taken up firing positions and opened rapid fire. Ivan replied in like manner. It was clearly his intention to knock these guns out but his shooting was atrocious, and all of it came down on our heads. 'We should have stayed back there where we were!' Clods of earth and splinters whirled above me. Nose to the ground and lie as flat as possible. Now and again I shouted forward, 'Akteris! Fritsch! Everything OK?' 'Yes, but very shitty here!' After a while when Ivan had a rest Akteris stood up and ran to the rear, one hand wrapped in a bloody bandage. 'I am wounded. Where is a *Sanitäter*?[1] A splinter had cut his hand to ribbons. The firing started again – tanks or anti-tank. This was not all like the summer offensive. Then we often had crazy assignments, the outcome balanced on a knife-edge, but we had always come through and without serious losses. 'Mortar! Get moving there! We're going forward!' We went forward under cover of the bushes. Grenadier Gerdes was missing. Two men went back and found him sitting in a foxhole, head resting on his knees, dead. A splinter had killed him. For a moment we stood dumb. One direct hit had left four of us relatively severely injured, I was walking wounded but could not bend one knee and we had one man dead at the beginning of the attack. We had imagined it otherwise. '*Los!* Mortar follow us!' We came under tank fire: the impact preceded the report of the gun firing. Often these shells would sweep through the scrub, rebound somewhere and eventually come harmlessly to rest. We came to swampy terrain. I was wearing my summer laced shoes which filled up immediately. There was no advantage in wearing jackboots, for the water got in through the top. We came under fire from artillery of all calibres. In the morass one could not lie down for cover. 'Mortars dig in!' Here in the morass? Before I began digging I looked around for ready-made holes. I was lucky and found a fairly deep and dry infantry trench on ground with much grass laid around it. I got in and fell asleep. For how long I have no idea. I simply 'switched off' somehow. When I awoke the sun stood fairly low near the horizon! One may not think it possible but it is true. We had not been able to sleep properly in recent days. It was growing dark and cooler. First of all I had to orientate myself: MG tracer flitted to over there, Ivan's Maxim MG 'blabbered'. I heard artillery fire which grew less as the evening wore on. We were all fairly exhausted. The Russians must have a huge quantity of artillery here, I thought, only very rarely had I experienced so much. The whole Front gradually fell silent and we began to recover our normal hearing. I lit up a first cigarette. The first flares rose, from the Russian side also. With the onset of darkness the artillery fire died down, just a few desultory rounds, even the infantry fire grew less. We dared to stand up, walk about freely, socialize, remembering the events of the day and fallen comrades-in-arms. The company gathered after having become widely dispersed during the course of the day. In the endless running here and there we had never once fired our mortars. Here we were allotted firing positions and dug the pits. Deeper than before. Water entered and we had to build an earthwall around the mortars. Our slit trenches were dug deeper too. The rations carriers came back from the field kitchen at the battalion command post so far distant that the food had grown cold on the way though even cold noodles and goulash tasted good. While still eating: 'II Battalion make ready to change position!' We had dug the mortar positions, our foxholes were ready, we were looking forward to sleep. With a silent curse we took up our belongings, careful not to leave anything hanging, lying or standing. Our new position was 3km away. We walked there in silence, the only noise the clatter of a mess tin or entrenching tool. The mortar carriers arrived there gasping for breath as did we ammunition runners carrying two cases with three mortar bombs each, hanging by a leather strap from the shoulder. The baseplate weighed 18.3kg, the bipod 23kg. The barrel was 113.4cm long and weighed 22kg. An ammunition runner carried two cases each with three mortar bombs each weighing 3.5kg, total 21kg. An infantryman had only his rifle to carry. All movement ceases when flares go up. In the whitish glare any movement can betray you. Finally we arrived. Our new position was pointed out to us and we dug another mortar pit. This may be difficult depending on the ground conditions. The depth was to be 2m and the radius 1m. The munitions were stored in two nooks, our foxholes logically close to the firing position. There would be a telephone line to the spotter's post, less often radio contact and often only a human chain in emergencies. We always had to listen out for 'sewing machines' overhead, even conceal the glow from our cigarettes. It was always a weird feeling when the crate, never very high up, was almost overhead. They flew very slowly. Today they left us in peace and dropped their bombs well to the rear. After establishing the roster for sentry duty we fell asleep dead tired.

11 September 1942

'Rehfeldt! Get up! Sentry duty!' I hung my carbine from my shoulder, took possession of the field glasses, put two hand grenades behind my belt strap and joined my No. 2 at the position. We never talked much so as to stay focused. It was a clear night of half-moon and cold. The infantry and observation post was at most 100m ahead. Usually the latter would ring up to confirm that the line was operational and the mortar ready to fire immediately. Now and again both sides fired up flares and an MG would rattle. If both sides sent out scouting parties into No Man's Land it could often get 'lively'. At night, artillery only fired in the event of a known danger.

'Hallo. Where is the 9 Company command post?'

'Here!' we replied and then two men appeared bringing in a wounded soldier from 4 Company. I showed them the way to the *Sanitäter* and then recognized the casualty was Hein. He had a through-and-through wound in the thigh. In response to my question he told me:

I was taking wounded men to the main dressing station and coming back in the dark but didn't know the location of 9 Company. I met up with a messenger from 14 Company who was going to the battalion command post. We strayed into No Man's Land and ran into a Russian scouting party. We thought there were only a couple of them and said they were our prisoners. At that they opened fire, killed the messenger and I got shot in the thigh. The Russians then ran off. I lay in the cold almost five hours, I couldn't walk. At first I didn't dare shout out but finally did so.

Hein told me his story with pauses, it was probably too much for him and he passed out. 'We heard the groaning and cries for help, the two of us crawled out, found him, and then the messenger, who was dead,' the 14 Company men said before taking their leave and disappearing into the darkness. Hein was shipped out on an artillery limber which had brought up ammunition. In our position were stored cases of rifle ammunition, hand grenades, balled charges, belts of MG ammunition and mortar bombs, Pak and Flak ammunition was kept in the ground hidden from view. After my two hours on watch I slept until 0900hrs when woken by the sun. '*Fertig machen!*' A new attack was in the offing. With dismantled mortars and ammunition we joined the MG crews at the departure line. Our artillery had shifted positions during the night. The Russians had not detected the new venue and so they fired random rounds across the terrain. We were 'only' 800m from their trenches. Our artillery, which included massive 21cm howitzers, destroyed the Russian infantry lines and defensive positions, enabling our grenadiers to reach an elevation receiving only isolated infantry fire. Just as we thought it was all over, the Russian artillery replied, round after round in quick succession exploding 60m ahead into our infantry. In a few minutes it became a 'black wall' – a wall of exploding shells of all calibres, a barrage such as we had never seen before. The ground trembled and shook, splinters and fragments of shell whizzed. It was impossible to go through it and emerge unscathed, but a few brave souls tried, and paid with their lives or finished up wounded and immobile. We mortar crews lay ourselves flat where we were and, having no cover, as flat as it is possible to lie under such a bombardment. Close by me lay my 21-year-old group leader, an Unteroffizier with whom I had served the same mortar at Tula in the 1941 winter when he was still a Gefreiter. Suddenly, lying amidst flying clods of earth and shell splinters, I felt a sharp pain in the calf. There was no rip in my trousers or blood (but in the evening I found the haematoma). The curtain of fire advanced towards us with a bestial howl. 'We can't stay here,' the Unteroffizier said, 'if we can, best return to our foxholes and wait for the counter-attack.' A warning came that the Russians were about to fire Stalin organs. I looked up, saw the rockets falling in their flight, apparently straight for me, but they missed narrowly, throwing up a cascade of earth and whirring splinters. The barrage was creeping ever nearer and then abated. I raised my head and heard it resume. New gun batteries? How many could they have brought up? Ivan had increased the range, the black wall now falling on our departure point. Wordlessly we watched the hurricane of fire. The wind drifted the smoke towards us, stinging our eyes, scratching the throat, sticking to the lungs. Our own artillery had not remained silent, we had not heard them firing, being almost deafened. The Russians maintained their fire: batteries shooting salvoes without end, on the receiving end an uninterrupted howling, screaming, crashing and bursting, whistling and whirring, an intolerable noise. Finally the wall of explosions had advanced far enough behind us to risk the run back. Men were being carried away from the worst of it. We retreated down the slope pursued by sporadic shellfire. Once back in my foxhole I felt safe. The bombardment had wandered to the left. I took a swig from my field flask and then prepared to defend. But the Russians didn't come.

12 September 1942

Our instructions to fire came by telephone, in the firing position it was almost impossible to hear shouted commands. My hole in the ground was 2.5m deep and as a step to get out I had a 1.5m-long panzer shell casing which also served as a pisspot, and a wooden artillery basket. When it rained I pulled my groundsheet over the hole. The artillery fire had slackened somewhat, the Russian infantry had retired from their forward trenches. They would not have been strong enough to repel our attack had it not been for their artillery. At dusk we advanced quietly and without a fight occupied the elevation we had not been able to take during the day. It was only a few hundred metres ahead. We dug in deep at once. It had been a hot day and despite the enormous artillery barrage the mortar team had suffered no losses. 'Hallo, 9 Company. Fetch cooked food and provisions!' This required two men from each group, one would have all twelve mess tins in both hands, half the tins per hand, the handles practically fitting neatly together, the other carried the groundsheet for carrying all the bread, sausage, cheese, butter and the so-called 'cold fare'. I took up my groundsheet and we set off. We needed only to follow along the deep track impressions of our panzers to pass through the depression where yesterday's attack had come to grief. The 'way' to the battalion command post was very rutted and littered with empty ammunition cases, equipment, artillery shell baskets and some wrecked vehicles. Flares were being fired continually and in the distance one could hear the shooting of both sides' long-range batteries, the shells of which roared through the night and fell far in the rear. When darkness fell over the battlefield the 'sewing machine' came into its own, dropping parachute flares to better see its targets. Our company's rations wagon lay in a small depression behind the battalion command post. The hot soup was poured from canisters into the mess tins, the quartermaster issued the cold fare after first having checked how many men were to be fed with it. When the 'sewing machine' released a parachute flare, we could use its light to fill the field flasks with coffee. The mess tin carrier has these on a strap around his neck. My companion, holding twelve full mess tins, said, 'All we need now is another artillery barrage', and just as I slung the full groundsheet over my shoulder like a sack an anti-tank or tank round exploded nearby. I ducked, but we were protected by being in the depression. We got back safely, shared out the rations, smoked the obligatory cigarette, the men wrote letters and then we went to our foxholes to sleep. At 0315hrs against a grey sky Ivan's infantry attacked with sub-machine guns without artillery support. I was alongside a 6 Company MG gunner who opened fire at a range of 100m, spewing death and injury into the ranks of the attackers. I had my carbine to my cheek when I heard my mortar being fired. I ran to the pit, primed the bombs and fed them into the barrel. 'Good! Good!' our Unteroffizier shouted. 'The fire is on target. Now break off. Range 50m, fire at will!' The Russians had come up fairly close, but in collaboration with all infantry weapons the attack was beaten off. The excitement died down and now more ammunition had to be fetched. I prepared for this and joined Gottfried Fritsch by a large bomb crater. It was good to be able to stand in the fresh air and exchange a few words. Suddenly a violent explosion rent the silence – a tank or anti-tank shell. Fritsch and I fell to the ground – I was uninjured but I heard Gottfried cry out, a terrible cry. I looked and saw that his whole leg was almost severed at the thigh. My hands were covered in blood, I opened a dressing pack and tried to stem the blood. It was not yet light enough to see what I was doing. Gottfried was groaning, 'Shoot me dead!' He must have been in dreadful agony. I cried out for our *Sanitäter*, who came at once: I was holding the dressing with both hands against the wound. As we both set to binding it, he died. During the day we carried him back to the company command post and wrapped his body in a groundsheet with those of the fallen of other companies. I remembered the traditional Dead Soldier's Song:

> *Ich hatt' einen Kameraden, einen bessren findst Du nicht,*
> *Er ging an meiner Seite in gleichen Schritt und Tritt.*
> *Eine Kugel kam geflogen, gilt sie mir oder gilt sie Dir?*
> *Sie hat ihn weggerissen, er liegt zu meinen Füssen*
> *Als wär's ein Stück von mir.*

> Translation: 'I had a comrade, a better you'd never find;
> He was at my side constantly.
> A bullet came flying, was it meant for me or you?
> It tore him away, he lies at my feet
> As though he were a part of me.'

then under Russian fire continued to the battalion command post for ammunition and hand grenades. More than once I had to throw myself flat when shells exploded very close. Then I would jump up and run for our foxhole. From there we saw two soldiers returning from ahead carrying a wounded man. We watched their progress on tenterhooks. The enemy shelling was falling very close. Suddenly clods of earth and smoke rose up, the two carriers threw themselves to the ground to seek cover: when they stood up again, one held his arm, the other was limping. *Sanitäter*! And the original wounded man? Two men jumped up from my mortar, two more of us followed, and despite the fierce enemy fire we carried him back cross-country to the depression. Whenever we had to dive for cover, or one of us tripped and fell, the poor fellow hit the ground hard. There was nothing for it, we had to drag him. Finally we came to a spot under enemy surveillance from about 500m. We put the casualty on the groundsheet, made the corners as upright as possible for a good hold and then we ran with it. We had not got far before the first shells exploded 20m to our rear and short. 'Keep going!' Now the shells were exploding ahead of us! Shit!!! Halfway to the other side we got to a deep rut made by a panzer track and collapsed face down into it, clods of earth and splinters whizzing above us. A sudden concentration of artillery fire! 'Don't leave me here, stay with me,' the helpless casualty begged us. He needn't have worried, we didn't dare stand up. After a rest finally we took a chance over the last 100m to the main dressing station. We couldn't find it but after much shouting we found the earth bunker. Many wounded inside it. A *Sanitäter* accepted the casualty and I took the opportunity to collect some ammunition. We walked back stiffly upright, unable to run. Ivan was shooting well to our rear but improving, and we got a move on back to our mortar pit. Now I had begun to notice that whenever I ran a bit or had to kneel a lot, my right knee gave me hell. The bandage was pressing on the wound which was now swollen.

Ivan's mortar bombs are of heavier calibre than ours (his 12cm, ours 8.4cm): we fire from cover into cover, our bombs falling almost vertically. Ivan hammered away all day with every calibre, for some reason raining Stalin-organ rockets on an elevation not occupied by ourselves. Six assault guns arrived between the battalion command post and our company sector as reinforcements and protection for us. Happy to see them on the one hand, we were worried that they might draw down Russian artillery fire on themselves and us. One of them drove up with a great roar directly in front of my foxhole. I could no longer see forward and feared that while manoeuvring it might accidentally run over me. I shouted a warning to the panzer's commander, a Hauptmann, and he called back I should look out, he was going to park overhead. Now I worried that the weight of the panzer might collapse my hole. The motor started up and the heavy steel box rolled into position above me. I supposed that it was an advantage to have this panzer as a roof, but I just hoped that the commander did not forget that he had a neighbour beneath him! And not turn either. The hours passed and Ivan seemed reluctant to attack. It was not boring, because the assault gun commander advised our MG people of rewarding targets which he could see from his high perch with his panoramic telescope. I could hear his radio conversations with other panzer commanders. Suddenly there was a violent boom above me, the ground trembled, the panzer recoiled a little, powder smoke infiltrated my foxhole. 'Hurrah! He's on fire!' I felt a bit uneasy but the assault gun moved forward slowly and fired a couple more times. Now a tank duel began. I curled up small in my foxhole, for Ivan was firing at 'my' assault gun. The others on the main battle line also fired. The final score was six of theirs destroyed without loss to ourselves. There was some damage to the wall of my foxhole but this was quickly shovelled out. The battle went on all day and sounded worse than it was. Now and again I looked out 'to assess the situation'. I could hear shells impacting as though only a few metres away when they actually exploded 100m away. The Stalin organ bombarded the unoccupied elevation all day and gave us a good laugh. In the evening we ran around to loosen up, conversed and looked at the newest shell craters. 'Man, you were lucky there. One metre more and . . .' After hot soup and cold fare by the pale light of a Hindenburg lamp (a cardboard box with stearin candle) we read the letters received from home. The British and Americans are bombing our cities. Not only military targets like bridges, stations or factories but the residential districts too by 'carpet bombing'.

I had just stood my two hours' sentry duty when I was awoken by a crazy tumult. MG sentry: 'Ivan, weapon down, hands up!' Another sentry: 'There they go, there they go!' Rifle shots rang out, flares soared up. I looked across the foreground then saw a figure near me, behind our positions, an indecisive Russian. I pointed my carbine at him and shouted in Russian, 'Halt! Rifle down, lie on the ground!' He threw his weapon aside, knelt and said something which I couldn't understand followed by '*Spassibo, pan, spassibo.*' (Thank you, sir, thank you.) I threw his rifle into my foxhole and searched him, then we both ran to the company command post where an interpreter interrogated him. He said something like: 'We were a scouting party with orders to blow up any bunkers we found. The sentry spotted us, the others ran away and I was left alone between the German positions. I thought about running away but found myself looking into the muzzle of a rifle and gave up.'

13 September 1942

Ivan seemed unaware it is Sunday and kept firing all day. Slowly it grinds you down. In order to take my mind off it I decided to make my foxhole safer. My knee wound interfered with the work. First I increased the depth to 2.7m. The bottom is about 30cm deeper than the 1.8m-long gallery for my legs. Now I have a covered 'bunker'. A roof of earth 1.5m thick protects me against light shellfire and mortars – so I believe and hope! I feel safer now. Occasionally I stopped digging and had a look outside. Whilst most of my colleagues are freezing in their holes I have already begun to sweat. Towards midday the Russian artillery fire was stepped up. I curled up deep in my 'bunker'. Often the shells landed nearby and I received a shower of earth, dirt and grass lumps; splinters went into the earth roof. Maximum alarm preparedness was ordered: once the artillery fire died down, or the range was lengthened, it could mean a Russian attack. I listened out hopefully for our Stukas, but instead Russian bombers came and dropped their loads on our rearward positions. Two other machines droned above our main front line drizzling a greyish-green liquid. Gas? Too bad for us if it was, our gas masks were in our lorries. It turned out to be a wall of smoke, not gas. Suddenly our own artillery opened fire, many batteries of all calibres, most of it falling directly ahead of our lines. The smoke from the explosions mixed with Ivan's artificial fog to form a pea-souper through which nothing could be seen. This was *our* barrage, and the splinters came *our* way! Then the wind changed and drifted it all towards Ivan's lines, and the range of our artillery lengthened to pound the Russian positions. There was no sign of Ivan's infantry, no attack intended. The day came to an end with mutual artillery fire.

'Four volunteers to the platoon leader!' It was always the same four 'volunteers' if you could call us that. He led us forward and pointed to two dead comrades of our company about 30m ahead of our lines. We went out and laid the first in a groundsheet. His hands still clutched his carbine and we carried him like that, first to a bunker to catch our breath and then to the battalion command post where we usually saw six and more dead laid out when we went to fetch ammunition. We looked at the faces and recognized good comrades, mostly grenadiers but some from the other mortars. Yesterday we had had a laugh with them: today they lay here in their bloodied uniforms shredded by splinters. Men of 18 to 20 years who had had no time to live their lives. We brought back the other corpse under MG fire, the foreground lit in the bright light of Russian flares. Every night we had to do this, the company's gravediggers. But this was war, murder which must be lived and experienced in order to understand what it means to be an infantryman in the front line under heavy fire for days on end, daily seeing friends die.

14 September 1942

The night passed relatively quietly but dawn came with dark, low-hanging rain clouds. I dug a ditch with drainage channel and stretched a groundsheet over the entrance to my foxhole. Torrential rain fell and defeated all my efforts. I tried to bail out the water with my mess tin and a can but ended up soaked through and shivering. Only my raised 'leg gallery' remained dry. Today post had arrived. If only the people at home knew what it was like. Despite the weather, the artillery, rocket launchers and Stalin organs kept it up all day: high above us aircraft, near us our panzers and assault guns. Panzers and Pak make an extremely loud and harsh report when fired. The worst is when one of our own panzers or assault guns fires from close behind us. The noise is deafening. Though we are glad to have our panzers near us, they do attract enemy artillery, anti-tank and tank fire. Our provisions official Lüdecke had the job of dividing up our food and rations. He would call each man by name, and then we would scamper over to him. Today the first man had gone and came under mortar fire on the way back. Both he and Lüdecke were wounded by splinters to the face, arm and hands. Now we were two men short. Cursing their bad luck, they ran back to the main dressing station with long strides. I had intended to report sick there myself tonight because my knee is very swollen and throbbing but decided to postpone it for one more day. Our group now has only seven men fit for duty, the remnants of sixteen! In the evening I went to fetch the rations. The wagon failed to arrive. Finally I joined a group of radiomen in a bunker on the slope of the depression and soon fell asleep shivering.

15 September 1942

I awoke at 0300hrs. The morning was relatively bright which meant I would have difficulty in getting back to my firing position unseen. Just then a motor car drove up with yesterday's rations. We had time only to fill the mess tins, flasks and groundsheet and then go hell for leather back to the firing position before Ivan's artillery began its morning greetings. This eternal artillery fire wears one down. Knowing the toll of our many dead and wounded we can more or less see that statistically our number will be up soon. We have the feeling that our artillery is the equal of the Russians. Then another of our batteries fired – a different sound. These salvoes fall well to our rear. They were firing too short! 'Shit!' Flares were sent up. 'Increase range!' Black columns of smoke arose 200m behind us. The battery fired again. Still too short!

Messengers ran to the battalion command post. Our messenger returned with the sad news that our platoon leader, Unteroffizier Stedtler, had fallen. He had been in our battalion command post when it received a direct hit from our own artillery battery. Besides Stedtler, Hauptmann Hönes (battalion leader), Leutnant von Mitzlaff and Leutnant Schlenga died in the same incident, Gefreiter Lüdecke was wounded. Unteroffizier Martin Scharfenberg is now mortar platoon leader.

A flight of Stukas arrived directly overhead and began to circle. From our earlier experience in the south this did not look good! Often the respective front lines were impossible to distinguish. Flares went up, orange-red smoke drifted out from various positions. Now the Stukas knew the German positions. The first machine tipped over into a steep dive, the second following. The other aircraft followed them down, 'Jericho sirens' howling. The Russian light and heavy anti-aircraft guns unleashed a furious response! We saw quite clearly the release from each Stuka of three bombs, felt the ground tremble with the explosions, saw the first machines pull out and climb. Clouds of black smoke hung over the Russian positions. Once all Stukas had re-formed they began the strafing run.

About 200m ahead of our line some snipers were nesting in the burned-out wreck of a T-34. One of the Stukas decided to attack the wreck at the same time as one of our assault guns was approaching it. Three large bombs detonated very close to the two vehicles. My groundsheet was torn by a splinter from Ivan's anti-aircraft fire, and when I went up to inspect it I saw the commander of the assault gun running back towards us. One of the Stuka bombs had exploded 10m from his panzer. Had he been misidentified as enemy? With smoke and fumes reducing visibility it was very possible. His assault gun had reversed but needed to be towed out. After a while another assault gun arrived, chains and steel hawsers were attached and the job done. After the Stuka attack the Russian artillery had fallen quiet and only his mortars were firing. We could hear the report of each at discharge! Now we also saw our He 111 and Ju 88 bombers returning from the Russian rear. They had attacked the artillery emplacements but the noise here had been so deafening that we had not heard the bombing. Once they had gone, however, the Russian artillery started up again. One of our MG42s rattled. Theoretically they could fire 1,500 rounds per minute, but mostly only a 'burst': a tug at the trigger fired fifty rounds in two seconds.

16 September 1942

At 0400hrs the maximum possible alert preparedness was advised. Everybody stood at his post. We shivered with cold and excitement. Defectors had said that the Russians were going to make another attack against us here and it was going to be the last. Well, let them come. During the night we brought up ammunition, prepared hand grenades, our assault guns waited in ambush in the depression. The Luftwaffe had been notified. In the evening our artillery zeroed-in: for some time we have had three concentration points at 600m, 300m and 50m. Now at 0355hrs we waited feverishly in our foxholes or huddled close together in the firing position. The mortar bombs had been given additional propellant charges and were covered over with a groundsheet to avoid contamination with dirt. The Russians began their softening-up process with five rounds from their long-range guns. We never heard them being fired and then it fell quiet. Finally with 'Urrah! Urrah!' their infantry attacked with bayonets fixed. Without artillery preparation or tanks! We let them approach unmolested to 100m and then opened fire with heavy and light MGs, carbines and naturally our mortars. The attackers threw themselves to the ground and fired a few rifle rounds. Suddenly we were shocked by a great thunderclap to our rear and only 50m from our No. 2 mortar. A great cloud of flying earth and smoke rose up. Up until then the heaviest-calibre artillery they had used was 15.2cm, but this was something new. Without further artillery support Ivan's infantry had stopped short of our lines and when we fired had turned and run. Two or three of them were shot down from behind. It was mere target practice. It seemed that the lives of their own men were of little consequence to the Russian commanders. On the way back the *soldatski* entered our 300m barrage zone. Our job was done: the artillery and Luftwaffe did the rest. From our No. 2 mortar came the report that our Karl Viole had fallen victim to the Russian super-heavy artillery. His foxhole had suffered a direct hit and was now a gaping crater several metres wide and deep. My mortar teams had lost five dead and eight wounded in six days, I was lightly wounded but had not reported it yet, thirteen casualties from a total of forty, a third of our platoon.

Here are the casualties from our mortars:

Wounded: Adelpoller, Barth, Hein, Rehfeldt (I hung on until 17th), Lüdecke, Spiegel.
Fallen: Gerdes, Fritsch, Unteroffizier Stedtler, Viole.

We lay what remained of Karl Viole – strips of bloodied uniform, some body parts, a foot wearing a laced-up shoe – in a groundsheet and carried them back. We were unable to find any papers or Soldbuch, not even his ID tags. Gefreiter Konrad was buried under earth and rubble and dug out dead. The Russians had shown us their determination to succeed no matter what the cost in their own lives, and we had to stop them with all we had. All we know is that this accursed war must go on until Bolshevism is wiped out. Not the Russian people! They deserve better.

17 September 1942

The night remained quiet. I sat on an empty ammunition case in my foxhole. My thickly swollen, inflamed knee caused me terrible pain. At 0800hrs we awaited the customary artillery greeting but to our great surprise it never came. The Stalin organs were silent too. Now the loud noise of engines and shouting from their side last evening made sense. They had taken their artillery elsewhere. Defectors told us that their troops over there found it very gruelling and were only kept at it by the Commissars and officers. Many more would cross over to us but they were fearful of the new German MG. I could see their point (unfortunately the ammunition consumption is very high).

18–20 September 1942

During the day some of our fighters flew over and dropped leaflets. As a result fifteen Ivans defected to us in our sector waving these leaflets which are also 'surrender passes'. I was with the *Sanitäter* when these Russians were being interrogated. My through-and-through splinter wound was very inflamed, the knee very painful and swollen and in the evening I went back and forth with the rations wagon. After the distribution we drove through conditions of thick mud, rain and cold and reached the closer rearward *Tross* at 2300hrs, 20km from the front line. At the *Tross* I had to fill MG belts and help bury the dead. I stayed three days before seeing the surgeon. He wrote me a wounded label: 'Urgent! Shell-splinter infection, through-and-through. Field hospital Artinov.' I was awarded the Wound Badge in Black (first wound).

21–24 September 1942

Today, the 21st, I arrived at Artinov in a field ambulance. The label read: 'Infantry shell-splinter in front of right kneecap. Urgent! Tetanus injection. Send sitting to . . .' I had to *walk* 8km to the field hospital where my right leg was put in a splint. The pain was still awful. After treatment we were housed in Russian cottages but with real field beds. We were still in range of the Russian artillery. We were well fed and a chaplain who visited brought a choice of cigarettes or chocolate for everyone. He told us about 'the hell of Rzhev'.

25 September 1942

Today they changed my dressing. 'You were damned lucky with this kneecap,' the surgeon said. We had bean coffee and cakes, white bread and chocolate. Outside a storm raged.

29 September–5 October 1942

The sun shone. On the 30th Russian aircraft bombed the hospital and we also came under artillery fire. It was a very uncomfortable feeling to lie in bed with no protection. The surgeon removed my splint.

6 –14 October 1942

Because of the large numbers of wounded arriving from the Front, some of us were moved back 5km to the village of Leonov, classified as a 'convalescent home'. No field post was delivered here, only ever more wounded. We could hear the fighting at the Front. Space was at a premium and we were always being moved to annexes farther back. My knee was still swollen and very painful.

15 October 1942

Some names were read out, including mine! We were conveyed by lorry to Sytchevka and from there by train to the wounded collection point at Vyasma.

16–17 October 1942

Things were looking up. The surgeon wrote me a label 'l.R' (lying in bed. Reich). After a night's stay a chaplain held a short service and at 1400hrs an ambulance train took us to Smolensk where we spent the night.

18–19 October 1942

The train passed through Orsha–Minsk heading westwards. We felt like holidaymakers!

20–21 October 1942

The stations at Baranowitshi and Byalistok lay behind us. We had escaped from the war! On the second day we reached Warsaw. The train stopped a long way outside the station. One could see much residential destruction. Poles carried us piggyback down the railway embankment to a waiting tram. Scarcely were we inside it than they wanted to trade – many zlotys for a woollen blanket!

22 October 1942

We were taken to Reserve Military Hospital VIII in the Ulica Pasteur. In the cellar were many bathtubs – and so into the glorious warm water! It felt like Christmas!

23–24 October 1942

We newcomers were admitted, registered and given a checkup. The building was a former chemicals concern. We lay in a large hall in the care of Red Cross nurses who gave us a dose of castor oil and the explanation, 'We must get all the filth of Russia out of you first.' This kept us occupied for several hours and blocked the toilets. Later we had tea and biscuits and in the evening a proper meal. In the afternoon we were visited by the local NSV (National Socialist Welfare) and everybody got 'a full plate'. My wounds were responding to treatment, soon I could even stand and I got 'town leave'. I saw two films in the Warsaw Soldiers' Cinema. In Marschall Strasse one could buy anything but only for a lot of money.

25–26 October 1942

The surgeon gave me a damp Rivanol dressing. Warsaw is deceptively 'calm' but one can sense the unrest. Hand grenades go off in cafés and trams. On 27 and 28 October partisans fired on Polish auxiliary police.

29 October 1942

Bad atmosphere here! The NSV women visited us again bringing reading matter and food. Great joy – we got our first post since 17 September at Rzhev. We saw a film in the hospital.

1–5 November 1942

Touring the city we saw a poster on the advertising boards: 'Attack with Hydrochloric Acid!' The city of Warsaw had to pay a fine of one million zlotys. Fifty names were listed of persons taken hostage. 'An eye for an eye, a tooth for a tooth.' *C'est la guerre.* Over the next few days I saw a film at the Warsaw Theatre and the NSV called again with food.

6–7 November 1942

My parents sent me a letter dated 11 October from my company leader Hauptmann Schmidt informing me that the regimental commander had awarded me the Infantry Assault Badge in Bronze. I pinned it to my uniform with pride. The mortar crews were always well forward with the infantry.

8 November 1942

Today we listened with very close attention to a 'Führer-speech', mainly about Stalingrad. Apparently we had quite small assault groups there. The town was in our hands, the enemy held a very narrow strip of the riverbank.

9–12 November 1942

Thursday was an NSV day as usual, whipping up enthusiasm on the trams, then a fight in the Hotel Mazur. Just what we needed after months at the Front. After that we saw two films.

13–16 November 1942

Those able to walk have to do sentry duty in pairs in the hospital in the evenings and at night: only a single sentry was posted during the day. A light MG is set up in the large entry hall as a precaution against partisan attack. All visitors are subjected to stiff controls. By chance I met a 9 Company *Grossdeutschland* comrade-in-arms (Wolf) with whom I watched the film *Panzerabwehr* at the YMCA. People might think that all I ever did was watch films.

18 November 1942

NSV day and Thursday. A match was held in the Warsaw football stadium between Schalke 04 and a Soldiers' Eleven. The soldiers led 1–0 at half time, but lost 1–2. It seemed as though the entire German occupation force was present to watch.

19–22 November 1942

Over these four days I saw seven films.

24 November 1942

Thursday, NSV day again: we don't mind because they bring us cake, biscuits and cigarettes. Today was my last appointment with the surgeon, my wounds have almost healed. Soon I shall be with the reserve unit. The 'Grossdeutschland Ersatzbrigade' has arrived at Cottbus. I expect to receive my orders at any time.

26 November–3 December 1942

On the 30th I took the 1450hrs train from Warsaw main station for Berlin, where I changed trains for Cottbus and reported to the Sachsendorf Barracks. We 'convalescents' were given special duty. We find that we have become strangers to barracks routine. The important thing is revising weapons training *ad nauseam*. At Cottbus we went to the cinema once.

4–6 December 1942

I went for a dental check-up. Toothache destroys concentration at the Front. Then I went to the cinema and afterwards submitted my request for convalescent leave. On 9 December I took the 2009hrs train from Cottbus to Hagen via Berlin and arrived at Hagen at 0834hrs.

28 December 1942– 8 January 1943

Back at Cottbus on 28 December 1942, I joined Ersatzbrigade *Grossdeutschland* 1, Convalescents' Company, Sachsendorf Barracks. Between 2nd and 4 January 1943 I saw two films and the surgeon passed me 'Fit for the Front' and 'Fit for Tropical Duty'. On 5 January I was attached to the 'Trained Replacement Company' on light duty in quarters at the village of Gross Ossnig. On 7 January 1943 at Gallinchen (near Cottbus) we were issued new uniforms and slept in private houses under thick eiderdowns. This was followed next day by roll call in our new things and a speech about duty.

9–16 January 1943

My light duty consisted of weapons training which returned us 'veterans' very quickly to the raw reality. We also had a 15km march through the snow carrying all equipment (heavy MG and heavy mortar). Then we returned to Sachsendorf Barracks.

17–18 January 1943

The 'Trained Replacement Company' prepared to move out on the 17th and amidst a fair amount of excitement next day the commanding officer of the Reserve Battalion held his parting speech: 'You are called upon to fill the gaps which the enemy steel has torn in the ranks of our proud Division *Grossdeutschland*.' The parents of some of the young soldiers also attended. I saw a mother crying, some young girls stood silent and waved. Cottbus, railway station, load! We were ninety-four 'recovered convalescents' (of *Grossdeutschland*) and others from Wittenberg and Coburg. In all about half a 'Trained Replacement Battalion'. We travelled in goods trucks, thirty men per truck.

Notes

1. *Sanitäter* = 'paramedic', but covers everything from ambulance driver to first-aid man, stretcher bearer and male nurse. (TN)

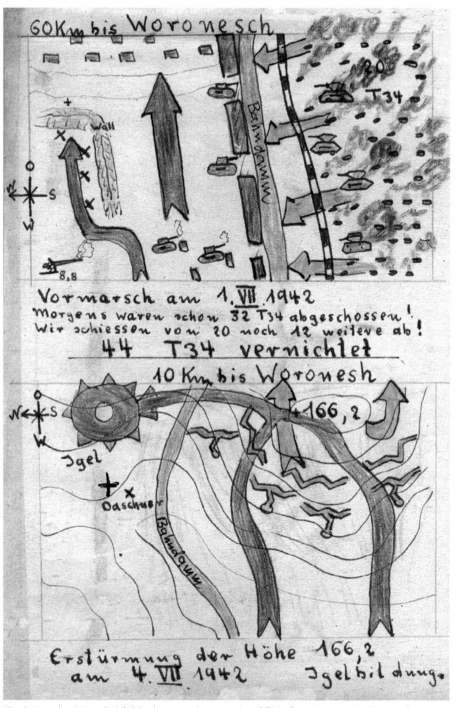

(*Top*) Map by Hans Rehfeldt showing the situation 60km from Voronezh during the advance of 1 July 1942. '32 T-34s were knocked out during the morning. We knocked out another 12 from 20! <u>44 T-34s destroyed</u>'. Bahndamm = railway embankment.

(*Bottom*) Map by Hans Rehfeldt showing the situation 10km from Voronezh on 4 July 1942, the attack on spot height 166.2, and the setting up of the 'hedgehog' all-round defence.

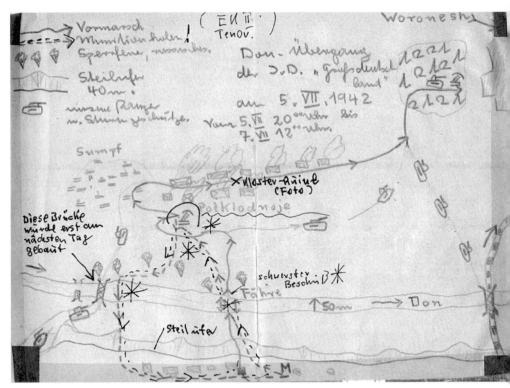

Map by Hans Rehfeldt.

General Hörnlein (with stick) approaching an observation post near Voronezh.

Oberst Köhler leading other officers in the approaches to Voronezh, 5 July 1942.

Grossdeutschland grenadiers moving up in pursuit to the central Don.

4 July 1942: road sign to Voronezh. Another 9km!

A bridge for panzers over the Voronezh. Before it was completed, the author was awarded the Iron Cross Second Class.

A mixed unit of assault guns and armoured personnel carriers leading an advance.

The effective Sturmgeschütz III Ausf F with the long-barrelled 7.5cm gun being re-ammunitioned.

Several mortar teams crossing the Don in an inflatable boat. The base plate of a mortar can be clearly seen.

Shortly after this photo was taken the riverbank received fire from a Stalin organ.

A multi-barrelled wheeled rocket launcher Do-Werfer being supplied with ammunition. This weapon was much feared by the Soviets.

A shot-down Russian Boston bomber supplied by the United States.

This T-34 was destroyed at Yassenki.

Self-propelled assault guns were often the saviours of infantry under attack by tanks and heavy weapons.

Moving on a dusty road.

A pause for rest at Gazinka, 12 July 1942.

Our faithful Opel-Blitz 3-tonner showing the divisional symbol of a steel helmet on the mudguard, below it the '9' for 9 Company.

Remains of the ruined convent at Potklodnoiye, 6 July 1942.

Our general's Fieseler Storch at a command post.

Bathed in sweat, covered in dust and sunburned — and always advancing! 4 Platoon/9 Company/ II Battalion/Grenadier Regiment *Grossdeutschland*, summer 1942.

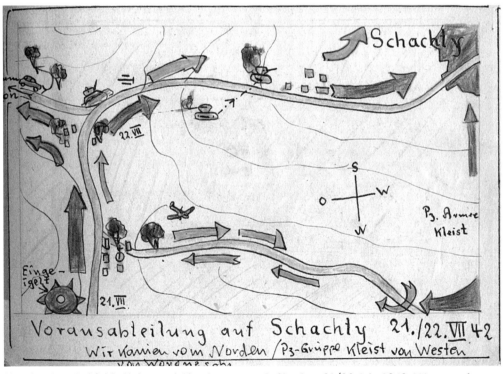

Map by Hans Rehfeldt. 'Advanced Abteilung towards Shachty, 21/22 July 1942. We came from the north from Voronezh, Pz.Gruppe Kleist from the west.' (This map can only be made out in parts. Bottom left, 'eingeigelt' = we formed a hedgehog, top left is probably the motor car which intervened and then fled.)

Grossdeutschland Division moving up to Stalino across the bridge over the Don built by the pioneers.

Vehicles of *Grossdeutschland* Division heading for Stalino after crossing the makeshift Don bridge.

Fritze Barth from Oranienburg.

Platoon leader Feldwebel Rhedanz, summer 1942.

Feldwebel Rhedanz and Hauptmann Schmidt eating eggs, milk and honey.

Gefreiter Gottfried Fritsch with MP40 and horse. He fell at Chermassovo on 12 September 1942.

Jupp Dörfler posing with the same horse.

Jupp Dörfler was a barber by trade and his services were therefore much sought-after!

A lorry on the makeshift bridge over the Don on the way to Stalino.

Gefreiter Fritsch and Unteroffizier Stedtler during a pause in the advance.

A column of panzers heading for Stalino.

1943

Chapter 13

Defending East of Kharkov

Author's note: On 19 January 1943 the Ukrainian city of Kharkov was held by German forces but had come under increasing threat as the catastrophe at Stalingrad neared its conclusion. The main area defended by *Grossdeutschland* Division, with fearsome losses, was to the north of the city and along the Byelgorod–Kharkov Rollbahn.

19–21 January 1943

The train took us via Sagan (Silesia) and Glogau to Lodz, then through Poland to Warsaw, the fifth time I had been through the capital city. My earlier note on the tensions there remained valid. On the way to Bialystok the weather thawed. We rolled through partisan country: on a neighbouring track a train stood burning. Our locomotive had two wagons ahead of it as anti-mine protection.

22–26 January 1943

We passed Lida and Minsk, monotonous snow-covered wastes on both sides of the track. At Bobruisk we met other German and Hungarian troops. Here we saw some SS-*Leibstandarte Adolf Hitler*. At Gomel–Bryansk on 24 January where the track ran through dense woodland, we noticed that a broad protective strip had been felled either side to make it more difficult for partisans to approach unseen. It also gave us a better field of fire. On 25 January we reached Orel, the nearest station for Moscow and Tula, but we received no orders. The train headed south. Nobody knew our destination; we passed through Svoboda towards Kursk.

27 January 1943

The train finally screeched to a halt at Voltshansk, a place between Byelgorod and Kharkov, and we de-trained with all our equipment. It was bitterly cold. We were given quarters in a school, and were then addressed by General

Hörnlein. He greeted the 'Old *Grossdeutschland* Comradeship' personally before telling us something of the general situation in this sector of the Front. After the disaster at Stalingrad, the Russians had broken through north and south at our junctions with our Hungarian and Italian allies. The gap which had appeared east of Byelgorod was up to 200km wide and over 150km deep, and we had no cohesive Front. With great haste, the OKW was throwing Panzer Grenadier Division *Grossdeutschland*, SS-Division *Das Reich* and SS-Division *Leibstandarte Adolf Hitler* across this gap to seal it off and so halt the enemy advance. We could see at once that this was going to be no light undertaking.

28 January 1943

We slept in good, warm quarters waiting for our *Tross* vehicles. Meanwhile the men of the reserve battalion were split up into individual companies. Most of us 'veterans' went back to our former companies and the same platoon. I conversed with the owners of our quarters, Ukrainians, and explained the overall military situation to them. They made no comment. Matka – Babushka, rather – made us a good soup and baked us a cake. We were lavish with the coffee beans, and at midday we had cabbage.

29 January 1943

Large groups of Hungarians are drifting back. The strain and anxiety on their faces is evident. *Grossdeutschland* will close the gaps and act as fire brigade again! Today we reached II Battalion and our company, where they greeted us joyfully. Only a few of my old mortar colleagues remained. Naturally they were the gladdest of all to see us! We received the new issue of winter clothing: steppe trousers, steppe jacket, thick mittens, fur boots and a large hood to cover the head. No complaints there!

30 January 1943

'Alarm!' The lorries took us via Voltshansk and Byelgorod to Baharotzka. There we set up our base and established a 'hedgehog'. The Russians were about 10km away.

31 January 1943

We advanced eastwards in the direction of Stary Oskol towards Belomestnoiye. The lorries brought us as far as possible along the Rollbahn and then we had to trudge for up to 10km through a snowy desert. We stopped in a long gully having seen Russians in a village to the right of us. Our scouting party saw Italian prisoners in the village. After some hesitation we attacked and took it after a short, violent action. Night was falling and it was damned cold. We heard a wounded man calling from the field and six of us carried him in on four carbine straps. All the wounded had to spend the night in the gully wrapped in woollen blankets, the Rollbahn was too far away.

1 February 1943

At dawn our fusiliers, Regiment *Grossdeutschland* 2, arrived. Nevertheless we were forced to give up Belomestnoiye; a new attack was ordered after we changed our position in the gully. Now another village was attacked: the infantry suffered heavy losses because the attack had to be made over a flat expanse of deep snow with no cover. The companies were almost wiped out. We had to economize on ammunition in case Ivan made a counter-attack and so the attack was broken off. Meanwhile reinforcements brought up ammunition loaded on Finnish *Muldenschlitten* – trough-shaped wooden sleds, of an outstanding design for travel through snow. Then they were used to convey the many wounded to vehicles waiting on the Rollbahn.

2 February 1943

We could not capture the village and went back to the Rollbahn through the long gully and some gorges. Two kilometres ahead of Baharotzka we set up a barrier about 100m in length along the Rollbahn.

3 February 1943

Ivan advanced to the Rollbahn. We spent the whole night in the open with our mortars in a small gully on a low hill. It was bitterly cold and windy. Ha ha! We captured some Russian lorries driving along the Rollbahn. A handful of Russian tanks appeared. Our panzers and tank destroyers climbed up a reverse slope to surprise them and after a short battle scared them off. We were apparently encircled and so formed another hedgehog. Our position was anything but tenable, however; the Russian artillery was shelling us from all directions and so we shifted to better secure the village.

4 February 1943

Ivan inveigled himself into a higher part of Baharotzka village but we still held most of it on the eastern side. From a small window at 800m range I shot a Russian MG crew. Our 15cm infantry guns began bombarding the Russian-occupied part of the village. Soon houses were burning. During the night we had four men standing sentry, relieved after every hour, three to listen out and the other a messenger between the other three. Our mortars had to relocate to the other side of a small bridge to my left. This was directly in Ivan's view and we needed to be fast crossing it. There were some dead civilians on the bridge whom Ivan had shot mistaking them for German soldiers.

5 February 1943

Alarm! Towards midnight we disengaged and went to the Rollbahn where Hungarians, mistaken for Russians in their similar-coloured uniforms, had come under our friendly fire. The Russians were close on their heels. We halted the Hungarians and showed them trenches from where they were to secure our right flank. Our 5cm Pak drove up and we secured in a village. An icy wind blew across the snowy plain. In the fighting we lost two heavy MGs (Hartmann).

6 February 1943

Scanty news reached us about Stalingrad. Sixth Army was totally wiped out, Feldmarschall Paulus has given himself up. Three days of mourning in Germany, flags at half-mast. With our trusty Opel-Blitz we reached Korotsha, then on to Voltshansk after a brief rest. The situation here is anything but stable!

7–8 February 1943

We were in action again today. SS-Division *Das Reich* and *Grossdeutschland* are attempting to stop the Russian advance. We fought off some Russian assault troops, then pulled back into the village of Ochrimoka to set up the main front line. We exchanged violent artillery fire with the Russians, some of our panzers, accompanied by a few armoured personnel carriers, advanced from our right: Ivan came from the left. Neither side had much success. We disengaged from the enemy.

9 February 1943

Yesterday the Russians took Byelgorod. We made a 'motorized advance' via Voltshansk to Kharkov, then were forced back. We are asking ourselves when will we ever stabilize the Front. In the night the lorries brought us to Dobina. It lies in a deep gully near the north–south Byelgorod–Kharkov Rollbahn. We secured along the higher edges of the village. Franz Schlossbauer and I took two men to reconnoitre a radius of several kilometres. As soon as we put our heads above the edge of the gully we came under Russian mortar fire, and soon afterwards Ivan attacked Dobina. We let Ivan have the village, then made a smart counter-attack he hadn't expected and ejected him!

10 February 1943

The Russians wanted to get their own back and came with nine T-34s. Our 8.8cm Flak destroyed two of them and forced them to reconsider. Then we rested.

11 February 1943

It is important to keep the Kharkov Rollbahn free. We have secured it with 8.8cm Flak, heavy Pak, 15cm infantry guns, mortars and our heavy MGs.

12 February 1943

Our mortars were attached to 6 Company in a village left of the Rollbahn. Suddenly, 'Alarm!' Ivan reached the Rollbahn behind us from the east and cut it off, outflanking us to the north. He had mined the Rollbahn and shot dead the occupants of those vehicles immobilized by the mines. The Russians were on either side of the Rollbahn: we attacked and forced them back. Some remained, feigning death. They came alive again with a gun muzzle to the head and a kick in the backside. When one saw one's own troops strewn around dead like that, it made one hard. At the slightest suspicious movement we shot the Russians. Under Russian anti-tank, infantry and mortar fire we removed the wreckage of the vehicles and the dead from the Rollbahn, then shovelled away the snow so that traffic could move faster.

13 February 1943

To make the Rollbahn safer, we made a surprise attack on a large village to the right of it accompanied by panzers and 3.7cm Flak. We attacked with cries of 'Hurrah!' and at top speed. Our attack tempo, motivated by anger, resulted in a clean sweep after house-to-house fighting. We received fire from almost every window. We made a radical 'cleansing' of armed civilians.

14 February 1943

We held the village but could not bring out our wounded. Not even in the armoured personnel carriers. We were encircled, fired on from all sides. The night was illuminated by sky glow! A most unpleasant situation! We had our backs to the wall, weapons ready to fire. And then we were extracted.

On our retreat we saw again the monotonous expanse of Russia's snowy wastes. We are fighting our way back to Kharkov; Ivan is pressing forward, emboldened and heartened. We have still failed to establish a firm Front. The Russians went round our Rollbahn blockades using light horse-drawn sleds and set up their own roadblock in a village to our north on the Rollbahn. From there they can intercept and destroy lorries and supply vehicles going back to Kharkov. Our assault group is preparing. If the Russians to the north can be held back and our position there is maintained, we intend to force the breakthrough to Kharkov.

Our force is composed of five panzers, a 3.7cm Flak on a half-track chassis[1] which, in order to economize on fuel, towed our lorry with our group, two heavy MGs and two mortars. We drove off the Rollbahn since Ivan would certainly have mined it. The panzers rumbled through the snow while we rattled and shook behind the 3.7cm Flak. The canopy over the rear of the lorry was rolled back so that we could fire at once from the lorry in motion. The cold cut through our winter clothing, our hands were soon clammy and numb, for the rifle cannot be handled well with mittens. After about forty-five minutes a large village came into sight. Ahead of its first houses was a tree nursery with many long rows of fruit trees. Our panzers had arrived there without opposition. We surveyed the village through binoculars and saw movement beyond it; enemy vehicles and sleds attempting to flee into the nearby woods. After firing warning shots, the panzers set off straight between the houses firing their guns and MGs until reaching the far end, where they stopped. The Russians tried to flee past them, but were all shot down. Our lorry and the 3.7cm Flak had rolled to the village centre without paying heed to the shooting and halted. Some houses were already burning from the shelling by the panzers. We came under rifle fire from close range; we were unable to spot any of these household snipers though fire seemed to be coming from all the houses. We assembled our mortars, received our orders and now even the 3.7cm Flak began firing explosive shells at the fleeing Russians. We also had the range and our 'rebounds' had good effect.

'Both mortars, five rounds, fire at will!' When the last bomb left the barrel, the first had not yet arrived at the target (flight time about twenty seconds), but then all ten came down in the midst of the fleeing troops, either exploding with a black column of smoke on impact with the ground or, if a rebound, just above head height. Suddenly we came under fire from several hidden rifles and the rounds whipped up the snow near our mortars. One of the men saw from which house firing was coming and informed the 3.7cm Flak. The gun swivelled round, the barrel depressed a little and then the gun barked three times. Later we found behind the window the body of a man, ripped to shreds, a civilian, a partisan. While our two mortars continued to bombard the fleeing Russians, the Flak protected us against the houses to our rear. The gun fired at any movement, even at individual Bolshevists, with two to three rounds. Some of the houses from which shooting had come had burst into flame. In the gathering darkness the smoke and fumes reduced the visibility to a dangerous level, and the shooting increased. Our panzers had pulled back, leaving us at the mercy of an unknown number of soldiers, partisans and armed civilians, but moved up in close support in the night. Sporadic shooting persisted, and we kept as close as possible to the hulls of the panzers or the house walls. We had radio contact with battalion through the panzers. The enemy ring closed around us. During the house searches several of our men had been wounded and were now laid out under blankets and greatcoats. They groaned often, for they felt the cold more than we did. An armoured car arrived to take them out to the battalion but fifteen minutes after its departure it returned having come under anti-tank and MG fire. Our outer ring of sentries reported hearing the sound of fighting and tank guns to the west. The noise increased and soon we heard our MG42 firing and a Russian tank replying, Ivan even fired his slower Maxim. Rounds chirped and whistled near us. Then we heard shouts fairly near of 'Hurrah!' and Ivan's reply of 'Urrah!' Our relief had arrived! The surviving Ivans in 'our village' slipped away silently. We fired flares and watched the arrival of our liberators. What a shaking of hands! It is difficult to put into words the feelings one has in such a moment. We sat on the panzer hulls and headed to the Rollbahn for Kharkov. We learned that Ivan was encircling the city from the north-east. Führer-order: 'The city of Kharkov is to be held at all costs.' We remembered Stalingrad. Was the same thing going to happen here?

15 February 1943

We lie in a suburb of Kharkov, preparing to abandon the city. The situation is totally confused. Pure chaos! Wehrmacht service offices are being hastily cleared out. Fires being lit. Our troops are being fired on by snipers hiding in houses (partisans but also civilians with guns) and shoot back. Our desire is to get out of this sea of houses. Bridges, compounds and rails, the entire station area is being blown up by our pioneers.

Surprisingly, German forces have been able to disengage from the enemy and (despite the Führer's order?) will leave Kharkov today. A new interception and security position is to be set up beyond the city. Our company lorries drew up ready to take us out. We stood around in small groups smoking and reading recently delivered field post. Despite the midday hour the sun shone pale, only a little above the horizon, fine white snowflakes glittered. A row of tall black wooden telegraph poles line the road leading into the city. We gaze at the buildings, often eight to ten storeys high, Party buildings for show, the GPU office in the morning mist: long rows of flats like fortress walls. A few kilometres outside the city is the tractor works. An icy easterly wind drifted fine snow horizontally over the Rollbahn. 'Mount up! Weapons at the ready!' Partisan riffraff are active in the city, so – watch out! We sat up in our trusty Opel-Blitzes, the canopies rolled back. The battalion rolled through the sea of houses. The city seemed deserted, only a few civilians running about. The great Wehrmacht supply compounds have been emptied or blown up, other buildings as well. We looked at them in silence as we passed. The Waffen-SS, the last demolition parties, occupied the bridges and crossroads. Crossing the railway bridge we saw what had once been the great station: its buildings now a heap of rubble across the tracks. Soon we came to the workers' settlements on the western outskirts: many small houses with a small garden. After the brickworks the road was more uphill. The convoy halted halfway up the slope.

On a road about 300m to our left, above a gully, we saw armed troops approaching dressed in white snow shirts. They halted, looked at us through binoculars and then we saw them bring up an anti-tank gun. 'Look out! Russians! Enemy anti-tank gun left!' The motors roared up, we were desperate to get off the exposed slope to the cover of houses higher up on the left. Our Opel-Blitz had difficulty making the climb and ran out of steam behind the first house. 'Dismount with equipment and hand weapons!' We leapt out. The drivers were to follow us in their vehicles but the icy ground was too smooth for the wheels to obtain a purchase. Now we came under fire from the brickworks at the foot of the hill: a Maxim MG by the sound of it and a 2cm Flak on a self-propelled wagon – a dangerous weapon. The anti-tank gun ahead obtained a direct hit on our 3.7cm Flak, destroying the gun: a wounded man was carried away by his crewmates to a waiting ambulance. The men and drivers of the vehicles which now lie immobile joined us. We could not fetch our mortars from our lorry! Enemy fire chirped around us, Ivan fired his anti-tank gun at us, but it did not appear to be aimed, just fired! The shells had the effect of driving everybody towards the shelter of a redbrick house about 100m farther on where the road rose over a small height to other houses. It was decided we would assemble there.

We made our way there individually or in small groups. Now I noticed that I had left my carbine on the lorry when we dismounted. I had only a stick hand grenade under my belt and one blue egg-type hand grenade in my haversack. I was running behind a damaged ambulance, Jupp Dörfler ahead of me, Franz Schlossbauer left of the ambulance. A shell exploded close by, splinters whirred and Jupp clasped his head shouting, 'My cheek!' He was bleeding heavily from a head wound. Franz grabbed him and ran. A splinter had struck him just below the left eye. 'A few millimetres higher and . . .' he would have lost the eye. *Soldatenglück!* The three of us ran abreast in long strides through the snow with bullets whistling all around. The snow was high and progress was slow. Near the redbrick house one of our Paks had driven up and returned fire, forcing the enemy anti-tank gun to change position. The company assembled – all out of breath. Since my mortar was on the lorry I had only grenades: as a mortar gunner, Obergefreiter Goga had a pistol and my carbine, which he had picked up when jumping down from the lorry, and so he lent me his pistol. We sought positions between the houses, a fairly unfavourable location: Leutnant Meyer said we should advance to a broad road about 500m away where we could defend ourselves better. Our group consisted of the heavy MGs led by Obergefreiter Schaepers, which split from us to the left, and the mortars under Sudeten German Franz Schlossbauer, to the right of the houses. Fighting among houses is very dangerous: fire can come from any window, cellar or garden. Several shots rang out and one of our men fell. When I peered around the corner of a house a bullet missed me by a fraction. 'Watch out, snipers!' shouted Schaepers. Giving each other cover we made it to a haystack and from there to the next house in line towards the road. The sniper was put out of action with MG42 fire and, bar one dead, our whole group had made it. A trail of dead Russians lay behind us, but twelve to fifteen of them, some in uniform, others in civilian clothing, made a run for it and all escaped. At the road we found a house under construction, all beams and empty window frames. From there we could monitor the road with a good field of fire but it left us isolated. The heavy MG joined us and, having noticed that other houses nearby were occupied by civilians, I decided to interview some of them. I found them naturally very anxious: the men were not all grandfathers, some were of military age. A girl speaking fairly good German stated that she had seen Russian troops about 3km north-west of here, and at the railway station many Russian soldiers with sleds and MGs. North-west? This meant that Ivan was coming from the north almost behind us, his intention probably being to cut off our route west. Our sentries focused primarily northwards. From the city we could hear the hard crack of anti-tank guns or panzers firing and see the night sky lit by flares.

Just after I checked the sentries I heard a burst of MG fire. The gunner told me, 'In the big house over there I saw people moving about.' When I asked the girl about the big house she said they were refugees from Stalingrad. I went over and shouted. The reply came, 'Hallo, are you 9 Company?' Our messenger emerged with the glad tidings that we were not totally cut off, there was a panzer or assault gun on its way to fetch us out. All hell was let loose in the city, everybody appeared to be shooting. A Tiger panzer appeared after half an hour and stopped about 200m short of us: one of its crewmen came with the message, 'Pack up silently and assemble by the panzer!' Leutnant Meyer was waiting by it and ordered, 'As many as possible of you on the hull, all the others follow behind on foot. Always keep close and keep an eye out to both sides.' In the rush to board I was unsuccessful and so had to stagger behind, holding a hook in one hand and my pistol in the other. The motor roared into life, the tracks screeched and crunched and with a jerk the vehicle moved off. I stumbled behind the steel colossus together with others. The tracks threw up snow and lumps of ice into our faces but we were happy for the protection: the empty roads with their piles of rubble, the tall houses with many dark windows, the occasional passing rifle round, these all made me shudder. In 'Red Square' the panzer stopped abruptly. In the light of burning houses, many lorries waited in columns between panzers and assault guns, soldiers ran busily here and there, commands ringing out. We could not determine where our own lorries were to be found and were directed instead to travel by a six-wheeled pioneer vehicle. The column set off, our vehicle tried to overtake, was pushed aside, left the road and bogged down in the snow. We all had to get off and push from the side. Despite the snow chains the wheels spun in vain: during various attempts I slipped and fell, trapping my left leg under the wheels of the two rear axles. I was lifted out and placed aboard the vehicle. Although my leg felt numb it was not broken: I was wearing thick fur puttees; the legs of my winter uniform were well padded and the snow lay deep. The column left this part of the city under panzer protection heading south-west. We broke out of the deadly encirclement to the sound of explosions and burning houses collapsing. The sky glowed red. Kharkov was on fire.

As we discovered later, after the Stalingrad disaster, Hitler had also ordered that Kharkov had to be held to the last man. The leader of the SS-Panzerkorps, SS-Oberstgruppenführer Hausser and our General Hörnlein assessed the situation more rationally and despite the Führer-order decided to pull out. 'No second Stalingrad!'

17 February 1943

We left Kharkov and disengaged from the enemy. I sat on a gun carriage. I had been reunited with my group, and since I could not walk, and there were few of us, I was given sentry duty. In the night I sat one-hour on, one off, wrapped in blankets and seated on a stool in front of our quarters. My leg was very swollen and bore the colourful imprint of the snow chain from knee to ankle. We had no water and so ate snow, which had the usual effect.

18–19 February 1943

The withdrawal continued. I rode on one of the rearmost assault guns. These rolled along the railway embankment to Lyubotin (west of Kharkov). While the remains of the company took up positions in front of the town, I was conveyed with the assault guns into town and shared the crew's quarters. From the huge provisions dumps at Kharkov they had helped themselves to quantities of preserves, butter, tins of meat, tins of sausage etc. I was offered my share but having the runs I did not feel like eating. He 111s, Do 17s and Stukas made bombing raids to give us breathing space.

19 February 1943

The Front is about 4km east of Lyubotin. Ivan attacked with T-34s but gave it up when confronted by the Luftwaffe, the remains of our panzers and assault guns and Pak gunners. The Mamuschka of our quarters noticed that I was not eating and made me a tea of short stalks. It tasted very bitter, but after twelve hours the diarrhoea dried up. It was very interesting for me that now when things were not going so well for us, the Ukrainian people showed sympathy to us poor Fritzes. When she asked me where I came from, I answered, '*Germaniya, Hagen*', to which she replied, 'No, you are a Ukrainian.' During my two years in Russia I had made great efforts to understand and speak Russian. There are good language guides with phonetical pronunciation: the Russians had them too. In the summer of 1942 I took one off a Russian soldier and learned Russian military expressions, commands and important terms of speech. I also learned the Cyrillic alphabet and can write almost correct Russian, though only in capitals. I found that it gave me many advantages. I had better contact with Mamuschka, her Malinki (children) and Russian prisoners. In heavy fighting lying in some bomb crater with a Russian prisoner, a cigarette and a few words of kindness in Russian made all the difference. Here in Reshetilovka a Mamka told me, 'You are Ukrainian.' When I told her '*Ya vas absolutno ne ponimaiyu*' ('I don't understand anything you say') she laughed and said I was only pretending, 'You will.'

19–20 February 1943

I was placed temporarily with the *Tross*. Our lorries are parked there, empty and always ready to cover long stretches of country when we move out. Here I kept myself busy loading MG belts.

21 to 27 February 1943

The weather is improving. It is fairly warm in the sun. On the way to Walki we were attacked by Ilyushin 2 'sewing machines': at Walki we were given quarters. The Front is 8km east of here. On 23 February I reported to the dressing station with a recurrence of the runs and the surgeon wrote me up eight days sick in the rear services (*Tross-krank*). My leg is getting better, the bruising is not so colourful. On his twenty-second birthday on the 24th Franz Schlossbauer was wounded. I visited him at the main dressing station. On this day the mass of the division was in the area about 30km south-west of Poltava. Reinforcements have arrived: IV Artillery-Abt/1 Company Tigers and replacement assault guns. We are much encouraged! On the 25th, thaw and slush. We changed location to a village about 35km from Poltava. There we changed quarters three times. On the 26th we were at Metroka. In the morning there was a hoar frost.

At least we have good quarters. On the 27th we continued towards Poltava as far as Digkanka where there is a supply base. Here we washed and deloused. It felt like Christmas again!

28 February 1943

Our entire *Grossdeutschland* Division has been withdrawn from the Front, and we are back at Reshetilovka, our main base. There are five of us lightly wounded in a Russian cottage. The snow melts here very quickly.

1–5 March 1943

The notorious mud *Rasputiza* ['time without roads'] has arrived outside. After our division assembled here with reinforcements, i.e. weapons and ammunition, Tiger panzers and thirty new assault guns, we are ready to roll. The SS-Panzerkorps brought out from France is preparing a powerful counter-offensive. They will advance to the right of us towards Kharkov. (Führer-order: The city will be encircled so as to avoid the feared high casualty rate from the expected street fighting.) We have moved to the main base at Poltava. Supply vehicles will drive up the '*Tross-krank*' to join the main fighting units. We have lodgings in a small village. We hear that the 'Popov' tank army, which has pressed forward too far, will be surrounded and annihilated in our counter-attack. The division has moved to readiness positions for the counter-attack on Kharkov and Byelgorod.

7 March 1943

'Ivan! We're coming back!' The Luftwaffe began rolling attacks against Ivan towards Walki and Kharkov. The SS-Panzerkorps is heading for Walki, *Grossdeutschland* is heading north-west for Lyubotin. Our Stukas are working on the Russians. We learn from prisoners that they are mostly fresh, Siberian troops. A cold wind is blowing, our motto is: 'Forward!' Ivan has taken one look at our panzers and assault guns and withdrawn hastily. We can even follow the main force in our lorries! I have been made i/c No. 1 mortar.

8 March 1943

We pushed north-west of Walki along the railway. Close behind our panzers we entered the lightly defended village of Perekop. The sight of our massed panzers gives us a boost. In his hurried flight Ivan left wrecked anti-tank guns and artillery, fully loaded sleds, mortars, dead horses, other weapons and materials and a few dead Russian soldiers.

9 March 1943

In his over-hasty retreat Ivan has kidnapped civilians for soldiers, both young and old, no uniform or training given. The women have to work. We are rolling forwards, an uplifting sensation. To our left and right over the broad expanses are motorized battlegroups. Panzers, assault guns, 2cm and 3.7cm self-propelled Flak-guns, single barrelled, twin- or quadruple-barrelled Flak, and armoured personnel carriers. The panzer main guns fire, and also the 8.8cm Flak, the best anti-tank gun. We came under fire from a railway linesman's house. The SS attended in amphibious Volkswagens and silenced the shooters. Now we made a turn to the north-east. We recognized where and how our flamethrower-panzers have been at work.

10 March 1943

Our motorcycle infantry descended upon Ivan, taking him completely by surprise. Now press forward, allow the enemy no opportunity to make a stand anywhere! Bogoduchov has been retaken! We reached a village and took up positions about 3km left of the Rollbahn.

11 March 1943

In the early morning we returned to the village which lies alongside a railway line. Ivan had some anti-tank guns and vehicles there which needed to be neutralized. Suddenly we came under attack from his Il 2 aircraft, but we had sufficient Flak for them not to worry us. One Russian aircraft was shot down. New task and orders: 'Establish contact with Regiment 2 (Fusiliers). There must be no gaps in the Front!'

12 March 1943

Abandoned on the rails we discovered a rail trolley. We loaded it with our mortars and ammunition, Two men work the lever, the thing rolls perfectly. This line goes to Bogoduchov (which was retaken yesterday). Our mortars have been seconded to two Pak crews of 7 Company. Our task now is to break down encirclements. The hunt begins! First we freed twenty-five to thirty civilians captured by Ivan. Next at a village about 5km west of Bogoduchov we worked in combination with the Pak gunners to prevent any Ivans escaping the trap. Our panzers set off in pursuit of fleeing Russians while we systematically searched all the buildings. We found twenty-two civilians in the cellars and holes, naturally very anxious, but no living Russian troops.

13 March 1943

We rejoined the push forward. In Bogoduchov we refuelled and re-ammunitioned and at 0415hrs set out with the division for Byelgorod. At a halt we were overtaken by our General Hörnlein. The columns are more bogged down than moving. The cause is a large pit of mud in the centre of the Rollbahn in which one of our panzers has become stuck fast. We stayed the night in Klodov.

14 March 1943

The general led the way out from Klodov. After the thaw parts of the terrain are flooded. The snow has thawed, but the ground is hard as iron. The mud is impeding our advance. When we halted we saw an abandoned anti-tank gun ready to fire. Some of the Pak gunners wanted to fire it just in case it was of value to the Russians in future; after some fumbling it fired 'by surprise', and the two 'gunners' fell on their hindquarters with the recoil. Best laugh of the campaign. Later we stopped again upon hearing the sounds of a fierce panzer/ anti-tank gun battle. We assumed that Russian massed armour had met our panzer spearhead! We heard that our aerial reconnaissance had reported about 120 Russian tanks ahead. Over the next few hours behind the woods where Borissovka lies there was apparently a fierce panzer battle in which our assault guns destroyed forty-three T-34s. We moved up a little and saw some of the wrecked tanks left and right of the Rollbahn, a number of them still burning.

15 March 1943

We took over and secured a remote village. Towards evening we advanced to another village in the woods and built a snow bunker. The village itself lies in a deep gully. When relieved we repaired to the village houses to warm up. We could hear a tank battle on the Rollbahn, Ivan was determined we should not pass. We spent six hours from 0500hrs in the bushy woodland position. We heard that twenty Russian tanks were destroyed today. The weather is sunny and clear. We can still hear tanks firing on the Rollbahn.

16 March 1943

The Rollbahn to Byelgorod, and the city itself, lie within range of our artillery. Our Stukas concentrate on destroying their tanks. Ivan has a huge force of armour here, but our assault guns and panzers have been very successful. The tank battle is continuing. We have now set up our positions in the village as infantry with heavy weapons on the outer ring in case the Russian infantry comes this way. At the moment all hangs on the outcome of the tank battle. Armoured Ilyushin 2 'sewing machines' have been attacking our panzers and vehicles with their cannon, MGs and rockets.

17 March 1943

We hear that the Waffen-SS has recaptured Kharkov! We have changed our position and made a hedgehog. We wiped out a Russian scouting party. Our Luftwaffe has been very active over Byelgorod! We have been standing around in the woods here so long they call us 'Waldheinis'. In the evening Ivan attacked our village with twelve T-34s. Gefreiter Schaepers destroyed three of them with the Pak, a fourth by close-combat methods. What a night that was in the village! When we got back from the woods we saw the mess. We formed a hedgehog again and spent a restless night, but Ivan never came back.

18 March 1943

The commanding officer of the *Grossdeutschland* Division, Generalleutnant Hörnlein, has been awarded the Oak Leaves to his Knight's Cross. We learn that Russian tanks have left Borissovka after the overwhelming defeat of their armour there. While securing at the edge of our village, a Russian ground attack aircraft dropped a bomb which landed 2m from our MG post but failed to explode. Our pioneers have mined the gully at the entrance to the village to prevent Ivan infiltrating. A scouting party had tried it, the bodies of two of them lie in the snow.

19 March 1943

Our panzer spearhead is attacking Byelgorod and apparently making good progress. We received new orders and have been relieved by the *Kleeblatt* [clover-leaf] Division. In warm spring sunshine we rolled through the Borissovka tank cemetery, the wrecks of the Russian tanks either line the streets or are shoved between the houses out of the way.

20 March 1943

We rolled through burning villages where our Luftwaffe had struck. Before noon we moved up to Tomarovka which our forces had taken the day before. We made the usual security arrangements, put the mortars in position and made ourselves comfortable in the houses, the small town being almost free of civilians. Our vehicles parked nearby, we had supper and then thought about bed. No such luck: Ivan began sending over his 'sewing machines' from 2000hrs until 0400hrs accompanied by aircraft we called 'Rollbahn whores', small, single-engined training aircraft with canvas-covered wings. The bombs dropped made large craters, the lightly built houses trembled with the blast, windowpanes shattered. We tried to play cards through it all and a guard posted at the door gave us early enough warning that a 'lame crane' was approaching at which we dowsed the candles. Then they started to arrive in droves. That was too dangerous!

21 March 1943

Only a few houses and lorries were damaged, but there were many delayed-action bombs with time-fuses which went off later. A dirty trick! This evening we moved our quarters to the outermost neighbourhood and parked the lorries separate from each other in the open field. I am occupying a cellar for root vegetables which is 3m deep, only one brave soul, Adolf V., elected to stay by Matka's warm stove upstairs! Tonight Ivan dropped phosphorous bombs which were soon burning in many areas of the town. Our Flak fired but claimed no kills. The 'Rollbahn whores' are very hard to shoot down because the shells go straight through the canvas on the wings. A second sleepless night for us. One is flying overhead. One has just dropped its bombs. One is heading towards the searchlight which guides it home. Another is arriving from the horizon. These aircraft are also known as 'nerve saws'.

22 March 1943

In daylight we looked at the large bomb craters. Many of the houses have been totally destroyed or are still burning. At the edge of town we discovered several Russian small-calibre artillery weapons with ammunition. We stood a spade upright in the ground as a target and fired one. *Donnerwetter*! It splayed the shaft and had an enormous recoil. We have to be prepared to move out.

Notes

1. 3.7cm Flak (Sf) on Zugkraftwagen 8t Sd.Kfz 7/2, the gun being on a half-tracked chassis. There were three versions, 36, 37 and 43, the latter built from 1942 until 1945, the main difference over the earlier versions being the rate of fire. The later model fired 230 to 250 rounds per minute. All versions could fire through 360° in the horizontal axis, the range in the vertical axis being between -7.5° and +90° Overall weight was 11 tonnes, top speed on the road 50km/hr. Alexander Lüdeke, *Panzer der Wehrmacht Band 2, Rad und Halbkettenfahrzeuge 1939–1945*, Motorbuch, 2012, p. 121. (TN)

Chapter 14

The Calm before the Storm

The division was relieved and withdrew into an 'availability area' north of Poltava, stretching from Achtyrka to Dikanka. There followed a reorganization with special training, weapons and field exercises, close-combat training, anti-tank and anti-bunker training.

23 March 1943

My unit left the unlovely town of Tomarovka for Kasakskaya 10km farther on and took up position. This was a quiet place and the population seemed really glad we were back. '*Kleeblatt*' Division arrived to relieve us. We were one company of infantry with two MGs and two mortars. '*Kleeblatt*' brought a whole battalion. We left for Diganka where we were given very good, clean quarters.

27–28 March 1943

The population is very well disposed to us and welcomes contact. We barter sugar for eggs and much more. We are a 'Prussian' unit, however, and as though back in barracks, reveille at 0600hrs, clean weapons! Weapons inspection! We are going to spend a longer period here than usual and receive special training. Our 9 Company/II Battalion is sending two groups of heavy MGs and two groups of mortars to the Front. I am to remain here with my heavy mortar group as a training instructor. Apart from myself, other 'veterans' or 'old soldiers', if you like, are to remain as instructors. We are to form the 'backbone'. For the present it is not exactly clear what we shall be doing. The important thing is, we get field post, and apart from weapons exercises and weapons care we get a lot of free time. From 1700hrs I stood sentry in town. Russian bombers visited Poltava.

29–30 March 1943

Now we have done something for our health and wellbeing and took a bath. Glorious! Then we went to the delousing centre at Poltava and took another bath. What else could one want?

31 March to 2 April 1943

During the night there was a violent storm. Our *Kampfstaffel* 9 Company has been merged with 10 Company. Today we went to the field hospital at Poltava for a medical examination from head to toe. In the evening we had hot food, pudding, liquor and other high-percentage drinks. Our company leader Leutnant Schmelter awarded me the Iron Cross Second Class in the name of our battalion commander. Promotions were announced, as for example Franz Schlossbauer became an 'Unteroffizier'. Therefore we had good reason to celebrate.

3 April 1943

I had to go to Poltava again, this time to see the optician because I had been 'snow blind' for a short period during the winter. No underlying condition was detected and so I had the chance to look around town.

At midday at a school I saw soldiers queuing for the field kitchen. I joined them and the young soldiers all ogled my newly awarded Iron Cross on its ribbon in the buttonhole. After the award, the recipient wears the medal for a short time and then later only the ribbon.

The leader of the Reserve Battalion asked me what it had been awarded for. He was quite disappointed when I told him that I had not taken the village of Potklodnoiye single-handed, but nevertheless I was introduced to the young soldiers as a modest hero and an example.

The citation for my award stated:

Gefreiter Rehfeldt took part in the Russian campaign as an ammunition runner for the heavy mortar platoon from October 1941 and always carried out his duties outstandingly. In the fighting at the Don bridge at Potklodnoiye on 6 July 1942 under heavy enemy mortar fire he carried ammunition from the transfer point to the weapon without a pause, allowing the mortar to wipe out a nest of enemy infantry. In the fighting at Chermassov south of Rzhev between 10 and 18 September 1942 he distinguished himself again as an ammunition runner paying no regard to the heaviest enemy artillery and mortar fire. Rehfeldt made an important contribution to the successes of his mortar team.

4–5 April 1943

I found that everything was scarce in Poltava and therefore expensive. Thus a loaf of bread cost 40 karbovanez. The *Tross* driver said to me, 'At home you could buy the bakery for that.' At midday we drove to Balnyasa where I was to be trained as an NCO, Prussian style! After settling into our quarters there was a roll call!

6 April 1943

On this training course we are going to be treated as raw recruits, all exactly as prescribed in Army Standing Orders. Everything we learned in barracks as recruits we are going to have to go through again, only harsher! 'Basic training', training on the mortar and 08 pistol. At battalion roll call the commander addressed us, his motto: 'Clear the eye, brave the heart and vitality from the stomach!' and he went on: 'What you are to do is show young soldiers coming here straight from barracks "war-similar conditions" from your own experience. Show them how to behave under enemy fire. Who digs deepest has more chance of survival. Courage and bravery credit the soldier, needless heroism can only do damage. Always be a model and example.'

7–8 April 1943

Today topography, description and assessment of the terrain. After that a conference. Then map reading and exercises, instruction on the new P.38 pistol. On the following day 'Commanding Officers' Guard' from 0800hrs to 1800hrs.

9 April 1943

Shooting training. Learning about the carbine and P.38. I fired the carbine at 100m: result 9, 9, 11. With the pistol, five rounds at 20m, four hits and one 'clipped bus ticket'. In the afternoon it rained and so we had instruction. Preparation of terrain sketches and report writing. We had learned all this in the Hitler Youth!

10 April 1943

Today mortar training: laying the barrel, zeroing-in. The *Herren* Training Staff (temporary officers) watched in fascination. In the evening we had an Unteroffiziers' Evening.

12 April 1943

Yesterday our *Spiess* Oskar Gellert received the rings for his lower sleeve. Leutnant Schmelter considers him to be 'the best *Spiess* in the entire Wehrmacht'. This meant an increase in pay and in the morning Gellert appeared in the best humour. Schmelter had had a drop too much during the festivities but Oskar had drunk him under the table! So we were all excused duty, and lazed the whole day awayexcept in the afternoon when we were immunized against typhus.

13 April 1943

Training against gas attack in the field! How to act in the face of gas attacks, instruction on gas masks. On the battlefield we almost never had a gas mask within reach. If we ever wore the container, it never had a gas mask in it.

14 April 1943

Today for various reasons we had strict barrack-square drill. Our company leader Leutnant Schmelter was promoted to Oberleutnant and I was awarded the Infantry Assault Badge for the second time. The first was awarded on 27 September 1942. Because the heavy MG and mortar groups were often switched between this company and that, the company leader of 6 or 7 Company of our battalion had submitted his recommendation for the award, not knowing that I already had it. There was no such thing as Infantry Assault Badge and bar and so Schmelter went through the ceremony again, and without batting an eyelid pinned the new badge on the patch left by my previous one. Some of my nearest companions raised a half-smile. At 2000hrs, 9 Company serenaded its promoted leader who responded with enough drink for a good celebration to be had by all!

15–17 April 1943

Weapons training in the field as almost every day. I was given the job of building a sandbox for instructional purposes. Everything was improvised, tanks marked by wooden sticks, minefields with stones etc. On the 16th, company watch duty, just like in barracks, on the 17th gas mask testing. We all had to go into a room filled with tear gas. My mask was tight, not so those of many of my colleagues. Ha ha ha!

Next a demonstration of a staged battle (heavy MGs and mortars). The situation: the troop is making a motorized advance to Village 'A' over a small bridge when it comes under MG and rifle fire from a gorge. Dismount! The heavy MGs return fire at once on the immediately recognized targets, we mortars fire blind into the gorge and on the known MG positions forcing the enemy to change position. If the enemy attempts to leave the gorge, bursts of our MG fire seal the exits. In the gorge the mortars can wipe him out.

This was an example of good cooperation using direct and indirect fire. After the exercise, a conference and company instruction. In the afternoon we went to Dikanka for a 'Front Varieté' at the Cocoloresbar.

18–21 April 1943

Today the weather was stormy and windy, just right for the firing range. Lying freehand at 150m I scored 6, 7 and 10. Pistol at 25m five rounds rapid fire (result, three hits). Shooting and exercises cross-country were continued over the next two days. The Führer's birthday was naturally celebrated on the 20th, but more importantly my own twentieth birthday on the 21st. Our quartermaster made some good-quality liquor available to all. Oberleutnant Schmelter congratulated me on my birthday and I returned the compliment regarding his promotion and we both wished each other *Soldatenglück*.

22–24 April 1943

Duties as previously but as I had to have my eyes checked for acuity of vision by a specialist at the military hospital. Having been given the thumbs-up I saw a film in Dikanka and another in Poltava.

25 April 1943: Easter Sunday

Days beforehand, the local inhabitants had begun their spring cleaning. The floors and ovens were painted and the ceilings whitewashed. They used mud, chalk, cowpats and something blue mixed in. Then they showed us how they distil schnapps from root vegetables and call it 'samogonka'. We watched with great interest and drank it warm from the apparatus. To thin it, we then mixed it with 96 per cent proof vodka from Poltava. Impossible to describe! All kinds of cakes ('*piroggen*') were baked and filled with maize or cabbage. On Easter Sunday the women wore clean, bright dresses with colourful ribbons from their trousseau, their hair carefully combed. The women and girls were often in traditional costume. They laughed a lot and I was impressed by their gaiety.

26–27 April 1943

The only males in the town were children and old men, the rest had been taken to serve in the Red Army. They wore handed-down suits which didn't fit and hung loose from their shoulders, but had stylish modern hats and boots. They also wore linen overalls with a bright border. The whole village assembled in a meadow, most arriving by small horse and cart. First they ate, then sat in the grass and sang to the balalaika. This continued in some of the larger houses throughout the afternoon and evening. As for their singing, one wonders from where there talent can have originated (my note made at the time).

27–28 April 1943

Training for the Battle Group, the remainder of 9 Company with elements of the Army Battalion, now all at Dikanka.

29–30 April 1943

New mortar groups are being formed, men from the grenadier companies acting as ammunition runners. Ivan has many more mortars than we do: we need to catch up. Two heavy MG platoons, two mortar platoons (a third is being planned) are being prepared for 9 Company. So far we have half of this.

1–6 May 1943

The roads have dried out. Every day we have exercises: overcoming obstacles, close combat, shooting and moving in the field. Collaboration between heavy MGs and mortars. On the 6th we had an exercise with practice ammunition at Achtyrka. Everything as per the battlefield. Hard weeks of training were to follow. We bathed occasionally but attended one roll call after another. 'There's definitely something in the air,' the grenadiers said.

7–16 May 1943

Evenings and nights Russian bombers fly over our area, their targets being railway stations and suspected troop concentrations. At Achtyrka about 75km north-north-east of Poltava I wandered through the market stalls. Shortages and high prices. Sunflower seeds in wartime are a supplementary food, known locally as 'Stalin's chocolate'. Roasted on the oven they are very tasty. Often in action I had my pockets full of roasted sunflower seeds to augment my rations, or lack of them.

17–24 May 1943

We spent the whole day of the 17th in the field practising with the mortar, interchanging with the heavy MG crews. This culminated in a night exercise on the 20th, and on the 24th after these many exercises we practised with live ammunition.

27–31 May 1943

Hard exercises in the field every day. Preparation for a major offensive? We still know nothing for certain. Everything has to be kept secret so that the civilians cannot betray us.

1–2 June 1943

The weather is glorious and in our free time we bathe in the Vorskla. One of our men got entangled under water in the reeds and only with great difficulty did we get him out. In desperation we stood him on his head several times in the attempt to clear the water from his lungs and he survived. ('You're not dying here, Grenadier, you've here to fight!')

3–6 June 1943

Hard training with the weapons every day including firing by night.

8–9 June 1943

We mortar crews are now being trained on the heavy MG. We had gone through this as recruits at Neuruppin. The MG men had to struggle with our mortar. They did not like its weight (base plate – tripod – barrel).

10–15 June 1943

Ever more hard training, mostly in the field. Suddenly at 2300hrs on the 15th, 'Alarm!' II Battalion is to proceed by lorry to Martinovka where a Ukrainian militiaman has been shot dead. Partisans? Our mortars are at Yuravnoiye and so we receive a light MG to better defend ourselves than with the NCOs' sub-machine guns and the carbines of the ammunition runners. Partisans make us cautious!

16 June 1943

Up to 1100hrs we had normal duties to cover our real purposes, and at 1130hrs went back to Martinovka to 'cleanse' the village. Our relief came at 1500hrs. We know that partisans are in the woods: fresh partisans are being parachuted down from Russian aircraft.

17–18 June 1943

We arrived back at Martinovka towards 0230hrs. In a very short time the entire location was surrounded on all sides. We made a search of all houses, earth bunkers used as cellars, and shacks. All males were herded together, weapons searched for: then all inhabitants including the women had to assemble on the road where they were informed that their livestock were being confiscated. Where these people were taken I could not discover. In the afternoon we drove back to Yuravnoiye, taking honey and a pig with us as booty. Until 1030hrs next morning we attended to our weapons in the terrain; at 1100hrs a motorcycle rider arrived with orders for the 'Second mortar group to make ready immediately'. We boarded the lorry and set off to Martinovka again as occupation troops. We made our quarters there near the military building fronting the village square. Civilians were still being fetched out. The empty village was searched unceasingly. Our orders were to search all houses for civilians twice a day morning and evening. It seemed to me that the reason for this action was to prepare and occupy villages for the imminent major offensive. Villages along the future Front are evacuated in order to provide an assembly area, quarters for troops, storage for ammunition, provisions and fuel. However, this is all supposition, not a word has leaked out. On 18 June we were relieved at 1500hrs and drove back to Yuravnoiye, but we would have preferred to remain where we were, since while there we lived on the fat of the land.

19–22 June 1943: Sonnenwendfeir

Today we had a very impressive experience! On a hill west of Yuravnoiye, in the direction of the setting sun and the Reich, a large pyre of wooden boards and stakes was prepared. At dusk our II Battalion/Grenadier Regiment/Infantry Division *Grossdeutschland* paraded to celebrate *Der grosse Zapfenstreich* ('The Great Tattoo'), the annual German custom of gathering around a blazing bonfire of wooden stakes on the evening of the midsummer solstice in order to give expression to our joy that finally the might of winter has been broken and summer has emerged victorious. All being properly turned out with steel helmets, now we heard the ponderous, steady tread of our regimental band approaching, come all the way from Cottbus. Leading the way the Honour Company, followed by the drum major, jingling johnnies and the Music Corps playing a brisk march, and all accompanied on the flanks by torch bearers. The Honour Company halted at the pyre, the music stopped and the ceremony began. The grenadiers of *Grossdeutschland* are not only great fighters but also perfectly drilled on the parade ground! The torch bearers then lit the pyre, swore together the oath of racial loyalty and tossed their torches into the fire, which then flared brightly. Then we removed our helmets for the old prayer of the German soldier – *Ich bete an die Macht der Liebe, die sich in Jesum offenbart* ('I pray to the Power of Love which revealed itself in Jesus'). Afterwards I was reflecting on the fact that two years ago to this very day, the Führer had given the order to advance across the eastern border. I was remembering with pride the many battles we had won when suddenly, blinded by the flames, at the limit of bright and dark, I saw the mystical, ghostly vision of all our *Grossdeutschland* Fallen, an immensely long column in field grey with steel helmets and rifles, standing at attention and replacing the Honour Company. When finally the long ceremony ended, and the regimental band had departed to its next scheduled location, I thought to myself, 'What a wonderful feeling it would be to have a *Grosser Zapfenstreich* to celebrate both peace and as the crowning conclusion to our victory.'[1]

23–27 June 1943

Three days of routine with beer and wine in the evenings and then on the 26th a big regimental sports day at Achtyrka. So now we now that the offensive is imminent. Where and when remain a mystery. On the 27th 'Make ready! Pack up everything!' Told you so!

28–30 June 1943

Entraining and loading exercises. The grenadiers had fallen off somewhat in the many weeks of 'quiet' living in village houses and it seems that a shaking-up is urgently required.

1 July 1943

'Alarm!' We left Achtyrka at 2100hrs for Tchernetshino. There must be a military hospital there, for the Red Cross nurses gave us a big kerbside send-off. 'Auf Wiedersehen!' they called to us. It was obviously well meant but many of us must have thought 'How long before we need you again?'

2 July 1943

The whole division rolled along a railway embankment heading north-east. The landscape came to life with movement. In the darkness we saw well-camouflaged Tigers, large squarish-looking colossi. And how many of them! At Novo-Borissovka more panzers and the new tracked self-propelled guns. Also other kinds of panzers in great numbers. Our own well-camouflaged resting area is about 6km from Borissovka.

3 July 1943

From our camouflaged vehicles lying near the Rollbahn we saw the new Panther tanks pass, all with the long barrel and looking very stylish. It is incredible the huge amount of material here: panzers of all kinds, assault guns, anti-tank panzers and armoured artillery on tracks. We have never seen so much armour and might on tracks before! We must be going to push through to the Urals!

Notes

1. Because the chapter relating to his induction into and training with *Grossdeutschland* as from mid-July 1941 appears to have been censored from the original volume published in Germany, the author leaves us in the dark as to certain aspects of indoctrination which *Grossdeutschland* recruits must have undergone. The regiment was an elite unit which provided the security at the Führer-HQs, therefore its loyalty to Hitler would have been beyond question. The *Grosser Zapfenstreich*, included in National Socialist solar mysticism, appears to have been celebrated at the Front only by *Grossdeutschland* and the Waffen-SS. Therefore the Waffen-SS, who bore the name *Sig*, the object of their devotion,

on their collar patches and flag, had a closer affinity with the *Grossdeutschland* Regiment than with any other.

Author SS-Obergruppenführer Fritz Weitzel explained that since time immemorial the German tribes worshipped only the visible Sun. 'For five thousand years, Nordic folk have used the runic alphabet to express symbolically a sacred idea. One of the oldest symbols is the swastika, the symbol of the sacred cycle of the sun, to be understood today as the sacred symbol of the Nordic racial ideology, and our Third Reich . . .' The rune *Sig* (the single lightning flash) signifies The Victorious Sun. The double rune *Sig-Sig* on the SS collar patch expresses the old motto *Sig und Sal* (the Victorious Sun and Salt), i.e the redemption which comes with the victory of the Sun.' The book mentions the two occasions for lighting fires of praise to the Sun as being Easter (*Ostern*, which is itself of German origin), and the *Sonnenwendfeir* on 21 June. Source: Fritz Weitzel, *Die Gestaltung der Feste im Jahres- und Lebenslauf in der SS-Familie* as authorized for publication by the Reichsführer-SS in 1939. (TN)

At Shachty a statue of Lenin appears to be welcoming German infantrymen.

A self-propelled 2cm Flak at Shachty.

Pontoon bridge over the River Manytsh.

The ferry over the Donetz was repeatedly targeted by Russian bombers.

The confluence of the Don and Manytsh, 5 August 1942.

Exhausted, they slept where they dropped during a halt near Gedoloff on the Manytsh.

Grossdeutschland graves along the route of the advance, 1942.

20 July 1942: the ferry service over the Donetz.

The shield indicates the demarcation line between Europe and Asia on the Manytsh embankment, summer 1942.

Captured guns along the permanent way awaiting collection.

The railway station at Makeyevka.

A training day on the mortar, September 1942.

A group photo before an operation.

Mortar troops on an exercise.

Feldwebel Rhedanz taking leave of his men.

The mortar captain at the gunsight of a heavy mortar.

A peaceful meal before the heavy defensive fighting at Rzhev.

A rest period shared with a family near Stalino.

A graveyard at Rzhev by no means full yet. Most of the losses at Rzhev were suffered by *Grossdeutschland* Division.

Very many *Grossdeutschland* comrades found their final resting place here.

Josef 'Jupp' Dörfler in a trench near Rzhev, autumn 1942.

Jupp after his award of the *Nahkampfspange* (Close Combat Clasp) in Bronze, worn above his jacket left pocket.

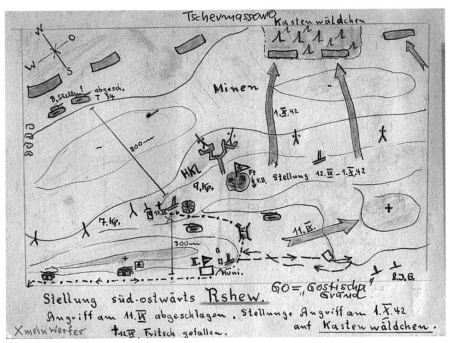

Map by Hans Rehfeldt, 'Position south-eastwards of Rzhev, attack 11 September beaten off, attack trench position 1 October 1942. on Kasten woods. X = my mortar +12 September, Fritsch fell. HKL = main front line'.

Sie sahen "das Weiße im Auge des Gegners"

Die Verleihung des Infanterie-Sturmabzeichens setzt voraus, daß sein Träger an drei Sturm-
angriffen in vorderster Linie mit der Waffe in der Hand einbrechend, und zwar an drei ver-
schiedenen Kampftagen teilgenommen hat, also an Nahkämpfen, in denen er „das Weiße im Auge
des Gegners" zu sehen bekam.

'They Saw the Whites of the Enemy's Eyes'. The Infantry Assault Badge was awarded to soldiers who had proved themselves in close combat.

Letter from his company commander notifying Hans Rehfeldt of the award:

'My dear Rehfeldt! It is with great pleasure that I can award you today the Infantry Assault Badge as notified by the Herrn Regimental Commander for the attacks in the Russian campaigns in which you have taken part. On behalf of the entire company I express my heartiest congratulations on this proud distinction. I hope that you will soon be feeling right enough again to make an early return to the company. Heil Hitler!'

Felddienststelle
Feldpostnr.09964 E
O.U., den 11.10.1942

Mein lieber Rehfeldt !

Zu meiner grössten Freude kann ich Ihnen heute das Infanterie-Sturmabzeichen, welches Ihnen durch den Herrn Regiments-Kommandeur für die im russ. Feldzuge mitgemachten Sturmangriffe, übermitteln. Im Namen der ganzen Kompanie spreche ich Ihnen zu dieser stolzen Auszeichnung meine herzlichsten Glückwünsche aus.

Ich hoffe, dass es Ihnen gesundheitlich wieder recht gut geht und dass Sie bald zur Kompanie zurückkommen können.

Heil Hitler !

Hauptmann und Kp.- Chef

Felddienststelle
Feldpostnr.09964 E
O.U., den 11.10.1942

Herrn

Hans Rehfeldt,

Hagen i. Westf.
Mackensenstr. 8

Anliegend übersendet Ihnen die Dienststelle das Infanterie-
Sturmabzeichen mit Besitzurkunde und Schreiben für Ihren
Sohn Hans, mit der Bitte um Weiterleitung an seine augen-
blickliche Lazarettanschrift, die infolge der Postschwie-
rigkeiten bei der Dienststelle nicht bekannt ist.

Heil Hitler !

Hauptmann u.Kp.- Chef

Letter with certificate regarding the award of the Infantry Assault Badge sent to the author's father for forwarding to the military hospital in which Rehfeldt was a patient and which could not be determined due to difficulties with the post at that time.

Front and back of the Wounded Label. Millions of German ground troops had one at some time during the six years of the war.

Stamp and signature of the senior surgeon authorizing admission to military hospital.

Following the wound he received at Rzhev on 13 October 1942, Hans Rehfeldt was brought to Reserve Military Hospital VIII in the Ulica Pasteur hospital, Warsaw.

Mansion and grounds near Warsaw.

The Warsaw Market Square before the destruction of the city in 1943/44.

A large Warsaw church.

Street scene in Market Square, Warsaw.

Hans Rehfeldt was given home convalescent leave after his recovery.

During the war the author collected leaflets and other Soviet propaganda material. This picture shows a collection of stamps with the hammer and sickle and a war lottery ticket.

Russian war lottery tickets with patriotic motifs.

Chapter 15

Operation *Zitadelle*

---

4 July 1943

At 1500hrs III Battalion advanced with Stuka support to take out the enemy forward outposts and so capture the high ground ahead of the enemy front line. This created the planned favourable starting point for the offensive next day.

In the evening we moved to Tomarovka via Borissovka. The Führer's order was read out to us:

> My soldiers! You are embarking on a great offensive whose outcome may be of decisive importance for the war. Your victory will reinforce throughout the whole world the conviction that any resistance to the German Wehrmacht is ultimately in vain. Another severe defeat for the Russians will strike ever more doubt in the wavering ranks of the Russian armed forces that victory for them is possible. The powerful blow which will hit them tomorrow morning will shake them to the marrow. You should be aware that everything may depend upon the success of this battle!

We moved up to the Front during the hours of darkness. Two hundred of the new Panthers are to be deployed with us. We also saw some of these Panthers immobile by the roadside with engines burning through overheating. A bad omen? We also saw our armoured and self-propelled heavy infantry guns. I Battalion mortars and heavy MGs have SPWs. Only II Battalion mortars and heavy MGs will be going into battle on foot and without armour protection!

4–5 July 1943

During the night 2 Company *Grossdeutschland* panzer pioneers entered the depression this side of Gerzovka in order to clear a mine-free corridor for the attack. My mortar group and one group of heavy MGs provided them with protection. Ivan noticed nothing. In a few hours our pioneers defused and removed 2,700 mines without incident. The mine-free lanes were then marked out. We returned exhausted and lay quiet so as not to alert Ivan. From our departure position we could not see the Russian advanced lines, first it was necessary to pass through the area ahead of Gerzovka to reach higher ground. The former German winter position had bypassed it. We had still not received any orders nor hour for the attack, which surprised us.

5 July 1943

1450hrs. Much aerial activity by our side. A lone German fighter shot down six Russian bombers out of a formation of eight! Our artillery has begun its softening-up bombardment. We are rolling! Ahead, behind and all around we see hundreds of vehicles breaking out from under their camouflage – countless panzers, tank destroyers, motorized Pak, 2cm quadruple Flaks, 3.7cm Flak and assault guns, including some with the long barrel. Many other armoured vehicles and ammunition wagons coming up from the rear. Amidst it all are ourselves with our mortars and the MG people with big spaces between us in the long single file. Everybody is making his way through the depression towards the mine-free corridors. It is thick with vehicles. Now Ivan is awake and his Il 2 'sewing machines' come to strafe the attackers. They also drop bombs and fire rockets. This is hellishly dangerous. We lost our regimental adjutant Hauptmann Gerhard Beckendorf to an aircraft bomb in the first hour, today Leutnant Werner Holzgrefe, III Battalion adjutant, fell at Tcherkassoiye. The panzers have first to get across a ditch and then the marked-out mine-free area cleared by the pioneers last night limits the width of the breakthrough gap. Pioneers forward! Everyone is crowding together in the depression. We hope and pray for no massive ground attack by aircraft. Wherever they dropped they would be bound to hit something. Where is the Russian artillery barrage? At the moment their fire is very scattered after we wiped out their artillery spotters. Our own heavy batteries are firing deep into the Russian rear areas. Our first panzers have crossed the ditch. Damn! More large minefields. Tread only in the footprint of the man ahead! We are pressing forward but only slowly, for there is danger everywhere. Meanwhile Ivan's artillery has come to life but we feared much more curtain fire initially. During the night we stayed ahead of the tank ditch and dug our foxholes and mortar pit deeper than usual. 'Whoever digs deeper has more chance of survival . . .'

5–6 July 1943

The pioneers cleared another corridor through the minefield while assault guns and 3.7cm Flak gave them cover. Then it started raining, the ground became as slippery as soft soap. Overhead the bombers rumbled, Ivan's anti-aircraft guns fired at them intermittently. At midday the advance continued and we reached the Russian main defensive line to the north-east. We saw and heard our panzers firing and received some of the fire meant for them. There is an occupied hill ahead of us which looks impossible to take. More anti-panzer ditches, barbed-wire entanglements and well-disguised field fortifications, bunkers and trenches: Ivan had to give them up finally after panzers managed to attack them from the flanks. Our mortar has not fired yet, we are spending most of our time with our noses to the ground. Fortunately for us the Russian defensive fire seems very haphazard. Possibly their batteries were cut down by our artillery bombardment and air attacks, otherwise it is inexplicable.

We are through. After much effort we have made our first breakthrough and now 'full speed ahead' is demanded. Cursing and swearing under the weight of the mortar parts, two ammunition cases, a pistol in the hand or carbine at the hip, we run forward gasping to keep up with the infantry. But what a magnificent sight when we look around us! Our panzers and assault guns dominating all the hilltops, in all the gorges and gullies our lorries, ambulances, ammunition wagons, radio wagons, panzers and artillery. Infantry reinforcements and support services trail behind as far as the eye can see. I have never seen so much material, not even at the beginning of our summer offensive in 1942. It looks chaotic, but the terrain dictates movement.

When the Russian firing abated somewhat the advance continued immediately. Our infantry attacked the village of Gerzovka. Ivan sent three T-34s to defend it. Our Panthers left two of these burning in front of the village: the other tank turned tail. Our lorries collected us and dropped us off forward. Ivan stepped up his artillery response, the air became filled with the rumble of panzer engines, the aircraft of the combatants, the crack and detonation of artillery shelling. Our target was an array of anti-tank guns, dangerous for our panzers. With our mortar bombs keeping his head down, Ivan could not aim and fire calmly: often we saw his ammunition exploding. When a known gun fell silent, we rejoiced loudly. The entrenching tool was often a lifesaver, for besides our personal foxholes we had to dig a larger and deeper pit with room for the mortar and five men: the three mortar crew, the mortar commander and at least one ammunition runner.

7 July 1943

The hilltop village of Dubrovka was very heavily defended and we made poor progress. Once we began firing from a fresh position we came under fire from a T-34. 'Dismantle mortar. Assemble around vehicles!' Obergefreiter Schleier and Grenadier Karge fell, Gefreiters Wagner and Köstler were wounded, all within a few minutes. We boarded the lorries and roared off in pursuit of our panzer spearhead, almost 2km ahead, passing field positions our troops had occupied. From our left as we passed by, Ivan concentrated all his firepower – anti-tank guns, mortars, MGs and sub-machine guns – on our lorries which were conveying, besides ourselves, our ammunition, the fuel canisters and four anti-tank mines. They got a hit on the radiator which made it difficult for our driver to see his way, and in the woods another lorry ran over a mine, front wheel left side. 'Dismount! With equipment!' We sought shelter in former Russian positions. Our panzers had assembled just inside the forward edge of the wood and we came in for the overspill from the heavy artillery fire they attracted. In the abandoned enemy trench system was a bunker built of wooden beams, already too packed for me to enter. Artillery rounds falling nearby made the bunker tremble. I crouched low by the entrance. Ivan was firing with 15.2cm calibre field guns or heavier; if the bunker received a direct hit I would have had a chance to get clear, but from a hit in the bunker entrance I would receive the full load of splinters. An incoming shell hit a corner of the bunker. The wooden beams splintered, the earth sprayed up, the noise deafened me for a while but I was unharmed and the first man to get clear of the bunker. Only two men were wounded – splinters and crushing. A section of trench was found 50m to our right.

The enemy artillery died down and our panzers advanced, followed by 6 Company and ourselves. Despite enemy MGs and mortars we ejected Ivan from his complicated and refined field installations which extended over 3 or 4km of flat ground and cornfields. The Russians liked to play dead, and it was essential to ensure that they *were* dead or they would fire at your back once you had passed. Therefore Russians whether alive or dead got one chance: '*Ruki werch a ne to budu strelyat!*' 'Hands up or I shoot!' We took a large number of prisoners. During this advance we had self-propelled 2cm and 3.7cm Flak and some armoured personnel carriers with MGs and flamethrowers as our escorts. The Russian field defences were very cleverly designed, well camouflaged and deep! We had a machine-pistol company to face ahead of us, their weapons chattering ceaselessly, but mostly firing too high. Our infantry had casualties but the pioneers smoked them out of their nests with the flamethrowers. The village ahead was Szyrzev and we took it quickly. We had a crazy front line: Ivan to the left of us, in front of us and at two o'clock from us. We had driven a wedge into his defences, however, and the day, though hard, had been successful. By sunset we had achieved our objective. This kind of attack often results in undesirable indentations in the Front, and so in the evening we assembled in the many gulleys and gulches offering at least enough protection to walk about in safety. The infantry was positioned at the edges of the hills, our mortars were in pits in the ground, our spotter forward with the infantry company leader to receive his wishes for transmission to us. The heavy MG groups likewise. The ammunition and provisions lorries and some ambulances occupied the narrow gorges. Our dead and the wounded unable to walk were looked for and brought in. The thought struck me suddenly: all the gulleys and gorges here are full of vehicles and people. Hurry, hurry! Look for positions, dig foxholes! Who knew when Ivan would not realize it too! And we had not long to wait.

We heard the typical sound of his Ilyushin 2 ground-attack aircraft arriving, 8.8cm Flak, 2cm and 3.7cm Flak, MGs and carbines fired a welcome. All night the bombing attacks went on! Without waiting for the order we dug our mortar pit and foxholes very much deeper remembering the motto: 'Who digs deeper . . .' The sky and the entire terrain were lit up by Ivan's 'good old sewing machines'. Dig deeper! In the early hours of the morning, after a few hours' exhausted sleep, we readied ourselves for the next attack. We have here a real battle of material, and a war of attrition.

8 July 1943

Our direction of advance was now to the north-west. 'Make ready! Take up equipment!' We followed behind our panzers on foot. The unpleasant side of this equation is that attacking panzers attract defensive fire from anti-tank guns and enemy tanks, and often artillery. The troops proceeding behind or between panzers or assault guns receive whatever fails to hit the armour. Ivan fired straddling salvoes. 'Don't lie down, keep going forward!' That required determination. We hastened forward, ducking low, threw ourselves down, jumped up, kept going, shells exploding all around us. The closer one can get to the enemy, the 'safer' one is against his artillery. We slipped through without casualties, always behind the panzers. We could hear their MGs and guns shooting at enemy infantry throwing Molotov cocktails and laying surface mines.

Thirty Stukas appeared in two waves. The noise made now by our own and the Russian artillery, panzer engines, panzer guns firing, aircraft above dropping bombs and firing on-board weapons, the chatter of MGs and sub-machine guns: add our mortars to all that and the 'pressure' on the ears is enough to render one deaf. Shouted orders, if heard at all, seem to originate from a very 'thin' voice.

Our objective was the village of Krasnoiye-Dubrova on a hill. Our panzers were already waiting to attack. We were to be east of the Rollbahn through long gulleys, protecting the flanks. Our artillery was very active. We were preceded by the self-propelled 15cm heavy artillery[1] and the 'industrious' Flak. The infantry company advanced, we mortar crews gasping under the weight and having to climb uphill. The attack on the defensive positions was successful. My mortars pinned Ivan down for as long as was necessary. Being under 12cm Russian mortar fire was very unpleasant, the bombs being almost inaudible until the very short hiss upon arrival. Our advantage was the ricochet mortar bomb which could get at Ivan in his trench, two-thirds of the bomb exploding 2–3m high after bouncing. The Russians didn't have these, but instead of the single standard mortar as we had, he came equipped with various sizes from the 'spade-size' mortar to the 12cm. (Until then our heaviest mortar was 8.14cm calibre.) As the war went on we copied the Russian 12cm mortar, but this had to be transported by vehicle.

After a fierce infantry fight we occupied the hill and set up our mortar pits in a field of rye where we could move about unseen. The night was very dark, the moon waxing and pale. To our left not far off we could see the elongated village of Werchopenye (werch = high) blazing in many places. To our annoyance it began to rain. Throughout my turn as sentry I watched the heavy fighting for this village. Our neighbour on our left to the west, Panzer Regiment 6/ Panzer Division 3, had difficulties because the Russians were making energetic attacks to get to the east for breathing space. Often Ivan attacked with packs of between twenty and forty T-34s. His leadership was inferior to ours, and unlike our panzers his tanks had no radio, and we were happy to leave him to our Pak or panzers and assault guns. We had an interesting innovation, an egg-shaped glass container filled with ammonia containing a test-tube with a salt/sulphuric acid mixture. When the glass was crushed, the two fluids combined to cause an irritating mist which 'blinded' the tank crew and put them out of action. However, we found that these eggs were very fragile and in the end they were never used by us in action.

9 July 1943

Today our objective was the capture of Werchopenye for which purpose we set out at 0700hrs with ten Tigers, ten Panthers and about twenty Panzer IVs, the proven workhorses, and air support from twelve Stukas and some He 111s. The ground troops entered the first houses at the north-east corner of the village, our mortars set up east of it. The Russians replied with heavy artillery, anti-tank and tank fire and their 12cm mortars. It was like being back at Rzhev. We crouched down filthy, wet and exhausted in our foxholes. The artillery of both sides fired without a pause, then the Il 2 'sewing machines' arrived and bombed the gullies where we had left the vehicles. The light Flak fired furiously, but these aircraft are armoured and not many of them get knocked down by a 2cm. The rockets with which these aircraft are equipped are something new.

We engaged the Russian mortar positions with some success. Unteroffizier Franz Schlossbauer was our spotter until he was wounded for the third time on this Front. In the afternoon we were relieved and went to Novosselovka where the sun beat down; the Russian positions were higher up and they could look down and see our every movement. They pounded us with their 7.62cm general-purpose guns: our MG42 rattled away at them from their right flank, then III Battalion made an all-out attack. Suddenly it started raining and so we sat in mud and filth. We looked like wild pigs, hands and faces black, unshaven since 4 July.

Ivan seemed to be growing in strength. Russian tanks were advancing from an easterly direction. This was very bad news because they knew our positions. The fields of wheat had been steamrollered flat so that we had no conceal-ment: every time we moved they subjected us to violent fire. We thought about digging deeper, but then Ivan began to fire salvoes of mortar bombs at us combined with missiles from the Stalin organ and so it didn't matter how deep we dug. We were nailed down at last! 'Shit position!' said the infantry. It was so serious that we could not return to the mortar pit. We fired back to show we were not out of action: finally the order came to decamp. These last few days with the infantry and other units had resulted in many losses for us.

10 July 1943

We withdrew individually at long intervals and assembled in a broad gully lying cross-wise to the village. Here we spent the night. I excavated a hole on the slope on the side nearer the village, fairly safe from artillery, and slept for eight hours. Then we began walking back with our equipment like a long drawn-out line of filthy pigs. We had not gone far before we came under artillery and anti-tank fire, which meant they could see us: we spaced ourselves out more generously and increased the pace. This made little difference and we had to suffer endless lying down and getting up for another kilometre. A heavy shell which landed 4m from us failed to explode. Finally we came to a deep gully, in glorious sunshine and, assuming ourselves to be out of sight, we rested, bathed in a stream and acted happy as sandboys. Rifle fire and MG bursts announced that Ivan could still see us: he followed this up with heavy mortar fire. He must have had a good spotter position. We set off again through a village to the Rollbahn where we knew our lorries were waiting. Once aboard we were driven northwards to our panzer spearhead. The lorries went into cover, we lay in a wood with our artillery positions in a gully directly to our rear. Based on my experience I built a 'bunker' in front of the artillery, the excavation being particularly deep and covered over with beams and earth. In the pallid light of a Hindenburg lamp (a candle in a tin can) I wrote a letter – sign of life – to my parents. The shooting went on all night without pause but we were so exhausted that we slept.

12 July 1943

We were awoken at midnight, 'Make ready with equipment for special assignment!' It was explained that we had to creep through the Russian field positions to a bend in the Rollbahn. We must make not the slightest noise but remain at instant readiness to fight should we be detected. We were successful, but we saw Ivan and he must have seen us but mistaken us for his own troops. We, that is to say our heavy MG groups, the 6 Company battlegroup and my mortar group, went right, east of the Rollbahn to Obayan, a good 75km from Kursk. We passed through small gorges and over hills unnoticed, arriving about 800m behind the third Russian defensive line and dug in, keeping a sharp lookout. The full moon was on the 17th, and so the nights were very bright. About 200m ahead to our right, a T-34 was positioned on an elevation and firing at traffic on the Rollbahn. We formed a hedgehog for all-round defence and then looked on – as if in a cinema – as our II Battalion, the panzer reconnaissance detachment and some panzers moved up and down the Rollbahn. We experienced a German attack from the Russian side! When the Russian infantry pulled back in front of our noses with their heavy weapons, mortars, anti-tank and light anti-tank guns in battalion strength, we opened fire with everything we had. Ivan had not expected that we could be nearer than his most advanced front line. After our surprise we heard the rattling tracks and loud engines of our assault guns climbing out of a gully to our right. After getting over their shock at finding German infantry so far forward, we pointed out the T-34 on the hill still shooting at II Battalion on the Rollbahn, the assault guns manoeuvred and after a few rounds the T-34 was burning. This was the signal for all the Russian tanks and anti-tank guns in the village to fire at us: our artillery, rocket launchers and mortars replied by bombarding their village from a deep gorge. For the rest of the day their artillery pounded the gullies and gorges where they rightly guessed our vehicles, artillery and panzers were. We discovered that in that village alone twenty-two T-34s had been stationed.

Ilyushin 2 aircraft came and set about the locality with bombs, rockets, cannon and MGs. Burning vehicles in the gorges marked their success. The Russian 'tank village' was a mass of flame. When dusk fell we moved to a better position: this was routine once the enemy knew our existing position and had fired at it accurately. Our seven mortars were placed on a hilltop. This was not ideal because the advantage of the mortar as a high-trajectory weapon is that it can fire from cover at the enemy in cover. Our best shooting positions were gorges, deep trenches or behind houses, from where we fired indirectly. On this occasion the advantage was that we could observe the fall of our own bombs. Ivan's tanks were feeling their way forward but then halted and the night fell quiet. We learned at the food wagon that we had taken 24,000 prisoners, destroyed 1,800 tanks, 250 guns and an additional 1,080 anti-tank guns destroyed or captured!

13 July 1943: Part One

We crouched low, dug in on our hilltop, panzers and assault guns on our flanks and behind us. In the first hours of daylight the artillery of both sides exchanged salvoes. Our mortars dropped a barrage before their infantry who were feeling their way forward. The weather was cool and rainy. Ivan persisted with his advance until 1600hrs when Russian infantry appeared suddenly in inexhaustible numbers from every imaginable gorge and gully. With their tanks they reached the first heights! Despite our fire, the Russians were making good progress, the range was ever decreasing, we had to crank the mortar barrels ever closer to the vertical, and they were getting damned hot! Because the enemy would soon have been able to see into our mortar positions we had to disassemble the weapons and pull back under infantry fire. We were out of ammunition! The baseplate of my mortar had almost sunk into the ground on account of the number of bombs fired! Our group leader Unteroffizier Kellner was feeding the bombs into the barrel himself while we cranked like crazy at the elevating and traverse gears under heavy fire. I was almost deaf in both ears. Our own infantry was running back. Kellner began firing his pistol wildly here and there upon hearing the shouts of 'Urrah!' coming from almost all around us. Sub-machine gun and MG fire whipped past my nose. I ducked, Kellner shouted: 'Dismantle mortar at once, assemble in the large gully!'

While the ammunition runners took to their carbines, our bipod gunner removed the bipod with the adjusting gears and ran off without first buckling on the carrying frame. Now I had to hold the red-hot barrel with both hands while Kellner dropped the last bombs inside it! Had I not been wearing asbestos gloves this would not have been possible. 'Rehfeldt! Go! Into the large gully!' Kellner shouted. I had to use the barrel as a lever to prise the baseplate out of the ground: the steel ribs of the lower plate were full of mud, which made the baseplate even heavier, but I had no time to clean it, I had to lift the carrying frame and strap the plate to my shoulders. This at least protected my back during my own 'withdrawal movement'!

13 July 1943: Part Two

The village from where Ivan had broken out was called Kalinovka. Upon my breathless arrival in the battalion's gully, bullets whistling around me, I searched for my mortar crews. They had slunk off into narrow side gullies with the heavy equipment. I sought cover there myself since chaos reigned in the gully proper. Our battalion commander Major Bethge was attempting to regroup II Battalion prior to a counter-attack! Suddenly T-34s appeared over the ridge and we jumped aboard a Flak panzer returning from re-ammunitioning which took us up the slope out of the gully and stopped at the edge of a wood. We had come 500m and there we sat and waited. We could see a host of our panzers standing on the Rollbahn waiting for the order to advance. General Hörnlein appeared and admonished Kellner for not remaining in the gully. He was quite dazed. Therefore we reboarded the Flak panzer and returned there. We were very irritated that Ivan had managed to eject us from our position, and with *Furor Teutonicus* our panzers now went for him. Roaring 'Hurrah!' at the tops of our voices we embarked on our counter-attack. Ivan's infantry turned tail. 100m to our left, Major Bethge led his men forward. Suddenly he fell, shot through the neck. A young lieutenant with pistol drawn shouted loudly, 'II Battalion, follow me!' The advance continued a few hundred metres with the men of the infantry company behind him. We mortars headed as fast as we could back to our former firing position. The counter-attack seemed to have been successful – then I saw the young lieutenant fall dead. A violent skirmish now erupted. We had not been able to reach our mortar pit and so, overburdened by the mortar components, we charged, firing our sub-machine guns, pistols or carbines wildly into the Russian throng until we regained the position we had lost just an hour before. Ivan kept on running, our panzers forcing him to retire to the left, western flank where he would run into our attack spearhead. Our infantry had also reached their former lines. Now we looked for a new spotting position with a much better field of observation for the mortars, not wishing to repeat the ugly surprise of a few hours previously. Gradually our men calmed down and worked to improve their foxholes. We moved cautiously, not wishing to betray our positions.

14 July 1943

A silence has fallen over the battlefield. Our long-range artillery and the enemy's fires overhead, but the shells explode far in the distance, probably where troop concentrations are suspected. During the day we observed the Russian positions and noted where he had put his MGs and mortars. Naturally both sides carry out this kind of reconnaissance. In the evening Ivan's tanks made an effort to attack but were deterred by our artillery barrage.

15 July 1943

At night one does not always sleep between the turns of sentry duty for fear of being surprised. In the hours of darkness the Russians often try to capture a soldier in his foxhole and 'spirit him away'. These are dramatic moments generally resulting in the Russians being driven off or shot. But many of our men have been lost in this way. Our scouting parties have the same task of capturing enemy soldiers for interrogation. Today I have been a soldier for precisely two years. Ivan is quiet, the sun is shining. From this position we shall embark on Operation *Roland*, a limited advance to the north either side of the Obayan Rollbahn. The Luftwaffe bombed the Russians in strips 15km broad.

Our Stukas and artillery are concentrating on targets far in the rear, of which we can hear only the effects. Ivan let us have some mortar salvoes, and we fired back at his infantry, not at single individuals but groups of about ten.

16 July 1943

The night was wet and cold and I sat in the narrow, muddy mortar pit. The groundsheets were tensed but the rain still dripped everywhere, under my collar and down my back. I bailed out the water with mess tins. (Radius of mortar emplacement 3 x 4m, 1–2m deep). My No. 2 and No. 3 gunners, exhausted, slept all through it partially submerged. In the morning Ivan fired his mortars at us occasionally. Russian bombers attacked the many gullies behind us where we park our vehicles. On their second run they bombed their own positions by mistake. That gave us something to cheer. We have heard that in Italy, Marshal Badoglio has gone over to the Western Allies. Mussolini has been deposed. So what will happen to our Operation *Roland*? News comes that 3 Panzer Division is to relieve us. Why? After we took all surplus ammunition to the battalion command post, Ivan attacked at 2000hrs. I heard the order shouted, 'Anyone with ammunition, fire at will!' After Major Bethge was wounded, Oberleutnant Konopka took over as battalion leader. Now a wild exchange of fire ensued for half an hour. The planned thrust to the north has been abandoned but our relief failed to appear. We lay shivering with cold (in July!) in our foxholes. At night, only sporadic firing. The word is, there has been a high-level Führer-conference.

17 July 1943

I woke this morning to bright sunshine. At the front today it remained fairly quiet, nobody fired all day except the respective artilleries. I went to the artillery and rocket observation posts from where one can watch Ivan 800m away. The Ivans are running around in the fields, almost on the horizon one sees Russian columns. The Ilyushins attacked our numerous vehicles in the gorges and gulches. When they went away I read my mail and dreamed of leave, peace, summer, Salzburg, Berchtesgaden, holiday trips, being happy, joy of living. Instead, here: war, fighting, filth and death. And the only liberating word – *Scheisse*! Shit! Three flights each of twenty-five Stukas with fighter cover came over and circled like vultures. We took cover just in case but they knew their target and unloaded the lot on Ivan's front sector. Approaching from the west, dark rain clouds.

18 July 1943

Sunday, full moon with much cloud. During the night we heard loud singing and music coming from Ivan, women's voices too. Probably rounded up from the villages to celebrate. Celebrate what? Later we learned of the Russian offensive on the Orel Bend. the so-called 'big relief offensive'. In the morning it was announced that Operation *Roland* has been called off. The SS-Panzer Divisions *Leibstandarte Adolf Hitler* and *Das Reich* have been withdrawn from the Front and all offensive plans here have been suspended. Russian aerial reconnaissance reported the roads to the rear as being crammed with German convoys and as a result sixty bombers and Ilyushin 2s bombed the columns and villages to the south. We were alert for a Russian attack but nothing came of it. During the day it became sunny and warm. I fired with a long Russian rifle at 'Ratas' (Russian fighters) and some damned 'sewing machines' but unfortunately without success. Then we fired on a gully where Russian mortar positions were suspected. 'Ten rounds at aiming point 3, fire at will!' Just as the last bomb left the barrel the first one exploded amongst the Ivans, and there were still nine on their way! Ivan responded promptly with forty to fifty rounds to our ten. We were already in cover, a couple came down close but the rest were all 100m over. I dug my mortar pit a bit deeper. Who knew if Ivan wouldn't improve? Otherwise the day passed all quiet.

19 July 1943

We are halted near the village of Kalinovka (5km south of Obayan and 50km from Kursk) in an advanced position on the north-western edge of our great attack wedge. More to the west-south-west are the companies of 3 Panzer Division; eastwards and north-eastwards to our right is 11 Panzer Division. Farther east still are the SS-Panzer Corps and 7, 19 and 6 Panzer Divisions. They make up the broad spearhead of the attack. For the moment, however, all has come to a standstill. We are told that the Anglo-Americans will be landing in Sicily. 'Badoglio's treachery'. Operation *Zitadelle* has been cancelled by Führer-order, Waffen-SS units are being taken out of the line for transfer to Italy. The official word is that we are being pulled back to the starting point at Gerzovka. We think that is nonsense. On watch for an hour from 0200hrs only aircraft could be heard, in the far distance and over our and the enemy's rear. Across No Man's Land I saw tanks and columns of lorries moving about and then stopping, searchlights blinking. After dawn everybody got an issue of a parcel 'For Front Soldiers in the Great Struggle' more generally known as 'Nazi Packets'. Contents: chocolate bars with filling, fruit paste, creamy caramels, biscuits, a roll of fruit drops and a packet of Juno, advertising slogan: 'All Berlin is smoking Juno – thick and round.' The edible parts are soon consumed, then we puff away on the Junos. Good for morale!

Still no news of our relief. The advance party came yesterday for briefing on the situation and our Front sector. It was fairly misty all day, at noon Ivan made a sort of very tentative attack soon beaten off with concentrated fire from our heavy MGs, mortars and light and heavy infantry guns. We still do not know 'the big picture'. From 5 July we advanced from Gerzovka for 45–48km northwards through the deeply staggered Russian positions to a point 5km from Obayan, and now we're going back? What's the point of that?

20 July 1943

Officers of 3 Panzer Division came again for a briefing. Across No Man's Land only light shooting all day. Through binoculars at the observation post one could see columns of Russian vehicles and tanks, artillery and support services moving back and forth. It looked fairly indecisive to me. Their attempts to break out to the east here, under pressure from all sides, are being frustrated. At 2300hrs our forward outposts were withdrawn and we disengaged silently from the enemy. 3 Panzer Division occupied different positions when they came to relieve us. After a difficult trudge we reached our vehicles. 'Load equipment, keep hand weapons with you, mount up.' We left heading south on the Rollbahn through Yakovlev, Tomarovka and Borissovka to Slehovi. There we washed, shaved and slept.

Notes

1. Here is meant the 24-tonne howitzer-panzer Hummel, 15cm sFH 18/1 on Gw.III/IV (Sf), Sd.Kfz 165. Although originally planned as an interim measure, it remained operational from 1942 until May 1945. The design was a combination of the Gw.III/IV Nashorn (Panzer IV chassis, Panzer III engine, gearing and steering) fitted with a 15cm 18/1 L/30 heavy field howitzer in an open-top 10–30mm armoured casemate. Only eighteen rounds could be carried on the vehicle. Source: Alexander Lüdeke, *Panzer der Wehrmacht Band 1, 1933–1945*, Motorbuch, 2014, pp. 112–13 (with photo and sketch).

Chapter 16

In the Karachev Woods:
Grossdeutschland – the Fire Brigade

_____

21–22 July 1943

Our lorries rolled along paths, roads and Rollbahns heading north-north-west to the woods at Karachev. Near here Ivan has infiltrated north of the large Rollbahn and railway line as part of his major offensive against Orel. We – *Grossdeutschland*, the fire brigade – have been called to the burning Front. Even our front-line newspaper is called *Die Feuerwehr* – 'The Fire Brigade'. At a fast pace we passed through Borissovka, Graivoron, Boromliya, Ssumi and Belopolye to Putivel, then Gluchow and Lugani trailing great yellow-brown banners of dust. The dust lies thick and sluggish on the Rollbahn. In one village children and girls threw bouquets of wild flowers on the lorries. We responded with a friendly wave. From the style of the houses we can see we are heading north. In the Ukraine the houses are of loam and brushwood, painted white; on the other hand here there are the typical block houses often with carved woodwork at the windows. We often passed through totally gutted villages, their former occupants living in misery in holes in the ground. Other elements of our division have been moved up by train.

23 July 1943

Today we reached Cheplokino. Speed is everything, we are told that Ivan is pouring into the woods at the sides of the Rollbahn. Squadrons of the Luftwaffe are overhead to assist the ground troops in the heavy fighting below. We spent the night in a village.

24 July 1943: Part One

Laundry, weapons cleaning, make and mend is our task for today. We are therefore certainly going to be busy. In the skies flights of Stukas going back and forth to the Front. For the first time I saw an He 111 towing a transport glider. 'Move out!' We passed through Karachev to Odrino, general heading north-east, and held up in a small wood, ready to fight because the situation remains fairly unclear. We have with us now Flak panzers, 15cm Hummels, tank destroyers and armoured personnel carriers. We still have no clear idea of what our intentions are supposed to be, though apparently we have to take two villages in which the Red Army and partisans are collaborating. Because our fighting elements are only arriving here 'as and when', we are going to be without the greater part of our tracked vehicles, including panzers and assault guns, from the outset. Our regiment is advancing in three battalions to Alechino, where the Russian infantry is dug in on a ridge. Our orders are to 'take this ridge and the guns!'

We advanced through a very dense wood and entered a village at top speed accompanied by tank destroyers and self-propelled quadruple Flak guns. There was little resistance. After a short pause and discussion we went on to the next village. Here there was more opposition, and half of it was burning already. We came under heavy fire from Ivan's 15.2cm 'Black Pig' and his general-purpose 7.62cm guns, while his heavy mortars aimed between the houses and bombarded the village square.

24 July 1943: Part Two

II Battalion is now led by Oberleutnant Konopka. A sign said the village was called Mertvoiye. It was burning fiercely, much smoke and fumes and great heat. We advanced, pistols in hand, mortar component on the back, sweat pouring from under the steel helmet down the face and into the eyes. We reached the end of the village with three dead: Unteroffizier Riedschewsky, Gefreiters Schleier and Stomberg. During the exchange of fire at the edge of the village square some beehives had been destroyed. The bees were buzzing round wildly and swarms attacked everyone whether German or Russian. The fighting was forgotten. Arms flailing, ducking low, we fought together to ward off the bees. Finally Ivan fled into the woods and we gave chase so as not to allow him any peace. We made contact with 6 Company.

After the conference there followed a brief preparation before proceeding to the third village. Luftwaffe bombers and Me 110s attacked Ivan from the air. In a clearing in the woods we came under attack by Stukas returning from a bombing raid who raked us with cannon fire until we released orange smoke to identify ourselves. After this fright we took the village of Alissov by storm and with loud cries of 'Hurrah!', then continued through these accursed Karachev Woods: to the left of us, therefore to the north-west, Russian heavy guns.

Pulses racing and bathed in sweat we even took the triangulated height. Unteroffizier Martin Scharfenberg was wounded. He was given a dressing and brought out. Company leader Oberleutnant Schmelter came past us from behind, heard our report and said to me, 'Rehfeldt! Take command of the mortars!' We advanced and were soon receiving anti-tank and tank fire from left and right. Dammit! Where the hell is the Front?

25 July 1943

Sunday. At 0400hrs a fresh attack, though at least we had our panzers back with us. The first village was taken relatively easily. Before the next we joined with other German units coming from our right and then entered. The Russians went to ground and the village fell to us! Now we searched all houses and cellars for Russians in hiding. The cellars were full of them. With weapons at the ready we stood clear and shouted down '*Russki! Poloshi oruyie i idi ssudan skorei!*' ('Russians, weapons down and come out quickly!'). If they didn't emerge within a reasonable time we lobbed two hand grenades inside. At the first cellar only one came out, a lightly wounded 20-year-old. On searching him we found German letters, belt and photos. He also had a German sub-machine gun. By his shoulder straps his rank was lieutenant, he wore decorations and a badge – Red Banner – therefore a Russian elite unit. In the other cellar were three Russian officers who came out with their hands up. They had on them German map cases, letters and sketches. I questioned them in my pidgin-Russian but was told nothing of value, only 'Orel offensive here' and 'What is going to happen to us?' All prisoners were taken back in a returning ammunition lorry. I took the decorations and badges from the dead Russians and, emulating the Russians, photos, snipers' badges and some of the big blood-red Commissar-Stars. The captured weapons included anti-tank and 7.62cm general-purpose guns, mortars, sub-machine guns and MGs. And we knew that we were facing the Russian 'Red Banner' Guards Division.

Next we remounted our vehicles and headed towards the Russian artillery positions. Meanwhile, it had begun to rain heavily: the advance continued through a dense pine forest providing poor visibility. Flak panzers preceded us with great caution on the narrow paths. Suddenly we came under fierce fire from the 15.2cm Black Pig, from tanks and anti-tank guns and naturally the heavy mortars. A hollow in the ground, an abandoned trench – these were the best hopes of cover. The noise was fearsome: trees crashing, shells splintering at head height: we had dead and wounded. We moved up to the edge of the wood. Here Ivan's barrage was impenetrable and so I took the mortars 150m back to a small clearing where we quickly dug a pit and then our own foxholes. My God! How much of Russia had we dug up already? Scarcely had we finished than came the shout 'Tanks ahead!' And Ivan's infantry with them. We fired our mortars and made the forest shake. Once that fright was over we had to keep advancing until 2000hrs: supposedly to the edge of the wood, and then the next village. It was not possible, Ivan resumed his barrage and forced us back. We lost one man dead but retrieved his body. It rained all night and we shivered in our holes in the earth. Freezing, hardly sleeping, we lay below ground with our wet groundsheets. The night passed quietly.

26 July 1943

At 0700hrs we attacked with a powerful force including eleven panzers. The mortars followed! It looked good until we came into tremendous defensive and barrage fire causing us many casualties. We selected a large bomb crater for our mortar position. A wounded man came back to us and was attended to by a *Sanitäter*. How the noise of firing resounded and echoed in those accursed woods! It was impossible to tell who was firing and from where. 'Change position forwards!' We leapt up and sprinted from the wood towards the village, taking cover behind a stack of timber. This attracted Ivan's fire and we tried to curl up as tightly as possible. A couple of men attempted to dig in but the ground was too stony for that. I noticed a large hole ahead and we scrambled towards it, finding it to be a squarish, sandy and not very deep cellar foundation for a house. Sooner than it takes to tell, my whole group was in it: we could hear and see our panzers and no matter how glad we might be to have them with us, we did not appreciate the enemy fire they drew down on themselves nearby. Finally they trundled forward. We had pressed ourselves against the excavated wall for protection and now Russian shelling began to fall very close. Raising my nose to assess our plight, I saw two Ivans running about distractedly and in a loud voice I shouted to them, *'Ivan! Sskoryei idi ssuda! ruki wwerch i poloshi orugyie!'* ('Ivan, come here quickly, hands up and weapons down!') They came to us at once in the mortar pit. We gave them a search and found a huge quantity of ammunition in their pockets and haversack, and some tubes of toothpaste but no toothbrush. When I asked the first Ivan what the toothpaste was for, by hand gestures he indicated that it was spread on bread as jam. We had a conversation about their families and peacetime jobs, and when the firing grew worse during our panzer attack, all of us huddled in the safest corner. Two enemies, common fears. Finally when the shooting abated, I lit a cigarette, at the first drag the Ivan stared at me, and I gave one each to him and his companion. They relaxed visibly: for them the war was over, although none of us knew if we were going to survive this. Ivan said to me: '*Gitler i Stalin kaputt – a potom mir budet*' ('If Hitler and Stalin are dead, then we shall have peace'). I had heard the same before often enough from prisoners, but also from Mamkas. And they believed it. As I handed over the two Russians to a returning unit, suddenly I heard tank fire: a T-34 and two smaller tanks. Reconnaissance? Our tank destroyers fired but without success, the tanks kept coming, went past our observation post and then halted. The turret hatch opened, the commander looked out briefly, and before we could shoot him with our carbines he went below and shut the hatch. The tank then moved forward a few metres and fired at the edge of our mortar pit. This attracted fire from a 15cm Hummel which forced him aside. The Russian infantry now attacked in regimental strength leaving our very weakened infantry companies little option but to pull back. Our mortars, being exposed in an advanced position, were dismantled for withdrawal into the woods, re-assembled near the battalion command post while Ivan sprayed fire into the firs and undergrowth of the wood. Leutnant Heinze fell. III Battalion, whose companies had recently suffered heavy losses, moved up to our left beside us as reinforcements together with a few panzers. The mortars provided covering fire for the infantry from the wood. Our dead and wounded were retrieved. The commanding officer's SPW received an anti-tank shell which killed two men although the vehicle remained battleworthy. All around us in the woods we could hear the sounds of fighting. When night fell, dead tired though we were, we dared not sleep. I lay wide awake, pistol at the ready, but must have nodded off for a couple of hours.

27 July 1943

At daybreak we came under artillery fire apparently from all directions. Had Ivan encircled us? 'Alarm!' Ivan was coming with tanks and infantry to our right while from our south, a T-34 appeared. Several enemy tanks were engaged by our panzers in front of our positions, projectiles which missed kept straight on for us at the mortars. So loud was the combined noise from tank and anti-tank fire and the resultant explosions that often our men would have to request orders to be repeated two or three times. 'Ivan's tanks are through! Tank destroyers forward!' We heard the engines of two Marder IIIs[1] start up and come through the wood towards us. In this difficult terrain the panzer drivers had plenty to occupy their attention and one of them overran my foxhole. I saw him coming and got out but all my things left ready to hand, my mess tin, field flask, hand grenades, were buried. Even our mortar pit was partially collapsed. At that moment all that mattered, however, was the two Marder IIIs! After a few rounds we heard, 'He's on fire! He's on fire!' The worst danger had been overcome, elsewhere the Russian attack had faltered and we fired at their retreating force with every barrel we had. The command panzer with the artillery spotter for our heavy infantry guns had drawn up near us while a second artillery spotter joined us at the mortars and set up telephone connections. The two spotters had a long and careful look at the battlefield and then began measuring the ranges. I heard their commands to fire. We had some panzers in the trees and bushes ahead of us, then came the edge of the wood and about 600–800m farther on in a cornfield a number of Russian anti-tank guns. After the zeroing-in it fell quieter. Suddenly a Russian MG opened fire and the spotter for the heavy guns fell near his command panzer. Where was the front line? Or was this a sniper in the woods? At dusk we heard nervous rifle and MG fire and mortar bombs exploding over at I Battalion. Whatever it was it soon blew over but was unpleasant while it lasted.

28 July 1943

The morning was relatively quiet, but just after returning to my foxhole at 0800hrs, the Russian artillery began firing whole salvoes into the trees, many splinters flying and whirling from shells exploding against the trunks. Our panzers moved up to the edge of the wood to do battle, the Russian artillery shifted their target to the panzers! Our artillery laid down a barrage and we fired with all our mortars at the attackers. As quickly as the hubbub started, it died down. We had destroyed three of the eight attacking T-34s. Ivan's infantry stood down.

I was chatting with the panzer people after they pulled back into the wood. There was a Panzer IV near my mortar pit. Ivan resumed shelling with his artillery, some of it falling close: Ivan's infantry came out again. The panzer commander, an Unteroffizier, jumped down into my foxhole. There wasn't much room in it for two but at least it offered protection against splinters. Then our Stukas arrived and Ivan's infantry went back. The Stuka bombs made the earth shake. Watching the cornfield we saw that Ivan had nevertheless got that far forward again. We took counter-measures. Six well-camouflaged Panzer IVs, quadruple flaks and single-barrel 20cm Flak moved up to the edge of the woods to receive Ivan but he declined to come. Our II Battalion leader Oberleutnant Konopka telephoned to express his fullest recognition and sent his greetings.

29 July 1943

In the evening it rained again: I slept until 0200hrs then climbed out of my foxhole and did exercises to warm up. I had decided to convert this foxhole into a firm bunker. Panzer IVs had an apron of side-armour about 8mm thick. From the neighbouring panzer I obtained a damaged one of these armour plates for use as my roof. I laid over it some wooden beams and then earth. Nearly all our foxholes had groundwater: we carpeted the ground with brushwood, moss and then our groundsheet but despite that it was always damp.

During the day Luftwaffe ground-attack aircraft strafed and bombed identified Russian positions and assembly areas. The Russian anti-aircraft fire responded wildly but were in luck and shot down one machine. The pilot bailed out successfully. In the evening four Tigers came forward for briefing then headed out into No Man's Land. One ran on a mine but suffered only minor damage.

In the night I crept out to the stack of timber near Ivan's village to fetch some beams for my bunker. The stack was 60m from our positions at the edge of the wood and 40m from the enemy-occupied village. It was a night of a new moon, pitch black, and while returning after taking my four beams I became disoriented. Things look so different at night! This situation was very dangerous. After a while I decided to chance a shout. 'Hallo, 9 Company?' I listened out. Finally came a voice from the woods, 'II Battalion here!' I had gone too far right and was happy to hear a voice say, 'For heaven's sake, Rehfeldt! What the hell are you doing wandering about out there?' Thus I was 'saved'. I laid my four beams on the roof and then slept soundly.

30 July 1943

The mortar platoon leader at that time was Oberfeldwebel Sass. Usually when one had just built the perfect bunker the order came to move out. Suddenly Ivan attacked from our left again. We heard tank fire, artillery and his mortars. We were very alert but took no action. It all died down after two hours. Our Panzer IV radioed to Battalion: 'Main battle activity terminated. Light exchange of fire. Otherwise nothing to report. Weather: sky heavily overcast. 1130hrs. Out!'

31 July 1943

During the night we set up an all-round screen of trees and bushes because we think Ivan might be able to observe us from anywhere. Our panzers and tank destroyers had run down so many fir trees that now especially from the left side we were coming increasingly under fire from that side. We recognized a Russian assembly position from where without doubt Ivan intended to break out to the main Rollbahn. We were told that our ground and air forces had destroyed twenty-four of the fifty T-34 tanks within a 3km radius of Karachev. Almost forty Stukas knocked out the Russian readiness positions and tank assemblies. Defectors tell us that a battalion now counts as fifty men. When our Marder IIIs attacked we saw the new projectiles known as *Stielgranate* [a muzzle-loaded projectile used against bunkers and fortifications]. Their effect is so tremendous that we have to take cover against the blast effect and splinters.

My spotter position is on the security panzer. I could see my opposite number's scissors telescope 300m away. Our artillery fires at it occasionally but only to startle Ivan. I zeroed-in with three bombs 50m left near the recognized observation point on a stack of wood. I knew the range exactly, for effective fire all I needed to do was give the order. I had three mortars fire seven rounds each. The Unteroffizier i/c mortar position reported the three mortars fired and soon we saw the explosive clouds rising. The forward artillery spotter reported that some of our bombs had dropped directly into Ivan's trenches. I had seen that for myself through my 7 x 50 glasses. In the evening the advanced spotter of an Army long-range artillery battery came with radio operator and messenger to zero-in – with good effect!

1 August 1943

The eye of our heavy guns is established in our corner. For the first time Russian bombers flew over, continuing far into our rear to be engaged by our heavy Flak (8.8cm to 15cm). The tremendously noisy 21cm mortars of our heavy artillery are aiming to wipe out the remainder of the houses in the village of Alissov. The earth trembles with each round fired. When the second formation of Russian bombers came over they were intercepted by our fighters: we saw one bomber burning but did not witness the crash because of the cloud cover. The infantry are sunning themselves near their 'foxhole bunkers'. We have had no post since leaving the *Zitadelle* battlefield but cigarettes in plenty, I am almost a chain-smoker! Because my lighter is empty and my matches wet, I light up from the previous fag-end.

In the evenings Ivan likes to fire on our communications paths or vehicle assemblies, particulary with his mortars. Thus when a rations carrier suddenly receives mortar fire while holding twelve full mess tins or carrying a groundsheet with cold fare and throws himself low for protection, nobody complains if upon his safe arrival the mess tins are not brimming over with soup, or the potatoes have picked up some earth in transit. A few days ago one of them was killed and another wounded. The same applies to the ammunition runners. The signallers too have a dangerous equivalent task, often leaving cover to strip cabling from damaged panzers and assault guns. This has cost many of them their lives. Or they were 'only' wounded.

After a careful survey of Ivan's positions I had four mortars fire twenty-five rounds each. The loader drops the next bomb into the barrel as soon as the previous bomb is fired. The gunners have to maintain reports because each recoil presses the baseplate deeper into the ground which brings the barrel more upright (shortening the range). No. 1 and No. 2 gunners are constantly cranking the elevating gear while holding the bipod steady with the other hand. With much firing often the mortar pit begins to cave in if the walls are sandy. My pit was half collapsed! The noise is deafening. Once the last bomb was away we all went into 'full cover' for Ivan will not take this lying down. In the event he failed to reply because of the damage and casualties inflicted. That night on sentry duty Ivan's artillery bombarded the edges of our wood and we took cover against splinters. I got behind our panzers. Otherwise the night passed quietly.

2 August 1943

I was just about to let Ivan have twenty-five more rounds each from two mortars when I was ordered to take cover. Rumours abounded. Now I heard the forward artillery spotter give his orders to fire at the edge of the village of Alissov. It was good flying weather, our Stukas were up with fighter escorts. This was the state of my 2 Group heavy mortars, 1 Battlegroup:

Unteroffizier Franz Schlossbauer, group leader, wounded.

Obergefreiter Becker, gunner (bipod), fully fit.

Gefreiter Rehfeldt, acting mortar leader, fully fit.

Obergefreiter Schleier, gunner (barrel), fallen.

Gefreiters Preuss and Wagner, Grenadiers Köstler and Husemann, all wounded.

We were sitting on the panzer watching Ivan through binoculars. When his mortars opened fire, we replied with twenty-five rounds each from four mortars. This bought us some peace and quiet for a while. Then a messenger came: 'Obergefreiter Spiegel, Gefreiters Ahlburg and Rehfeldt to report to the company command post in the evening. With steel helmet!' When we responded to this mysterious summons as ordered, our company leader Oberleutnant Schmelter came from his bunker limping (his leg had been crushed when the turret of the panzer on which he was sitting turned). Schmelter addressed us: 'My dear Ahlburg, dear Spiegel, dear Rehfeldt. For special distinction and bravery in the face of the enemy I promote each of you to "*Tapferkeits* Unteroffizier". I know you are capable, for in the recent period of NCO training and here in action I have observed you and seen your commitment. I congratulate you! May you bring your well-deserved lace safely home! Stand at ease!' Now he offered each of us his hand and we received the shoulder straps of an Unteroffizier. We each handed in our Soldbuch for the promotion to be entered. Battalion commander Oberleutnant Konopka added: 'That is especially fine, promotion for bravery on the battlefield! Do well, men!' Another firm handshake and next moment we all dived into the nearest foxhole to receive Ivan's own opinion.

Now came a short briefing: we were told that our attack was planned for the coming day. 'Gentlemen, synchronize watches! It is 1835hrs precisely. At X hour artillery bombardment by all batteries supported by our heavy weapons. Then two waves of Stukas, first bombing and then strafing. On the right our I Battalion will advance with Panther support, veer right to the north to the village of Alissov and then beyond to the "Yellow Height". Our infantry will race forward 400–600m at the second artillery bombardment, dodging enemy fire as best they can. Then our panzers will advance from the wood to the "Yellow Height". Once there, they will wheel to the north-west. That will conclude our objective for the day. After that, dig in at once and set up firing positions.' We were also informed that this would be our last 'little push' in order to create better positions for the units relieving us, then we would be relieved. We were dismissed and ran back to our positions to be heartily congratulated by our comrades.

3 August 1943

The last night before the 'little push' I did not sleep well. The artillery spotters had built a small wooden bunker. I went there as spotter for my mortars. Our Stukas arrived. All artillery and mortars were zeroed-in. The bombardment began. 'Fire at point zero. Six rounds per mortar!' The artillery observers give their fire commands. The ground trembled as they fired. Our heavy artillery was firing short, the shells falling 50m to our rear in the wood. 'Battery halt! Cease fire, fresh orders, up 400m!' The artillery spotter had gone pale. Had the barrels cooled too much during the night, or was it the same old story about worn-down rifling? Our wooden bunker tottered and shook at the impact of the rounds falling short. The next salvo was good and fell at the edge of Alissov village. Luckily we had suffered no casualties. I aimed our mortars at the known Russian artillery spotter positions. I saw many direct hits and also silenced an MG.

Our infantry companies advanced with the panzers. This resulted in bitter close combat. In the thicket almost nothing could be seen of the enemy, only shooting betrayed his position. At some places the woodland was on fire due to our flamethrower panzers.[2] We had decided to change our position when the enemy fire died down. Some way along a woodland path we stopped to consider. How far should we proceed? We had lost contact with the infantry company: I received the order to go forward with a messenger to restore contact. Holding weapons in hand ready to fire we advanced through the wood to the sound of shells howling and exploding, and worst of all 'Baumkrepierer', shells impacting against trees to release showers of whizzing splinters at head height. Acrid, suffocating smoke and fumes swept through the splayed and split tree trunks. Firing was coming from all directions. I followed a telephone line which ended in a small Russian-built earth bunker. A lieutenant with messenger and 'line stripper' were in occupation, looking for bunkers for the company and battalion command posts. They could not tell me about any infantry. We went on and bore right to the edge of the wood, finding ourselves in the great cornfield codenamed 'Yellow Height', full of Ivans all running around. From the cover of a bomb crater we watched a duel between a Tiger and T-34. After the second Tiger round (8.8cm), the T-34 exploded: half-axles with iron wheels and other metal parts of the T-34 came flying past. Immediately after, two more T-3s were destroyed. We were unwillingly in the midst of a tank battle and retired to the woods, by chance meeting up with the infantry company together with our heavy MGs. A large area of the wood was on fire, the ground glowing red with burning boughs and branches, pine needles and hot ashes up to 15cm high. We had to pass through it in leaps and bounds, I was worried that it might burn our boot leather. Even under the heaviest fire one could not throw himself flat here. I ran back to our mortar group and led it forward, the enemy fire being such that we sought cover in Ivan's former bunkers earmarked for our command posts. Our own artillery replied with salvo after salvo: we abandoned the wood for the field of wheat. 'Yellow Height' was ours, the Russians had been ejected from a well-developed defensive position – at the edges of the wood were many bunkers, firing positions, observation posts – all in and under the ground with thick felled tree trunks above them for cover. We nested in them at once, though now facing the other way.

Evening was approaching and I went with Obergefreiter Becker into the 'Yellow Height' to find a good spotting position for myself. The wheat had been flattened and was burning in places. I found what I thought was a good position and Becker stayed there as observer while I returned to the mortars. Standing on the hull of their vehicles, the panzer crews obtained a good view of Ivans moving about in the wheatfield. Some of the Ivans were very near and others were suspected to be lying low. When Unteroffizier Spiegel went forward to the spotter position to 'study the situation', a shot rang out from the wheatfield and mortally wounded Obergefreiter Becker in the throat. We carried him back to the edge of the wood, and decided to have our spotter post in a bunker at the edge of the wood and not in the cornfield. Thus, despite our painful losses, we were proud and happy to have ended the advance with success. The day's objectives had been achieved, and now our panzers and armoured personnel carriers went through the cornfield to cleanse it of Ivan while the flamethrowers smoked the village of Shudre, which continued to burn all night.

We concluded by making our daily report – munition stock and requirements, dead and wounded, loss in weapons and equipment – then after the evening meal – hot and cold – a cigarette, drew up the sentry roster, whoever wasn't on it went to sleep. That night swarms of 'sewing machines' came over but I slept exhausted through it all. Come daybreak I was awoken by the shouts of my people, 'Unteroffizier, get up! We are being relieved!' It was the best kind of morning greeting.

4–6 August 1943

We were driven to a village 'base' and left at 0045hrs next morning heading for an assembly point at Bryansk. It was very warm. On the 6th, Russian bombers attempted to destroy the railway line at Bryansk but our Flak drove them off. Battalion roll call! Oberleutnant Konopka is wounded, therefore Hauptmann Adler has taken over II Battalion, Grenadier Regiment. Tomorrow they are taking us somewhere by train, probably as 'fire brigade' again?

7 August 1943

At midday we travelled along an asphalt road to the Bryansk-South railway station, a big supply centre. Our vehicles were put on flat wagons with our tents erected between the lorries. This is partisan territory, and so all hand weapons at the ready. Along the track there is a fortified base every 200m. On both sides of the embankment a broad strip of trees has been removed for a better view and field of fire. Railway 'guards' and anti-partisan fighters armed with Russian Maxim heavy MGs and other captured weapons sit there, soldiers of the Russian Liberation Army. Their uniforms have a blood-red collar patch and look rather 'German'. Are they Mongols, Cossacks? In any case 'eastern-looking' types. We wave and they wave back! Maybe the Vlassow Army? The train headed south: the woodlands grew less frequent, we saw wide, open spaces, the wheat already harvested. The houses have small gardens and instead of the wood-beamed construction they are made of stone or loam on brushwood bound to wooden posts. Whitewashed, they look very new.

8 August 1943

The train passed through Ssumi station and when it halted we heard the growling and thundering from the Front not too far distant. At a small station a single Russian bomber appeared through the clouds, dropped a bomb quite near and then raked us with his guns before disappearing as swiftly as he had arrived. At Boromlya(?) we de-trained. Here we could hear the Front very clearly. We headed for Achtyrka, making poor progress on account of the

Rollbahn being clogged, columns and single vehicles moving in nervous fits and starts. One could see that 'here it *really* stinks!' We heard that Ivan had nearly broken through with sixty to eighty T-34s and had gone round our panzer divisions while they were in the process of being relieved. The head of our southern attack wedge is just short of Obayan, but the Front is being pulled back to the departure point. The Russians have now arrived between A and B so that the Front no longer hangs together. 'Well this is another fine piece of shit we've been landed in!' We sat up in the lorry all night but didn't get far.

9 August 1943

In the early morning we reached somewhere we knew, the little town of Tchernetshino, where at the beginning of July the Red Cross nurses had waved to us and thrown wild flowers on our lorries. They had shouted, 'Come back safe and sound!' but there had been many amongst us then waving back with a carefree laugh who had since fallen or been wounded, remembered by the empty places on the lorry benches. I saw roadsigns with the name Achtyrka. Ivan had got to the outskirts there yesterday evening but been repulsed by III Battalion. Our column rested in a wood north of Achtyrka where our company was reorganized. I went into the Leaders' Reserve as Unteroffizier zbV (for special purposes) at the *Gefechtstross* Tchernetshino. There I talked to an Ivan and his Mamka about the great 1933 famine. In their village half the population died of hunger! I could scarcely believe it. In the granary of Europe, in the midst of wheatfields thousands of people simply died of hunger? I asked, 'Did the harvest fail? Where were the reserve stocks from the previous year?' They replied '*Kommissar e soldati zaprali!*' The Ukrainians were punished for not doing as they were told. The Bolshevists with their Commissars and Red Guards took everything. The grain, the potatoes and the cabbage. The only food left was grass and leaves. I found it incredible. Wherever I looked around me the corn waved golden yellow on the haulm. Other villagers confirmed it. Each had buried several members of their own family. The dead were taken in cartloads to the cemetery. The people cried telling me. I found this story confirmed in other villages and regions of the Ukraine, at Kranoszilka, between Krementchug and Kiev, for example.

The *Spiess* said I was probably going to be detached on 1 September for a course of study. Our *Tross* has withdrawn into woods south of the town. In the neighbouring locality is an Army provisions compound which we cleared out so as to prevent the contents falling into the hands of the Russians. All of the *Tross* units in the district are hard at work 'organizing'. I was told that our II Battalion had made a counter-attack. The intention is to hold the Russians as long as possible here until our division is up to strength back from Karachev. We also heard that SS units have been surrounded.

10 August 1943

Russian bombers never linger once our fighters appear. The situation here is chaotic: stragglers collect at Achtyrka. Indication signs everywhere for these troops. A sorry sight. Fighting morale has sunk very low in some units.

11 August 1943

On the drive to the Front we were passed by lorries filled with soldiers flooding back who, when they saw our *Grossdeutschland* cuff titles, shouted 'Clear off, you division of warmongers! It's all shit here!' We could hardly believe our ears – and that in the summer of 1943. All I can say in explanation is that after nearly all SS units and *Grossdeutschland* had been withdrawn from the attacking wedge at Obayan on Hitler's order, the Russians used this weakening of the Front to launch a counter-offensive. It was often their superiority in tanks and artillery which resulted in simple infantry divisions, not well endowed with heavy weapons, being overrun. Unfortunately we had to face the fact that after the *Zitadelle* offensive was broken off, causing us serious losses in panzers and men, the Wehrmacht was no longer capable of going on the offensive. All that was left was to ward off enemy attacks until such time as the 'new miracle weapons' would be ready for deployment. And we had to believe in them, because now almost everything else was lost. Furthermore, the Allies had agreed amongst themselves that the only terms acceptable were Unconditional Surrender. This was simply out of the question. *Vae victis* – Woe to the Vanquished!

Notes

1. There were three versions of the Sd.Kfz 138/9 Marder III of which the last model, version M, appearing in April 1943, was considered by far the best. This was a Panzerjäger (tank destroyer) 38t (t = Czech capture) with 7.5cm Pak 40/3

mounted on a Panzer 38t tracked chassis. The battle room was open-top but otherwise well protected with an armoured casemate up to 25mm thick situated at the rear of the vehicle. Top speed, road, 45km/hr. Alexander Lüdeke, *Panzer der Wehrmacht Band 1, 1933–1945*, Motorbuch, 2014, p. 81. (TN)

2. The only flamethrower panzer turned out as such appears to have been the Wegmann conversion PzKpfw.III (Flamm) version M, Sd.Kfz 141/3, one hundred of which were converted between February and April 1943. The 5cm cannon was replaced by a 1500mm long tube of 14mm diameter. A thousand litres of flamethrower fuel were carried in two tanks, sufficient for 125 short bursts of fire over a maximum range of 60m. Crew was three men, armament 2 x MG34s. Alexander Lüdeke, *Panzer der Wehrmacht Band 1, 1933–1945*, Motorbuch, 2014, p. 45. (TN)

In Volume Two, the continuation of this work, Dr Hans Heinz Rehfeldt publishes his war memoir from August 1943 to his return home in July 1945.

MORTAR GUNNER
ON THE
EASTERN FRONT

VOLUME II:
RUSSIA, HUNGARY, LITHUANIA
AND THE BATTLE FOR EAST PRUSSIA

THE MEMOIR OF
DR HANS HEINZ REHFELDT